SystemsToolKit>™

UNIX Reference Manual

Table Of Contents

Table of Contents

Table of Contents

Preface

Purpose and Audience

Systems<ToolKit> is an ANSI-compliant C++ library that includes classes for data structures, utilities, portable error handling, portable runtime type identification, binary streaming and systems programming. This reference manual contains a concise description of every class and algorithm in Systems<ToolKit>, and is intended as a tool for programmers who already have a basic working knowledge of the product.

For examples and an overview of each class, consult the *Systems<ToolKit> User's Manual*. The user's manual is more appropriate for new users of Systems<ToolKit>.

How to Use this Document

This manual is divided into three sections:

1. *Class Catalog:* a description of the public members of every class in Systems<ToolKit>.

2. *Algorithm Catalog:* a description of every STL algorithm, including the ObjectSpace helper algorithms.

3. *Appendix:* a list of the error and panic events that can be generated by Systems<ToolKit>.

The introduction sections to the Class Catalog and Algorithm catalog should be read prior to using the catalog itself. These introductions provide information on conventions used throughout the catalog.

To locate a specific catalog entry, use the table of contents as an index.

Associated Documents

Information about how to install, compile and link to Systems<ToolKit> is provided in the *Systems<ToolKit> Installation Guide* document.

Examples and an overview of the classes in Systems<ToolKit> can be found in the *Systems<ToolKit> User's Manual*.

General Conventions

This document uses the following conventions:

Code   Example code is shown in 10 point monospaced courier.

Output   Example output is shown in 10 point bold monospaced courier.

For conventions specific to a catalog entry, refer to the catalog introductions.

Class Catalog

This section contains a concise description of every class in Systems<ToolKit> in alphabetical order. The os_ prefix is omitted from the title of each catalog entry for the purpose of readability. However, it is shown in the types of the member signatures themselves. Classes that are part of the ANSI standard are not shown with an os_ prefix.

Every entry contains the following information:

- *A Description.* This description is a brief overview of the class; for more information and examples of usage, consult its corresponding chapter in the *Systems<ToolKit> User's Manual.*

- *A Declaration.* This lists the name of the header file that contains the declaration of the class, together with the class declaration. Inheritance is indicated using standard C++ notation.

- *A list of associated enumerators, typedefs, and constants.*

- *A list of constructors and destructors.* For convenience, these functions are grouped at the start of the member function list.

- *A list of member functions.* The class's public member functions are presented in alphabetical order. Inherited functions are not shown. Non-alphabetical functions are listed first. Static and non-static functions are combined into the same list. If a function is virtual or static, a comment precedes the function signature that indicates these attributes (e.g. /* static */, /* virtual */).

- *A list of non-member functions.* The class's non-member functions are presented.

Error Codes

Many of the functions in Systems<ToolKit> can generate errors. The mechanism used to report an error may be configured based on your preferences and compiler. Refer to the section on error handling in the *Systems<ToolKit> User's Manual* for more details on error handling mechanisms.

Each function that can generate an error has a separate line labeled "Events:" followed by the category of event that it can generate. There are three categorizations of events:

- `syscall`: errors generated by underlying system calls.
- `memory`: errors generated due to heap allocation failures.
- `other`: Systems<ToolKit> internal errors.

For a detailed list of the error codes in each category, refer to the appendix of this manual.

If an error occurs, it is often useful to know information about the state of an object following the error. This information is listed in an optional line labeled "On Resumption:." If you are not using C++ exception handling, functions return in the event of an error. The return value in the presence of an error is listed in the resumption line of the function entry.

Common Typedefs and Class Compatibility

Systems<ToolKit> defines several common `typedefs` to isolate its source code from the underlying operating system. In addition, several classes in Systems<ToolKit> define conversion operators that allow them to be used whenever their associated `typedef` is expected.

For example, `os_sig_t` is used to indicate a UNIX signal code and is compatible with the class `os_signal`. You can pass an `os_signal` object anywhere a function take `os_sig_t` as a parameter. Similarly, you can assign to or construct an `os_signal` object from any `os_sig_t` type.

The following table summarizes the `typedefs` and class compatibility for Systems<ToolKit>. To promote decoupling of library components, most interfaces take the primitives instead of their class equivalents.

typedef	Represents	Type	Compatible Classes
os_desc_t	A file descriptor.	int	os_file, os_named_pipe, os_unnamed_pipe, os_tcp_socket, os_tcp_connection_server
os_dev_t	A device number.	short	–
os_flock_t	A file lock structure.	struct flock	os_file_lock
os_gid_t	A group id.	unsigned short	os_group
os_ino_t	An inode number.	unsigned long	–
os_ioctl_t	An I/O control code.	int	os_io_control
os_key_t	A System V key.	long	os_key
os_lim_t	A hard/soft limit.	int	–
os_mode_t	A UNIX file mode.	unsigned short	os_mode
os_nlink_t	Link count.	short	–

`os_off_t`	A file offset.	`long`	–
`os_open_t`	A UNIX open mode.	`int`	`os_open_control`
`os_pid_t`	A process id.	`int`	`os_process,` `os_process_group`
`os_rlimit_t`	A resource limit structure.	`struct` `rlimit`	`os_resource`
`os_sig_t`	A signal code.	`int`	`os_signal`
`os_sigaction_t`	A signal action structure.	`struct` `sigaction`	`os_signal_action`
`os_stat_t`	A status structure.	`struct` `stat`	–
`os_thread_t`	A thread id.	`unsigned` `int`	`os_thread`
`os_uid_t`	A user id.	`Unsigned` `short`	`os_user`

`os_vid_t`	A System V id.	`int`	`os_shared_memory,`
			`os_message_queue,`
			`os_sysv_semaphore`

adapter

Description:

When a binary stream (`os_bstream`) or text stream (`os_tstream`) is constructed, it is associated with a particular I/O device via an intermediate adapter object called an `os_adapter`. When an item is streamed, it is sent to the I/O device via the adapter. This technique allows the streaming mechanisms to be fully decoupled from details of any particular I/O device.

Systems<ToolKit> contains adapters for the following Systems<ToolKit> I/O objects:

- `os_file`
- `os_named_pipe`
- `os_unnamed_pipe`
- `os_tcp_socket`

In addition, it contains adapters for IOStreams, allowing you to create binary streams on the following:

- `fstream`
- `strstream`
- `ostream` (like `cout` and `cerr`)
- `istream` (like `cin`)

There is no need to use the adapter interfaces directly unless you are adapting Systems<ToolKit> for an unsupported device.

For IOStream based objects, use the global function `os_adapter_for()` to create the appropriate adapter for use with `os_bstream` or `os_tstream`. See the chapter on "Binary Streams" in the *Systems<ToolKit> User's Manual* for more information.

Declaration:
```
#include <ospace/io/adapter.h>
class os_adapter
```

back_insert_iterator, back_inserter

Description:
A `back_insert_iterator` is an iterator that always inserts at the end of its associated container.

Declaration:
```
#include <iterator.h>
template< Container >
class back_insert_iterator : public output_iterator
```

Adapter:
```
template<class Container>
back_insert_iterator< Container >
back_inserter( Container& container )
```

Constructor	*back_insert_iterator(Container& container)* Construct myself to be associated with `container`.
=	*back_insert_iterator< Container >& operator=(const value_type& value)* Insert a copy of `value` at the end of my associated container.
*	*back_insert_iterator< Container >& operator*()* Return a reference to myself.
++	*back_insert_iterator< Container >& operator++()* Return a reference to myself.
++	*back_insert_iterator< Container > operator++(int)* Return a copy of myself.

Example <ospace/stl/examples/binsert1.cpp>

```
#include <stl.h>
#include <iostream.h>

char* array [] = { "laurie", "jennifer", "leisa" };

int main ()
{
  vector<char*> names;
  copy (array, array + 3,
    back_insert_iterator<vector <char*> > (names));
  vector<char*>::iterator i;
  for (i = names.begin (); i != names.end (); i++)
    cout << *i << endl;
  return 0;
}
```

laurie
jennifer
leisa

Example <ospace/stl/examples/binsert2.cpp>

```
#include <stl.h>
#include <iostream.h>

char* array [] = { "laurie", "jennifer", "leisa" };

int main ()
{
  vector<char*> names;
  copy (array, array + 3, back_inserter (names));
  vector<char*>::iterator i;
  for (i = names.begin (); i != names.end (); i++)
    cout << *i << endl;
  return 0;
}
```

laurie
jennifer
leisa

binary_compose, compose2

Description:

binary_compose is a unary function object that returns the result of executing its three operations in a specific sequence. Its associated adapter function compose2() allows you to conveniently construct a binary_compose object directly from three functions.

Declaration:
```
#include <function.h>
template< class Operation1, class Operation2, class Operation3 >
class binary_compose : public unary_function
  < Operation2::argument_type, Operation1::result_type >
```

Adapter:
```
template< class Operation1, class Operation2, class Operation3 >
binary_compose< Operation1, Operation2, Operation3 >
compose2
  (
  const Operation1& op1,
  const Operation2& op2,
  const Operation3& op3
  )
```

Constructor	*binary_compose(const Operation1& op1, const Operation2& op2, const Operation3& op3)* Construct myself with associated operators op1, op2 and op3.
()	*Operation1::result_type operator()(const Operation2::argument_type& x) const* Return op1 (op2 (x), op3 (x)).

Example <ospace/stl/examples/bcompos1.cpp>

```cpp
#include <iostream.h>
#include <stl.h>

struct odd : public unary_function<int, bool>
{
  odd () {}
  bool operator () (int n_) const { return (n_ % 2) == 1; }
};

struct positive : public unary_function<int, bool>
{
  positive () {}
  bool operator () (int n_) const { return n_ >= 0; }
};

int array [6] = { -2, -1, 0, 1, 2, 3 };

int main ()
{
  binary_compose<logical_and<bool>, odd, positive>
    b (logical_and<bool> (), odd (), positive ());
  int* p = find_if (array, array + 6, b);
  if (p != array + 6)
    cout << *p << " is odd and positive" << endl;
  return 0;
}
```

Example <ospace/stl/examples/bcompos2.cpp>

```cpp
#include <iostream.h>
#include <stl.h>

struct odd : public unary_function<int, bool>
{
  odd () {}
  bool operator () (int n_) const { return (n_ % 2) == 1; }
};

struct positive : public unary_function<int, bool>
{
  positive () {}
  bool operator () (int n_) const { return n_ >= 0; }
};

int array [6] = { -2, -1 , 0, 1,, 2, 3 };

int main ()
{
  int* p = find_if (array, array + 6,
   compose2 (logical_and<bool> (), odd (), positive ()));
  if (p != array + 6)
    cout << *p << " is odd and positive" << endl;
  return 0;
}
```

binary_function

Description:

`binary_function` is the base structure of all binary function objects. It defines three useful `typedefs` that are used by most of its derived classes.

Declaration:

```
#include <function.h>
template< class Arg1, class Arg2, class Result >
struct binary_function
  {
  typedef Arg1 first_argument_type;
  typedef Arg2 second_argument_type;
  typedef Result result_type;
  };
```

binary_negate, not2

Description:

`binary_negate` is a binary function object that returns the logical negation of executing its binary predicate. Its associated adapter function `not2()` allows you to conveniently construct a `binary_negate` object directly from a predicate.

Declaration:
```
#include <function.h>
template< class Predicate >
class binary_negate : public binary_function
  < Predicate::first_argument_type,
    Predicate::second_argument_type, bool >
```

Adapter:
```
template< class Predicate >
binary_negate< Predicate > not2( const Predicate& pred )
```

Constructor *binary_negate(const Predicate& predicate)*
Construct myself with predicate `predicate`.

() *bool operator()(const first_argument_type& x,*
const second_argument_type& y) const
Return the result of `predicate( x, y )`

Example <ospace/stl/examples/bnegate1.cpp>

```
#include <stl.h>
#include <iostream.h>

int array [4] = { 4, 9, 7, 1 };

int main ()
{
  sort (array, array + 4,
    binary_negate<greater<int> > (greater<int> ()));
  for (int i = 0; i < 4; i++)
    cout << array[i] << endl;
  return 0;
}

1
4
7
9
```

Example <ospace/stl/examples/bnegate2.cpp>

```
#include <stl.h>
#include <iostream.h>

int array [4] = { 4, 9, 7, 1 };

int main ()
{
  sort (array, array + 4, not2 (greater<int> ()));
  for (int i = 0; i < 4; i++)
    cout << array[i] << endl;
  return 0;
}


1
4
7
9
```

binder1st, bind1st

Description:
binder1st is a unary function object that allows you to apply a binary function to an operand and a predefined value. Its associated adapter function bind1st() allows you to conveniently construct a binder1st object directly from a function and a value. The reason that it's called binder1st is that the operand is used as the first parameter to the binary function since the second parameter is supplied. Use binder2nd if you wish the operand to be used as the second parameter.

Declaration:
```
#include <function.h>
template< class Operation >
class binder1st : public unary_function
  < Operation::second_argument_type, Operation::result_type >
```

Adapter:
```
template< class Operation, class T >
binder1st< Operation > bind1st( const Operation& op, const T& x )
```

Constructor

binder1st(const Operation& op,
const Operation::first_argument_type& value)
Construct myself to be associated with operation op and value value.

()

Operation::result_type operator()(
const Operation::first_argument_type& x) const
Return op(value, x).

Example <ospace/stl/examples/bind1st>

```
#include <stl.h>
#include <iostream.h>

int array [3] = { 1, 2, 3 };

int main ()
{
  int* p = remove_if (array, array + 3,
    binder1st<less<int> > (less<int> (), 2));
  for (int* i = array; i != p; i++)
    cout << *i << endl;
  return 0;
}

2
3
```

Example <ospace/stl/examples/bind1st2.cpp>

```
#include <stl.h>
#include <iostream.h>

int array [3] = { 1, 2, 3 };

int main ()
{
  int* p = remove_if (array, array + 3, bind1st(less<int> (), 2));
  for (int* i = array; i != p; i++)
    cout << "** " << *i << endl;
  return 0;
}

2
3
```

binder2nd, bind2nd

Description:
> binder2nd is a unary function object that allows you to apply a binary function to a predefined value and another operand. Its associated adapter function bind2nd() allows you to conveniently construct a binder2nd object directly from a function and a value. The reason that it's called binder2nd is that the operand is used as the 2nd parameter to the binary function since the 1st parameter is supplied. Use binder1st if you wish the operand to be used as the 1st parameter.

Declaration:
```
#include <function.h>
template< class Operation >
class binder2nd : public unary_function
  < Operation::first_argument_type, Operation::result_type >
```

Adapter:
```
template< class Operation, class T >
binder2nd< Operation > bind2nd( const Operation& op, const T& x )
```

Constructor	*binder2nd(const Operation& op,* *const Operation::second_argument_type& value)* Construct myself to be associated with operation op and value value.
()	*Operation::result_type operator()(* *const Operation::first_argument_type& x) const* Return op(x, value).

Example <ospace/stl/examples/bind2nd1.cpp>

```cpp
#include <stl.h>
#include <iostream.h>

int array [3] = { 1, 2, 3 };

int main ()
{
  replace_if (array, array + 3,
    binder2nd<greater<int> > (greater<int> (), 2), 4);
  for (int i = 0; i < 3; i++)
    cout << array[i] << endl;
  return 0;
}
```

```
1
2
4
```

Example <ospace/stl/examples/bind2nd2.cpp>

```cpp
#include <stl.h>
#include <iostream.h>

int array [3] = { 1, 2, 3 };

int main ()
{
  replace_if (array, array + 3, bind2nd(greater<int> (), 2), 4);
  for (int i = 0; i < 3; i++)
    cout << array[i] << endl;
  return 0;
}
```

bit_vector

Description:

A `bit_vector` is a kind of vector that is specialized for storing and accessing bits efficiently.

Declaration:
```
#include <vector.h>
class bit_vector
```

Constuctor	*bit_vector()* Construct myself to be empty.
Constuctor	*bit_vector(alloc_type& alloc)* Construct myself to be empty. Use `alloc` to allocate storage.
Constructor	*bit_vector(size_type n, bool bit)* Construct me to contain n elements set to `bit` (default 0).
Constructor	*bit_vector(alloc_type& alloc, size_type n, bool bit)* Construct me to contain n elements set to `bit` (default 0). Use `alloc` to allocate storage.
Constructor	*bit_vector(const_iterator first, const_iterator last)* Construct me to contain copies of all of the bits in the range `[first, last)`.
Constructor	*bit_vector(alloc_type& alloc, const_iterator first, const_iterator last)* Construct me to contain copies of all of the bits in the range `[first, last)`. Use `alloc` to allocate storage.
Constructor	*bit_vector(const bit_vector& x)* Construct myself to be a copy of x.
Constructor	*bit_vector(alloc_type& alloc, const bit_vector& x)* Construct myself to be a copy of x. Use `alloc` to allocate storage.
Destructor	*~bit_vector()* Destroy myself.
=	*bit_vector& operator=(const bit_vector& x)* Replace my contents by a copy of x 's.
==	*bool operator==(const bit_vector& x) const* Return `true` if I contain the same bits in the same order as x.
<	*bool operator<(const bit_vector& x) const* Return `true` if I'm lexigraphically less than x.

[]	*bit_reference operator[ ](int index)* Return a reference to my `index`th bit. Events: `other (os_illegal_index)`
[]	*bool operator[ ](int index) const* Return a reference to my `index`th bit. Events: `other (os_illegal_index)`
back	*bit_reference back( )* Return a reference to my last bit. Events: `other (os_empty_error)`
back	*bool back( ) const* Return my last bit. Events: `other (os_empty_error)`
begin	*iterator begin( )* Return an iterator positioned at my first bit.
begin	*const_iterator begin( ) const* Return an iterator positioned at my first bit.
capacity	*size_type capacity( )* Return the number of bits that I can contain without allocating more memory.
empty	*bool empty( ) const* Return `true` if I contain no bits.
end	*iterator end( )* Return an iterator positioned immediately after my last bit.
end	*const_iterator end( ) const* Return an iterator positioned immediately after my last bit.
erase[1]	*void erase( )* Erase all of my bits.
erase	*void erase(iterator pos)* Erase the bit at `pos`.
erase	*void erase(iterator first, iterator last)* Erase the bits in range `[first, last)`.

---

[1] Non-standard, unique to Systems<ToolKit>

front	*bit_reference front()* Return a reference to my first bit. Events: other (os_empty_error)
front	*bool front() const* Return my first bit. Events: other (os_empty_error)
insert	*iterator insert(iterator pos, bool bit)* Insert bit at pos and return an iterator pointing to the new bit's position.
insert	*void insert(iterator pos, size_type n, bool bit)* Insert n copies of bit at pos.
insert	*void insert(iterator pos, const_iterator first, const_iterator last)* Insert copies of the bits in the range [first, last) at pos.
max_size	*size_type max_size() const* Return the maximum number of bits that I can contain.
push_back	*void push_back(bool bit)* Add bit at my end.
pop_back	*void pop_back()* Erase my last bit. Events: other (os_empty_error)
rbegin	*reverse_iterator rbegin()* Return a reverse iterator positioned at my last bit.
rbegin	*const_reverse_iterator rbegin() const* Return a reverse iterator positioned at my last bit.
rend	*reverse_iterator rend()* Return a reverse_iterator positioned immediately before my first bit.
rend	*const_reverse_iterator rend() const* Return a reverse_iterator positioned immediately before my first bit.
reserve	*void reserve(size_type n)* Pre-allocate enough space to hold up to n bits. This operation does not change the value returned by size().
size	*size_type size() const* Return the number of bits that I contain.
swap	*void swap(bit_vector<T>& x)* Swap my contents with x 's.

bstream

Description:

A binary stream is an instance of `os_bstream`. When an `os_bstream` is constructed, it is associated with a particular I/O device via an intermediate adapter object called an `os_adapter`. When an item is streamed to an `os_bstream`, it is converted into a binary format and then sent to the I/O device via the adapter. This technique allows the binary streaming mechanism to be fully decoupled from details of any particular I/O device.

Declaration:
```
#include <ospace/stream/bstream.h>
class os_bstream
```

Constructor	*os_bstream(const os_adapter& adapter)* Stream items to the device associated with `adapter`. Events: `memory` On Resumption: I will be in an unusable state.
Destructor	*~os_bstream()* Destructor.
<<	*os_bstream& operator<<(os_bstream& stream, char value)* Write `value` to `stream`.
<<	*os_bstream& operator<<(os_bstream& stream, char* value)* Write `value` to `stream`.
<<	*os_bstream& operator<<(os_bstream& stream, double value)* Write `value` to `stream`.
<<	*os_bstream& operator<<(os_bstream& stream, float value)* Write `value` to `stream`.
<<	*os_bstream& operator<<(os_bstream& stream, int value)* Write `value` to `stream`.
<<	*os_bstream& operator<<(os_bstream& stream, long value)* Write `value` to `stream`.
<<	*os_bstream& operator<<(os_bstream& stream, long double value)* Write `value` to `stream`.
<<	*os_bstream& operator<<(os_bstream& stream, short value)* Write `value` to `stream`.

<< *os_bstream& operator<<(os_bstream& stream, unsigned char value)*
Write value to stream.

<< *os_bstream& operator<<(os_bstream& stream, unsigned int value)*
Write value to stream.

<< *os_bstream& operator<<(os_bstream& stream, unsigned long value)*
Write value to stream.

<< *os_bstream& operator<<(os_bstream& stream, unsigned short value)*
Write value to stream.

<< *ostream& operator<<(ostream& stream, const os_bstream& bstream)*
Print bstream to stream.

>> *os_bstream& operator>>(os_bstream& stream, char& value)*
Read value from stream.

>> *os_bstream& operator>>(os_bstream& stream, char*& value)*
Read value from stream.

>> *os_bstream& operator>>(os_bstream& stream, double& value)*
Read value from stream.

>> *os_bstream& operator>>(os_bstream& stream, float& value)*
Read value from stream.

>> *os_bstream& operator>>(os_bstream& stream, int& value)*
Read value from stream.

>> *os_bstream& operator>>(os_bstream& stream, long& value)*
Read value from stream.

>> *os_bstream& operator>>(os_bstream& stream, long double& value)*
Read value from stream.

>> *os_bstream& operator>>(os_bstream& stream, short& value)*
Read value from stream.

>> *os_bstream& operator>>(os_bstream& stream, unsigned char& value)*
Read value from stream.

>> *os_bstream& operator>>(os_bstream& stream, unsigned int& value)*
Read value from stream.

>> *os_bstream& operator>>(os_bstream& stream, unsigned long& value)*
Read value from stream.

>> *os_bstream& operator>>(os_bstream& stream, unsigned short& value)*
Read value from stream.

adapter *const os_adapter& adapter() const*
Return a reference to my device adapter.

clear	*void clear()* Reset my state to good.
eof	*bool eof() const* Return `true` if I am at eof.
fail	*void fail()* Set my state to indicate failure.
good	*bool good() const* Return `true` if I am in a good state and not at eof.
ok	*bool ok() const* Return `true` if I am in a good state.
print	*void print(ostream& stream) const* Print myself to `stream`.
read	*int read(char& value)* Read a `char` into `value`.
read	*int read(char*& buffer)* Read a `char*` sequence into the heap and store the pointer to the memory region in `buffer`. Return the number of bytes read, or `-1` on error.
read	*int read(double& value)* Read a `double` into `value`.
read	*int read(float& value)* Read a `float` into `value`.
read	*int read(int& value)* Read an `int` into `value`.
read	*int read(long& value)* Read a `long` into `value`.
read	*int read(long double& value)* Read a `long double` into `value`.
read	*int read(short& value)* Read a `short` into `value`.
read	*int read(unsigned char& value)* Read an `unsigned char` into `value`.
read	*int read(unsigned int& value)* Read an `unsigned int` into `value`.
read	*int read(unsigned long& value)* Read an `unsigned long` into `value`.

read	*int read(unsigned short& value)* Read an `unsigned short` into `value`.
read_chunk	*int read_chunk(void* buffer, int bytes)* Read a chunk of data into `buffer` not to exceed `bytes` size. Return the number of bytes read on success, `-1` on failure.
read_chunk	*int read_chunk(void*& buffer)* Read a chunk of data into the heap and store a pointer to the data in `buffer`. Return the number of bytes read, or `-1` on failure.
write	*int write(char value)* Write `value`.
write	*int write(const char* string)* Write `string`.
write	*int write(double value)* Write `value`.
write	*int write(float value)* Write `value`.
write	*int write(int value)* Write `value`.
write	*int write(long value)* Write `value`.
write	*int write(long double value)* Write `value`.
write	*int write(short value)* Write `value`.
write	*int write(unsigned char value)* Write `value`.
write	*int write(unsigned int value)* Write `value`.
write	*int write(unsigned long value)* Write `value`.
write	*int write(unsigned short value)* Write `value`.
write_chunk	*int write_chunk(const void* buffer, int bytes)* Write `bytes` number of characters from `buffer`.

Other Non-Member Functions

In addition to the operators listed above, the binary streaming mechanisms in Systems<ToolKit> provide the non-member functions `operator<<` and `operator>>` for the following classes:

- `os_date`
- `os_event`
- `os_file_lock`
- `os_group`
- `os_host`
- `os_io_control`
- `os_io_status`
- `os_ip_address`
- `os_key`
- `os_mode`
- `os_network`
- `os_open_control`
- `os_path`
- `os_process`
- `os_process_group`
- `os_process_status`
- `os_resource`
- `os_resource_usage`
- `os_service`
- `os_signal`
- `os_socket_address`
- `os_stopwatch`
- `string`
- `os_time`
- `os_time_and_date`
- `os_tokenizer`
- `os_time_period`
- `os_user`

Any instance of these classes may be streamed into or out of an `os_bstream`. Refer to the catalog entries of each class for more details.

The following STL containers can be streamed in and out of an `os_bstream` if you declare the source macro for the container template instance in your code:

– `deque`
– `list`
– `map`
– `multimap`
– `multiset`
– `priority_queue`
– `queue`
– `set`
– `stack`
– `vector`

Refer to the *Systems\<ToolKit> User's Manual* for more information on using binary streaming with STL containers. Adding binary streaming macros to your own classes automatically declares the non-member functions `operator<<` and `operator>>`, allowing them to be streamed in and out of an `os_bstream`.

calendar_date

Description:
Represents a particular day in any given year. Instances of this class can be constructed to represent things like "the second Tuesday of March," "the fourth day of August," etc. The result is the proper date for any specified year.

Declaration:
```
#include <ospace/time/calendar.h>
class os_calendar_date
```

Constructor	*os_calendar_date(const os_time_period& time, os_month_t month, os_day_t day)* Construct myself to be the `day`th day of `month` with `time` elapsed.
Constructor	*os_calendar_date(const os_time_period& time, os_month_t month, os_which_one week, os_weekday_t weekday)* Construct myself to be the `weekday`th weekday of the `week`th week of the `month`, with elapsed time `time`.
Constructor	*os_calendar_date(const os_calendar_date& date)* Construct myself to be a copy of `date`.
=	*os_calendar_date& operator=(const os_calendar_date& date)* Assign myself from `date`.
date	*os_date date(os_year_t year) const* Return an `os_date` based on my values for the specified `year`.
day	*os_day_t day() const* Return my day.
day	*void day(os_day_t day)* Set my day to `day`.
month	*os_month_t month() const* Return my month.
month	*void month(os_month_t month)* Set my month to `month`.
print	*void print(ostream& stream) const* Print myself to `stream`.
time	*os_time time() const* Return my time.

week   *os_which_one week() const*
                   Return my week of the month as specified in constructor.

weekday   *os_weekday_t weekday() const*
                   Return my weekday.

weekday   *void weekday(os_which_one week, os_weekday_t weekday)*
                   Set my week to be week and my weekday to be weekday.

when   *os_time_period when() const*
                   Return my time.

when   *void when(const os_time_period& time)*
                   Set my time to time.

Non-Member Functions:

<<   *ostream& operator<<(ostream& stream, const os_calendar_date& date)*
                   Print date to stream.

catcher

Description:

An `os_catcher` prevents an event from propagating further down the handler stack by catching it and storing it for further processing.

A catcher cannot catch more than one event. You can obtain a pointer to the stored event using `event()`. If an event is propagated to a catcher that already is holding an event, the event is silently deleted instead of being caught. `clear()` causes a catcher's associated event to be deleted so that the catcher is free to catch another event. If a catcher is destroyed while it is still storing an event, a panic event occurs and the program terminates.

The conversion function `operator bool()` returns `true` if a catcher is storing an event.

Declaration:

```
#include <ospace/event/catcher.h>
class os_catcher : public os_handler
```

Constructor	*os_catcher()* Construct myself to catch all events with category `os_error` and domain `os_objectspace`.
Constructor	*os_catcher(os_filter* filter)* Construct myself to catch all events that pass through `filter`.
Destructor	*/* virtual */ ~os_catcher()* Pop myself from the handler stack. If I am holding an event, generate a panic event with code `os_unhandled_event`. Events: `other (os_unhandled_event)` On Resumption: I'm not usable
bool	*operator bool() const* Return `true` if I'm holding an event.
clear	*void clear()* If I'm storing an event, silently delete it.
event	*const os_event* event() const* If I'm storing an event, return a pointer to it, otherwise return 0.
print	*/* virtual */ void print(ostream& stream) const* Print myself to `stream`.
release	*void release()* Release any event that I am currently holding and propagate it to the next handler.

catcher

Non-Member Functions:

<<   *ostream& operator<<(ostream& stream, const os_catcher& catcher)*
                        Print `catcher` to `stream`.

class

Description:

Systems<ToolKit> has a portable runtime information facility that allows class hierarchy information to be accessed at runtime regardless of whether your compiler supports the new C++ RTTI mechanism. Every class that is enabled for portable RTTI has an associated `os_class` object that is automatically constructed during static initialization. When an `os_class` object is constructed, it registers useful information with the portable RTTI facility such as the class's name and immediate base classes. This information allows you to:

- obtain the `os_class` object associated with a particular object
- access a class's name
- access a class's derived classes
- access a class's base classes
- determine if an object's class is a specific class
- determine if an object's class is derived from a specific class

To obtain a reference to an object's associated `os_class` object, use `os_class_of()`. This function works correctly even when the object is accessed via a dereferenced pointer to one of its base classes.

To obtain a reference to a particular class object without instantiating the class, use `os_the_class()` with a pointer to the desired class type. One of the most convenient ways to obtain such a pointer is to cast a 0 to the required class type.

Declaration:
```
#include <ospace/rtti/class.h>
class os_class
```

<	*bool operator<(const os_class& x) const* Return `true` if my `name` is less than x's.
==	*bool operator==(const os_class& x) const* Return `true` if my `name` is the same as x's.
id	*int id() const* Return my unique `id` value.
is_base_of	*bool is_base_of(const os_class& x) const* Return `true` if I'm a base of x.
is_derived_from	*bool is_derived_from(const os_class& x) const* Return `true` if I'm derived from the class x.

is_kind_of	*bool is_kind_of(const os_class& x) const* Return `true` if I'm equal to or derived from `x`.
name	*const char* name() const* Return my `name`.
print	*void print(ostream& stream) const* Print myself to `stream`.
print_hierarchy	*void print_hierarchy(ostream& stream, int indent) const* Print myself and my derived classes in an indented format to `stream`, starting with indentation `indent` (default 0).

Non-Member Functions:

<<	*ostream& operator<<(ostream& stream, const os_class& class)* Print `class` to `stream`.

class_db

Description:
os_class_db is a class comprised of static member functions that allows you to access the database of class information. You may use os_class_db to find a class based on its name or its numeric id, as well as to obtain the derived and base classes of a particular class. Whitespace is ignored when looking up the name of a template class. If you have aliased the name of a class with a typedef, the alias cannot be used to locate a class.

Declaration:
```
#include <ospace/rtti/classdb.h>
class os_class_db
```

bases_inclusive_of   /* static */ vector< os_class* > bases_inclusive_of(const os_class& x)
Return a vector of pointers to x and all of its base classes.

bases_of   /* static */ vector< os_class* > bases_of(const os_class& x)
Return a vector of pointers to all of x's base classes.

derived_inclusive_of   /* static */ vector< os_class* > derived_inclusive_of(const os_class& x)
Return a vector of pointers to x and all of its derived classes.

derived_of   /* static */ vector< os_class* > derived_of(const os_class& x)
Return a vector of pointers to all of x's derived classes.

immediate_bases_of   /* static */ const vector< os_class* >& immediate_bases_of(const os_class& x)
Returns the immediate base classes of x.

immediate_derived_of /* static */ const vector< os_class* >& immediate_derived_of(const os_class& x)
Returns the immediate derived classes of x.

with_id   /* static */ os_class* with_id(int id)
Return a pointer to the class object whose id is id, or 0 if none is found.

with_name   /* static */ os_class* with_name(const string& name)
Return a pointer to the class object whose name is name, or 0 if none is found.

connectable_socket

Description:
   `os_connectable_socket` is an abstract base class that contains the functions common to
   `os_tcp_socket` and `os_udp_socket`, including read, write and connection behaviors.

Declaration:
```
#include <ospace/socket/connsock.h>
class os_connectable_socket : public os_socket
```

clear
   void clear()
   Reset my state to good.

connect_to
   void connect_to(const os_socket_address& address)
   Connect to the socket with IP socket address `address` (`AF_INET` only).

   > Events: `syscall`
   > On Resumption: I will be in an unknown state.

connected
   bool connected() const
   Return `true` if I'm connected to another socket.

eof
   bool eof() const
   Return `true` if I'm at the end of my input.

event_on_eof
   void event_on_eof(bool flag)
   If flag is `true`, I will generate an event on eof.

event_on_eof
   bool event_on_eof() const
   Return `true` if I will generate an event on eof.

good
   bool good() const
   Return `true` if I'm in a good state and not at eof.

ok
   bool ok() const
   Return `true` if I'm not broken or failed.

peer_address
   os_socket_address peer_address() const
   Return an instance of `os_socket_address` that represents the name of
   the peer connected to this socket.

   > Events: `syscall`
   > On Resumption: Return value may be invalid.

print
   void print(ostream& stream) const
   Print myself to `stream`. If I'm opened, print my descriptor and my peer;
   otherwise, print "UNOPENED."

read

int read(void* buffer, int bytes)
Read up to `bytes` bytes into `buffer`. Return the number of bytes actually read, or `-1` on error.

> Events: `syscall`
> On Resumption: Returns `-1`.

receive_from

int receive_from(os_socket_address& address, void* buffer, int bytes)
Receive up to `bytes` bytes and place them into `buffer`. Return the number of bytes that were successfully read and set `address` to the IP socket address of the socket that the bytes were read from (`AF_INET` only). [MT UNSAFE for Solaris]

> Events: `syscall`
> On Resumption: I will be in a failed state. Returns `-1`.

write

int write(const void* buffer, int bytes)
Write `bytes` bytes from `buffer`. Return the number of bytes actually written, or `-1` on error.

> Events: `syscall`
> On Resumption: Returns `-1`.

counting_semaphore

Description:

A counting semaphore is a generalization of a mutex semaphore that allows multiple resources to be locked and unlocked. All resource allocation functions such as `wait()` and `post()` take an optional parameter that is the number of resources to allocate/deallocate.

Unlike the `os_mutex_semaphore`, an `os_counting_semaphore` is not owned *by* a particular thread; it is simply owned. One thread can `wait()` and a different thread can `post()` to increase the available resource count and unblock waiters. Contrast this with an `os_mutex_semaphore`, where the same thread that waits (and acquires the resource) has to also post to release the resource.

Declaration:
```
#include <ospace/sync/counting.h>
class os_counting_semaphore
```

Typedefs:
```
typedef os_counting_semaphore os_semaphore
```

Constructor	*os_counting_semaphore(unsigned int initial)* Construct myself with `initial` resources available.
Constructor	*os_counting_semaphore(unsigned int initial, unsigned int maximum)* Construct myself with `initial` resources available and a `maximum` size.
Destructor	*~os_counting_semaphore()* Destroy myself.
count	*unsigned int count() const* Return my current count.
lock	*void lock(unsigned int count)* Decrement the number of my resources by `count`. If `count` resources are not present, block until they become available.
obtain	*void obtain(unsigned int count)* Equivalent to `lock( count )`. The default value of `count` is 1.
post	*void post(unsigned int count)* Equivalent to `unlock( count )`. The default value of `count` is 1.
print	*void print(ostream& stream) const* Printing myself to `stream`.
release	*void release(unsigned int count)* Equivalent to `unlock( count )`. The default value of `count` is 1.

size	*unsigned int size() const* Return my size.
try_lock	*bool try_lock(unsigned int count)* If I have at least `count` resources, decrement my resources by `count` (default `1`) and return `true`; otherwise, leave my resource count unchanged and immediately return `false`.
unlock	*void unlock(unsigned int count)* Increment the number of my resources by `count` (default `1`).
wait	*void wait(unsigned int count)* Equivalent to `lock( count )`. The default value of `count` is `1`.

Non-Member Functions:

<<	*ostream& operator<<(ostream& stream, const os_counting_semaphore& semaphore)* Print `semaphore` to `stream`.

date

Description:

An `os_date` can represent a date between Jan 1, 4713 BC and Dec 31, 32766 AD. You can compare, subtract, print and query dates for a variety of useful information. The strings used when accepting or displaying date descriptions are loaded from your operating system when the program starts. If you need to represent a specific time on a specific day, use `os_time_and_date` instead.

Declaration:
```
#include <ospace/time/date.h>
class os_date
```

Enums:
```
enum
    {
    invalid_weekday = 0,
    sunday,
    monday,
    tuesday,
    wednesday,
    thursday,
    friday,
    saturday
    }

enum
    {
    invalid_month = 0,
    january,
    february,
    march,
    april,
    may,
    june,
    july,
    august,
    september,
    october,
    november,
    december
    };
```

```
enum
   {
   min_month = january,
   max_month = december,
   min_day = 1,
   max_day = 31,
   min_year = -4713,
   max_year = 32766
   }
```

Constructor	*os_date( )* Construct myself to be Jan 1, 1970.
Constructor	*os_date(long julian_day)* Construct myself to represent the date with Julian value `julian_day`.
Constructor	*os_date(os_month_t month, os_day_t day, os_year_t year)* Construct myself to be a date using `month` (1-12), `day` (1-31) and `year` (-4713 (BC) .. +32766 (AD)).
Constructor	*os_date(const os_which_one& which, os_weekday_t weekday,* *os_month_t month, os_year_t year)* Construct myself to be the `which`th weekday of `month` in `year`.
Constructor	*os_date(const os_date& date)* Construct myself to be a copy of `date`.
!=	*bool operator!=(const os_date& date) const* Return `true` if I'm not equal to `date`.
+	*os_date operator+(const os_time_period& period) const* Return `period` added to myself.
++	*os_date operator++(int)* Post-increment myself by one day.
++	*os_date& operator++()* Pre-increment myself by one day.
+=	*os_date& operator+=(const os_time_period& period)* Add `period` to myself and return myself.
–	*os_time_period operator–(const os_date& date) const* Return the period between myself and `date`.
–	*os_date operator–(const os_time_period& period) const* Return `period` subtracted from myself.
—	*os_date& operator—()* Pre-decrement myself by one day.

—	*os_date operator—(int)* Post-decrement myself my one day.
–=	*os_date& operator–=(const os_time_period& period)* Subtract `period` from myself and return myself.
<	*bool operator<(const os_date& date) const* Return `true` if I am earlier than `date`.
<=	*bool operator<=(const os_date& date) const* Return `true` if I am earlier than or equal to `date`.
=	*os_date& operator=(const os_date& date)* Assign myself from `date`.
==	*bool operator==(const os_date& date) const* Return `true` if I have the same day, month and year as `date`.
>	*bool operator>(const os_date& date) const* Return `true` if I am later than `date`.
>=	*bool operator>=(const os_date& date) const* Return `true` if I am later than or equal to `date`.
ad_name	*/* static */ void ad_name(const string& name)* Change the string that is used to indicate an AD date to `name`. [MT UNSAFE]
ad_name	*/* static */ const string& ad_name()* Return the string that is used to indicate an AD date. [MT UNSAFE]
bc_name	*/* static */ const string& bc_name()* Return the string that is used to indicate a BC date. [MT UNSAFE]
bc_name	*/* static */ void bc_name(const string& name)* Change the string that is used to indicate an BC date to `name`. [MT UNSAFE]
calc_calendar_date	*/* static */ void calc_calendar_date(long julianDay, os_month_t* month_p, os_day_t* day_p, os_year_t* year_p)* Decode the Julian day `julian_day` and place its corresponding date into `month_p`, `day_p` and `year_p`.
calc_julian_day	*/* static */ long calc_julian_day(os_month_t month, os_day_t day, os_year_t year)* Return the Julian day that encodes a date using `month`, `day` and `year`.
date	*void date(os_month_t month, os_day_t day, os_year_t year)* Set my date to be `month` (1-12), `day` (1-31) and `year` (-4713 (BC).. +32766 (AD)).

date	*void date(const os_which_one& which, os_weekday_t weekday,* *os_month_t month, os_year_t year)* Set myself to be the `which`th weekday of `month` in `year`.
day	*os_day_t day() const* Return my day of the month (1-31).
day_of_year	*unsigned short day_of_year() const* Return my day of the year (0-365).
days_in_month	*/* static */ os_day_t days_in_month(os_month_t month, os_year_t year)* Return the number of days in `month` of `year` (1-31).
days_in_year	*/* static */ unsigned short days_in_year(os_year_t year)* Return the number of days in `year` (1-366).
default_format	*/* static */ void default_format(const string& format)* Set my default format to `format`. [not MTSAFE]
default_format	*/* static */ string default_format()* Return my current default format. [not MTSAFE]
is_ad	*bool is_ad() const* Return `true` if I occur on or after Jan 1, 1 A.D.
is_bc	*bool is_bc() const* Return `true` if I occur on or before Dec. 31, 1 B.C.
is_day_in_month	*/* static */ bool is_day_in_month(os_month_t month, os_day_t day,* *os_year_t year)* Return `true` if `day` is a valid day in `month` of `year`.
is_julian_day	*/* static */ bool is_julian_day(long julian_day)* Return `true` if `julian_day` is a valid Julian Day number.
is_leap_year	*bool is_leap_year() const* Return `true` if I am a leap year.
is_leap_year	*/* static */ bool is_leap_year(os_year_t year)* Return `true` if `year` is a leap year.
is_month	*/* static */ bool is_month(os_month_t month)* Return `true` if `month` is valid (1-12).
is_weekday	*/* static */ bool is_weekday(os_weekday_t weekday)* Return `true` if `weekday` is valid (0-6).
is_year	*/* static */ bool is_year(os_year_t year)* Return `true` if `year` is valid (4713 BC - 32766 AD). Use a negative value to indicate years BC. 0 is not a year; 1 BC is followed by 1 AD.

julian_day	*long julian_day() const* Return my Julian Day number (39-13688961).
max_date	*/* static */ const os_date& max_date()* Return the maximum date value.
min_date	*/* static */ const os_date& min_date()* Return the minimum date value.
month	*os_month_t month() const* Return my month index (1-12).
month_abbreviation	*/* static */ const string& month_abbreviation(os_month_t month)* Return the abbreviated name of the month with index `month` (1..12).
month_index	*/* static */ os_month_t month_index(const string& month)* Returns 1-12 if `month` is a string that matches either the abbreviation or full name of a month in the current locale of which the time and date subsystem is aware. Returns `invalid_month` if the string is not recognized.
month_name	*/* static */ const string& month_name(os_month_t month)* Return the full name of the month with index `month` (1..12).
next	*os_date next(os_weekday_t weekday) const* Return the next date that is on `weekday`. If I am already on `weekday`, return the day one week after me.
previous	*os_date previous(os_weekday_t weekday) const* Return the previous date that is on `weekday`. If I am already on `weekday`, return the day one week prior to me.
print	*void print(ostream& stream) const* Print myself to `stream`.
to_string	*string to_string() const* Return myself as a formatted string using the default format.
to_string	*string to_string(const string& format) const* Return myself as a formatted string using `format`.
today	*/* static */ os_date today()* Return the current local date.
week_of_year	*os_week_t week_of_year() const* Return the index of my week in the year.
week_of_year	*os_week_t week_of_year(os_weekday_t start_of_week) const* Return my week of the year, with `start_of_week` being the first day of a week (0-53).

weekday	*os_weekday_t weekday() const* Return my weekday.
weekday_abbreviation	*/* static */ const string& weekday_abbreviation(os_weekday_t weekday)* Return the abbreviated name of the weekday with index `weekday`.
weekday_index	*/* static */ os_weekday_t weekday_index(const string& weekday)* Returns 1-7 (1=Sunday) if `weekday` is a string that matches either the abbreviation or full name of a weekday in the current locale of which the time and date subsystem is aware. Returns `invalid_weekday` if the string is not recognized.
weekday_name	*/* static */ const string& weekday_name(os_weekday_t weekday)* Return the full name of the weekday with index `weekday`.
year	*os_year_t year() const* Return my year (-4713 (BC) .. +32766 (AD))

Non-Member Functions:

+	*os_date operator+(const os_time_period& period, const os_date& date)* Return a date that is `period` time after `date`.
<<	*ostream& operator<<(ostream& stream, const os_date& date)* Print `date` to `stream`.
<<	*os_bstream& operator<<(os_bstream& stream, const os_date& date)* Write `date` to `stream`.
>>	*os_bstream& operator>>(os_bstream& stream, os_date& date)* Read `date` from `stream`.

deque

Description:

A `deque` is a sequential container that is optimized for fast indexed-based access and efficient insertion at either of its extremities.

Declaration:
```
#include <deque.h>
template< class T >
class deque
```

Constructor	*deque()* Construct myself to be empty.
Constructor	*deque(alloc_type& alloc)* Construct myself to be empty. Use `alloc` to allocate storage.
Constructor	*deque(size_type n)* Construct me to contain `n` elements set to their default value.
Constructor	*deque(alloc_type& alloc, size_type n)* Construct me to contain `n` elements set to their default value. Use `alloc` to allocate storage.
Constructor	*deque(size_type n, const T& value)* Construct me to contain `n` copies of `value`.
Constructor	*deque(alloc_type& alloc, size_type n, const T& value)* Construct me to contain `n` copies of `value`. Use `alloc` to allocate storage.
Constructor	*deque(const T* first, const T* last)* Construct me to contain copies of all of the elements in the range `[first, last)`.
Constructor	*deque(alloc_type& alloc, const T* first, const T* last)* Construct me to contain copies of all of the elements in the range `[first, last)`. Use `alloc` to allocate storage.
Constructor	*deque(const deque< T >& x)* Construct myself to be a copy of `x`.
Constructor	*deque(alloc_type& alloc, const deque< T >& x)* Construct myself to be a copy of `x`. Use `alloc` to allocate storage.
Destructor	*~deque()* Destroy myself, erasing all of my items.

=	*deque< T >& operator=(const deque< T >& x)* Replace my contents by a copy of x's.
==	*bool operator==(const deque< T >& x) const* Return `true` if I contain the same items in the same order as x.
<	*bool operator<(const deque< T >& x) const* Return `true` if I'm lexigraphically less than x.
[]	*T& operator[ ](int index)* Return a reference to my `index`th element. 　　Events: `other (os_illegal_index)`
[]	*const T& operator[ ](int index) const* Return a reference to my `index`th element. 　　Events: `other (os_illegal_index)`
back	*T& back( )* Return a reference to my last element. 　　Events: `other (os_empty_error)`
back	*const T& back( ) const* Return a reference to my last element. 　　Events: `other (os_empty_error)`
begin	*iterator begin( )* Return an iterator positioned at my first item.
begin	*const_iterator begin( ) const* Return an iterator positioned at my first item.
empty	*bool empty( ) const* Return `true` if I contain no entries.
end	*iterator end( )* Return an iterator positioned immediately after my last item.
end	*const_iterator end( ) const* Return an iterator positioned immediately after my last item.
erase[2]	*void erase( )* Erase all of my elements.
erase	*void erase(iterator pos)* Erase the element at `pos`.

---

[2] Non-standard, unique to Systems<ToolKit>

erase	*void erase(iterator first, iterator last)* Erase the elements in range `[first, last)`.
front	*T& front()* Return a reference to my first element. Events: `other (os_empty_error)`
front	*const T& front() const* Return a reference to my first element. Events: `other (os_empty_error)`
insert	*iterator insert(iterator pos, const T& value)* Insert `value` at `pos` and return an iterator pointing to the new element's position.
insert	*void insert(iterator pos, size_type n, const T& value)* Insert `n` copies of `value` at `pos`.
insert	*void insert(iterator pos, const T* first, const T* last)* Insert copies of the elements in the range `[first, last)` at `pos`.
max_size	*size_type max_size() const* Return the maximum number of entries that I can contain.
push_back	*void push_back(const T& value)* Add `value` at my end.
push_front	*void push_front(const T& value)* Insert a copy of `value` in front of my first element.
pop_back	*void pop_back()* Erase my last element. Events: `other (os_empty_error)`
pop_front	*void pop_front()* Erase my first element. Events: `other (os_empty_error)`
rbegin	*reverse_iterator rbegin()* Return a reverse iterator positioned at my last item.
rbegin	*const_reverse_iterator rbegin() const* Return a reverse iterator positioned at my last item.
rend	*reverse_iterator rend()* Return a reverse_iterator positioned immediately before my first item.
rend	*const_reverse_iterator rend() const* Return a reverse_iterator positioned immediately before my first item.

size   *size_type size( ) const*
                   Return the number of entries that I contain.

swap   *void swap(deque< T >& x)*
                   Swap my contents with x's.

directory

Description:

An os_directory represents a file system directory. The os_directory class allows you to read an existing directory or create a new directory. To get a vector of all the filenames in a directory, use filenames().

Declaration:

```
#include <ospace/file/dir.h>
class os_directory
```

Options:

Legal open control: O_OPEN, O_CREAT, O_EXCL
Default open control: O_OPEN
Default mode: 0770 (read, write and search by user and group)

Constructor	*os_directory(const string& dirpath, os_open_t open_control, os_mode_t mode)* Construct myself to reference the directory with name dirpath and mode mode (default 0770) using the open flags open (default O_OPEN). See open() for more information, including error conditions.
Constructor	*os_directory()* Construct myself as closed.
Destructor	*~os_directory()* Destroy myself. If I'm open, close myself.
<	*bool operator<(const os_directory& directory) const* Return true if my handle is less than directory's. Note that this gives an ordering to open os_directory objects that is not based on their names.
==	*bool operator==(const os_directory& directory) const* Return true if my handle is the same as directory's.

chown_restricted   */* static */ bool chown_restricted(const string& dirpath)*
Return `true` if the system is configured to disallow the owners of any
non-directory files in `dirpath` to be changed by anyone except a
superuser, or `false` if the current process can change the owner of entries
of `dirpath` if it has file and directory access permissions. This calls
`limit` with an argument of `_PC_CHOWN_RESTRICTED`. See `limit()` for
more information.

> Events: `syscall`
> On Resumption: Returns `false`.

close   *void close()*
Close myself.

> Events: `syscall`

contains   *bool contains(const string& filename) const*
Return `true` if I contain `filename`. For repeated existence tests, you
might consider obtaining a list once with `filenames()` rather than
repeated use of this function, for efficiency.

> Events: `syscall`, `memory`, `other`
> On Resumption: The return value is unspecified.

create   */* static */ void create(const string& dirpath, os_mode_t mode)*
Create a new directory called `dirpath` with mode `mode` (default `0770`).

> Events: `syscall`, `memory`
> On Resumption: The directory is not created.

descriptor   *os_desc_t descriptor() const*
Return my UNIX primitive file descriptor, or `OS_UNDEFINED` if I'm not
open. See also `descriptor()`.

exists   */* static */ bool exists(const string& dirpath)*
Return `true` if `dirpath` is accessible by the current process. This is
`true` if the directories mentioned in `dirpath` exist and can be searched
(using the real user and group ID) and the rightmost name (the final
directory name or the file name) exists.'
This function is exactly equivalent to `os_file_system::exists()`.
Note that this function is not specific for directories, but will return `true`
if `dirpath` is a regular file, too.

> Events: `memory`
> On Resumption: Returns `false`.

filename_limit
/* static */ long filename_limit(const string& dirpath)
Return the maximum number of characters allowed in the base name if a file if placed in the directory `dirpath`. This calls `limit` with an argument of `_PC_NAME_MAX`. See `limit()` for more information, including error values.

filenames
vector< string > filenames() const
Return a vector of my filenames.

> Events: `syscall`, `memory`, `other`
> On Resumption: returns the list of filenames which had been read and processed up to the point of the error. The last entry may be blank.

is_open
bool is_open() const
Return `true` if I'm open. Contrast with `check_handle()`. This function simply tests for a non-zero handle. It does not actually validate that the handle is connected to a directory file.

no_truncate
/* static */ bool no_truncate(const string& dirpath)
Return `true` if the system is configured to error on filenames in `dirpath` longer that the maximum filename length, or `false` if the system is configured to truncate names in `dirpath` when they are too long. This calls `limit` with an argument of `_PC_NO_TRUNC`. See `limit()` for more information.

> Events: `syscall`
> On Resumption: Returns `false`.

open
void open(const string& dirpath, os_open_t control, os_mode_t mode)
Open a directory called `dirpath` with mode `mode` (default `0770`) using the open flags `control` (default `O_OPEN`).

> Events: `syscall`, `memory`
> On Resumption: Sets myself to a closed state.

os_desc_t
operator os_desc_t() const
This conversion operator is a synonym for `descriptor()`.

pathname_limit
/* static */ long pathname_limit(const string& dirpath)
Return the maximum number of characters allowed in a complete path name (including the base filename) interpreted as a relative path from the directory `dirpath`. To determine the maximum absolute path name length, call with `dirpath` of `"/"`. This calls `limit` with an argument of `_PC_PATH_MAX`. See `limit()` for more information, including error values.

pipe_buffer_limit	*/* static */ long pipe_buffer_limit(const string& dirpath)* Return the maximum number of bytes that may be atomically written to a named pipe placed in the directory `dirpath`. This calls `limit` with an argument of `_PC_PIPE_BUF`. See `limit()` for more information, including error values.
print	*void print(ostream& stream) const* Print my descriptor to `stream`. If I'm not open, print UNOPENED. See also `descriptor()`.
status	*os_io_status status() const* Return an `os_io_status` object constructed on my open file descriptor. See that class's constructor documentation for error information.

Non-Member Functions:

<<	*ostream& operator<<(ostream& stream, const os_directory& dir)* Print `dir` to `stream`.

divides

Description:

divides is a binary function object that returns the result of dividing its two operands.

Declaration:
```
#include <function.h>
template< class T >
struct divides : binary_function< T, T, T >
```

()   *T operator()(const T& x, const T& y) const*
                                Return x / y.

Example <ospace/stl/examples/divides.cpp>

```
#include <stl.h>
#include <iostream.h>

int input [3] = { 2, 3, 4 };

int main ()
{
  int result = accumulate (input, input + 4, 48, divides<int> ());
  cout << "result = " << result << endl;
  return 0;
}
```

result = 2

dropper

Description:

An `os_dropper` prevents an event from propagating any further down the handler stack by silently deleting it. For example, if you declared an `os_dropper` inside a destructor, it would silently delete all events that occurred during the object's destruction.

Declaration:
```
#include <ospace/event/dropper.h>
class os_dropper : public os_handler
```

Constructor	*os_dropper()* Construct myself to drop all events with category `os_error` and domain `os_objectspace`.
Constructor	*os_dropper(os_filter* filter)* Construct myself to drop all events that pass through `filter`. It is the user's responsibility to ensure `filter` stays in scope at least as long as I do. See `os_event_filter` for information about filtering.
Destructor	*/* virtual */ ~os_dropper()* Destructor.
print	*/* virtual */ void print(ostream& stream) const* Print myself to `stream`.

Non-Member Functions:

<<	*ostream& operator<<(ostream& stream, const os_dropper& dropper)* Print `dropper` to `stream`.

equal_to

Description:

equal_to is a binary function object that returns true if its operands match using ==.

Declaration:
```
#include <function.h>
template< class T >
struct equal_to : binary_function< T, T, bool >
```

()   *bool operator()(const T& x, const T& y) const*
                                 Return x == y.

Example <ospace/stl/examples/equalto.cpp>
```
#include <stl.h>
#include <iostream.h>

int input1 [4] = { 1, 7, 2, 2 };
int input2 [4] = { 1, 6, 2, 3 };

int main ()
{
  int output [4];
  transform (input1, input1 + 4, input2, output, equal_to<int> ());
  for (int i = 0; i < 4; i++)
    cout << output[i] << endl;
  return 0;
}

1
0
1
0
```

event

Description:

All Systems<ToolKit> components use the same consistent approach to error handling. When an event that requires special handling occurs, an `os_event` object is created with attributes defining the event. Each instance of `os_event` contains the following attributes:

– **Domain**—an `int` encoding the vendor of the component generating the event. The domain code of all events generated by ObjectSpace C++ toolkits is `os_objectspace`.

– **Category**—a `long` encoding the category of the event. Currently, the only two categories are `os_error`, which denotes an error event, and `os_panic`, which denotes a panic event.

Error events are recoverable. There are two ways to handle error events:

– If your compiler supports C++ exception handling and you enable this during library configuration, Systems<ToolKit> throws all instances of error events using the C++ keyword `throw`.

– If your compiler does not support C++ exception handling, or you choose not to enable it during library configuration, you can use the portable event handling mechanism.

Panic events are unrecoverable. A panic event is sent to a predefined global panic handler and then your program is terminated.

– **Code**—a `long` encoding the specific type of event within its category. For example, the code of an `os_error` denotes the specific kind of error. See the Appendix in the *Systems<ToolKit> Reference Manual* for a list of event codes in the `os_objectspace` domain.

– **Note**—A string describing the event.

See the "Error Handling" section of the Systems<ToolKit> User's Manual for information about how to handle events.

Declaration:
```
#include <ospace/event/event.h>
class os_event
```

Constructor	*os_event()* Constructor.
Constructor	*os_event(long category, long code, const char* note, int domain)* Construct myself from the attributes `category`, `code`, `note` and `domain`.
Constructor	*os_event(const os_event& event)* Construct myself to be a copy of `event`.

event

Destructor	*~os_event()* Destructor.
=	*os_event& operator=(const os_event& event)* Assign me from `event`.
category	*long category() const* Return my category.
code	*long code() const* Return my code.
describe	*/* virtual */ void describe(ostream& stream) const* Describe myself to the `stream`.
domain	*int domain() const* Return my domain.
note	*const char* note() const* Return my note.
print	*/* virtual */ void print(ostream& stream) const* Print myself to `stream`.

Non-Member Functions:

<<	*ostream& operator<<(ostream& stream, const os_event& event)* Print `event` to `stream`.
<<	*os_bstream& operator<<(os_bstream& stream, const os_event& event)* Write `event` to `stream`.
>>	*os_bstream& operator>>(os_bstream& stream, os_event& event)* Read `event` from `stream`.

event_filter

Description:
By default, a handler will process any error event that passes into it. You may use an event filter to restrict the kinds of error events that a handler will process.

To associate an `os_event_filter` with a handler, pass its address to the handler's constructor. The handler will then only process events that pass through the filter. Because the handler retains a pointer to the filter, the filter should not go out of scope before the handler. More than one handler can share the same filter.

Declaration:
```
#include <ospace/event/evntfltr.h>
class os_event_filter : public filter
```

Constructor	*os_event_filter()* Construct myself to pass all `os_objectspace` events with category `os_error`.
Constructor	*os_event_filter(long code, long category, long domain)* Construct myself to pass all events with error code equal to `code`, category equal to `category` (default `os_error`) and domain equal to `domain` (default `os_objectspace`).
Constructor	*os_event_filter(long lo_code, long hi_code, long lo_category, long hi_category, long domain)* Construct myself to pass all events with an error code in the range [`lo_code`, `hi_code`], category in the range [`lo_category`, `hi_category`] and domain equal to `domain`.
Constructor	*os_event_filter(const os_event_filter& filter)* Construct myself to be a copy of `filter`.
=	*os_event_filter& operator=(const os_event_filter& filter)* Assign myself from `filter`.

event_semaphore

Description:

To coordinate the actions of several threads based on a single event, use an event semaphore. For example, in a stockbroking system, you might want several different thread-controlled activities to occur when a stock price changes. An event semaphore can either be in an unposted state or a posted state. In an unposted state, all threads that perform a wait will block. In a posted state, no threads that perform a wait will block. If an event semaphore is pulsed when in an unposted state, all waiting semaphores will immediately unblock. If an event semaphore is moved to a posted state from an unposted state, all waiting semaphores will immediately unblock.

Declaration:
```
#include <ospace/sync/eventsem.h>
class os_event_semaphore
```

Constructor	*os_event_semaphore(bool posted)* Construct myself. `posted` (default `false`) indicates whether I am initially created in the posted or unposted state. Events: `syscall`
Destructor	*~os_event_semaphore()* Destroy myself, releasing any associated system resources. Events: `syscall`
post	*void post()* Set my state to posted. All threads waiting on me will immediately unblock, and subsequent threads that wait on me will not block. This is the antonym of `reset()`.
posted	*bool posted()* Returns `true` if I'm posted. Events: `syscall`
print	*void print(ostream& stream) const* Print myself to `stream`.
pulse	*void pulse()* Set myself to a posted state (thus allowing all blocked threads to awaken), then immediately reset myself.

reset

void reset( )

Reset my state. Subsequent threads waiting on me will block until I become posted again.

Events: `syscall`

wait

void wait( )

Wait until I become posted. If I'm already in a posted state, return immediately.

Events: `syscall`

file

Description:

An `os_file` represents a UNIX file. There are two ways to construct an `os_file`. One constructor accepts a filename and either creates a new file or opens an existing one. The other constructor offers a legacy interface and accepts an open file descriptor. In addition to the standard I/O facilities, `os_file` offers random access, record locking and truncation. By default, a file is automatically closed upon destruction.

The locking and seeking interfaces use the whence parameter from UNIX. This parameter indicates where the offset should be applied. Valid values are:

- `SEEK_SET`: apply offset relative to the start of the file.

- `SEEK_CUR`: apply offset relative to the current position in the file.

- `SEEK_END`: apply offset relative to the end of the file.

Conversions allow `os_file` and `os_desc_t` (UNIX descriptor) to be used interchangeably.

Declaration:
```
#include <ospace/file/file.h>
class os_file
```

Options:

Legal open control:	`O_OPEN, O_CREAT, O_EXCL, O_TRUNC`
Default open control:	`O_OPEN`
Legal I/O control:	`O_APPEND, O_CLOSE_ON_EXEC, O_RDONLY, O_WRONLY, O_RDWR`
Default I/O control:	`O_RDONLY`
Default mode:	`0660` (read & write by user and group)

Constructor
os_file(os_desc_t descriptor)
Construct myself to reference the file with descriptor `descriptor` (default `OS_UNDEFINED`).

Constructor
os_file(const string& name, os_open_t open_control,
os_ioctl_t io_control, os_mode_t mode)
Construct myself to reference a file with name `name` and mode `mode` (default `0660`), using open flags `open` (default `O_OPEN`) and control flags `control` (default `O_RDONLY`).

Events: `syscall`
On Resumption: My descriptor will be `OS_UNDEFINED`.

Destructor
~os_file()
Destroy myself, closing my descriptor if necessary.

<	*bool operator<(const os_file& file) const* Return `true` if my descriptor is less than `file`'s.
==	*bool operator==(const os_file& file) const* Return `true` if my descriptor is the same as `file`'s.

add_lock	*bool add_lock(const os_file_lock& lock, bool block)*
	Add `lock` to me. If `block` (default `true`) is `false`, return immediately if the lock cannot be made, else block until the lock can occur or a signal is received. Return `true` if the lock is obtained.
	    Events: `syscall`
	    On Resumption: Returns `false`.

auto_close	*bool auto_close() const* Return `true` if I close my descriptor on destruction.
auto_close	*void auto_close(bool flag)* If `flag` is `true`, close my descriptor on destruction.
clear	*void clear()* Reset my state to good.

close	*void close()*
	Close my descriptor and then set it to `OS_UNDEFINED`. If it's already closed, do nothing.
	    Events: `syscall`
	    On Resumption: My descriptor may be unchanged.

conflicting_lock	*bool conflicting_lock(const os_file_lock& lock, os_file_lock& conflict)*
	Check for locks that would block `lock`. If there is a conflicting lock, return `true` and set `conflict` to the conflicting lock, otherwise return `false`.
	    Events: `syscall`
	    On Resumption: Returns `false`.

descriptor	*void descriptor(os_desc_t descriptor)* Set my descriptor to `descriptor`.
descriptor	*os_desc_t descriptor() const* Return my descriptor.
eof	*bool eof() const* Return `true` if I'm at the end of my input.
event_on_eof	*bool event_on_eof() const* Return `true` if I will generate an event on eof.
event_on_eof	*void event_on_eof(bool flag)* If flag is `true`, I will generate an event on eof.

good	*bool good() const* Return `true` if I'm in a good state and not at eof.

io_control	*void io_control(os_ioctl_t control)*
	Set my I/O control setting to `control`.
	
	    Events: `syscall`
	    On Resumption: The I/O control may not have been updated.

io_control	*os_ioctl_t io_control() const*
	Return my I/O control setting.
	
	    Events: `syscall`
	    On Resumption: Returns `OS_UNDEFINED`.

is_open	*bool is_open() const* Return `true` if I'm open.
ok	*bool ok() const* Return `true` if I'm not broken or failed.

open	*void open(const string& path, os_open_t open, os_ioctl_t control, os_mode_t mode)*
	Open myself to reference a file with name `path` and mode `mode` (default `0660`), using open flags `open` (default `O_OPEN`) and control flags `control` (default `O_RDONLY`).
	
	    Events: `syscall`
	    On Resumption: My descriptor will remain unchanged.

os_adapter	*operator os_adapter() const*
	Return an `os_adapter` to myself.
	
	    Events: `syscall`
	    On Resumption: The attachment count of the adapter may be invalid.

os_desc_t	*operator os_desc_t() const* Return my descriptor.
print	*void print(ostream& stream) const* Print myself to `stream`.

read	*int read(void* buffer, int bytes)*
	Read up to `bytes` bytes into `buffer`. Return the number of bytes actually read, or `-1` on error.
	
	    Events: `syscall`
	    On Resumption: Returns `-1`.

remove_all_locks	*void remove_all_locks()*
	Remove all of my locks.
	
	    Events: `syscall`
	    On Resumption: File locks may exist.

remove_lock	*void remove_lock(const os_file_lock& lock)* Remove all locks for the region specified by `lock`. Events: `syscall` On Resumption: The `lock` may not have been removed.
remove_lock	*void remove_lock(os_off_t length, os_off_t offset, short whence)* Remove all locks in the region of `length` (default 0) bytes at offset `offset` (default 0) bytes from `whence` (default `SEEK_SET`). A length of zero indicates that the region extends to the end of the file. Events: `syscall` On Resumption: File locks on the region may exist.
resize_to	*void resize_to(os_off_t length)* Resize my length to `length` bytes. If I'm shorter than `length`, the resulting gap will set to zeros. For this function to work, I must be open. Events: `syscall` On Resumption: The file length will remain unchanged.
rewind	*void rewind()* Set my file pointer to my beginning. Events: `syscall` On Resumption: The file pointer may be unchanged.
seek	*void seek(os_off_t offset, short whence)* Seek to `offset` bytes from `whence`. If successful, clear my state. Events: `syscall` On Resumption: My position will remain unchanged.
status	*os_io_status status() const* Return my I/O status. Events: `syscall` On Resumption: Returned `os_io_status` will be invalid.
sync	*void sync()* Flush all of my modified buffers to permanent storage. When this function returns, all of the data will have been written. Events: `syscall` On Resumption: Modified buffers may not have been committed.
sync_all	*/* static */ void sync_all()* Schedule all "dirty" data in memory to be written to disk. This includes modified super blocks, modified inodes and delayed block I/O. The data will probably be written after this function returns.

file

tell   *os_off_t tell() const*
                            Return my file pointer as an offset in bytes from my first byte, or `-1` on
                            error.

                                    Events: `syscall`
                                    On Resumption: Returns `-1`.

write   *int write(const void* buffer, int bytes)*
                            Write `bytes` bytes from `buffer`. Return the number of bytes actually
                            written, or `-1` on error.

                                    Events: `syscall`
                                    On Resumption: Returns `-1`.

Non-Member Functions:

<<   *ostream& operator<<(ostream& stream, const os_file& file)*
                            Print a description of `file` to `stream`.

file_lock

Description:

An `os_file_lock` is used to represent a region of bytes in a file for locking purposes.

A process can request a read lock or a write lock for a region of a file. If granted, a read lock prevents other processes from obtaining a write lock for that region; a write lock prevents other processes from obtaining a read or a write lock for that region. If a process requests a lock that cannot be granted, the process blocks by default until the lock becomes available.

To place a lock or check for other existing locks, use the `os_file` class. For a definition of valid whence values, see the catalog entry for `os_file`.

Conversions allow `os_file_lock` and `os_flock_t` to be used interchangeably.

Declaration:
```
#include <ospace/file/filelock.h>
class os_file_lock
```

Typedefs:
```
typedef struct flock os_flock_t
```

Enums:
```
enum
    {
    os_read_lock = F_RDLCK,
    os_write_lock = F_WRLCK,
    os_no_lock = F_UNLCK
    };
```

Constructor	*os_file_lock(short type, os_off_t length, os_off_t offset, short whence)* Construct myself to be a lock of `length` (default 0) bytes of type `type` (default `os_read_lock`), starting at `offset` (default 0) bytes relative to `whence` (default `SEEK_SET`). If `length` is 0, extend the region to the current end of file.
Constructor	*os_file_lock(const os_flock_t& lock)* Construct me from the `os_flock_t` structure `lock`.
Constructor	*os_file_lock(const os_file_lock& lock)* Construct myself to be a copy of `lock`.
<	*bool operator<(const os_file_lock& lock) const* Return `true` if I'm considered to be "less" than `lock`, based on my attributes.

=   *os_file_lock& operator=(const os_file_lock& lock)*
                          Assign myself from `lock`.

==   *bool operator==(const os_file_lock& lock) const*
                          Return `true` if my attributes are the same as `lock`'s.

length   *os_off_t length() const*
                          Return the length of the locked region. The value 0 indicates the region always continues up to the end of the file.

offset   *os_off_t offset() const*
                          Return the start position of the locked region. The value is relative to the whence returned by `whence()`. For `SEEK_SET` and `SEEK_END`, the start is positive. For `SEEK_CUR`, the start is either positive or negative.

os_flock_t   *operator os_flock_t() const*
                          Return myself as an `os_flock_t` structure.

print   *void print(ostream& stream) const*
                          Print my lock type (read/write/no lock) to `stream`.

process   *os_pid_t process() const*
                          Return the `pid` of the process that currently has the lock.

read_lock   *void read_lock()*
                          Set my lock type to be a read lock.

set_lock   *void set_lock(short type, os_off_t length, os_off_t offset, short whence)*
                          Set my type to `type` (default `os_read_lock`) and my length to `length` (default 0) bytes, starting at `offset` (default 0) bytes relative to `whence` (default `SEEK_SET`). If `length` is 0, extend the region up to the current end of file.

type   *void type(short type)*
                          Set the lock type to `type`.

type   *short type() const*
                          Return the lock type: `os_read_lock`, `os_write_lock` or `os_no_lock`.

whence   *short whence() const*
                          Return my whence value: `SEEK_SET`, `SEEK_CUR`, or `SEEK_END`. This indicates the base for the relative start location.

write_lock   *void write_lock()*
                          Set my lock type to be a write lock.

Non-Member Functions:

<<   *ostream& operator<<(ostream& stream, const os_file_lock& lock)*
       Print `lock` to `stream`.

<<   *os_bstream& operator<<(os_bstream& stream, const os_file_lock& lock)*
       Write `lock` to `stream`.

>>   *os_bstream& operator>>(os_bstream& stream, os_file_lock& lock)*
       Read `lock` from `stream`.

file_system

Description:

The `os_file_system` class is comprised wholly of static functions that allow you to access and manipulate information associated with a particular path in a file system.

Declaration:
```
#include <ospace/file/filesys.h>
class os_file_system
```

executable   */* static */ bool executable(const string& path)*
Tests whether `path` has execute permission based on the real (as opposed to the effective) user and group ID.

exists   */* static */ bool exists(const string& path)*
Return `true` if `path` is accessible by the current process. This is `true` if the directories mentioned in `path` exist and can be searched (using the real user and group ID) and the rightmost name (the final directory name or the file name) exists.

limit   */* static */ long limit(const string& path, int limit)*
Return the limit of type `limit` associated with `path`. This is a wrapper around the `pathconf` system call—see your UNIX documentation for the various values for `limit`.

> Events: `syscall`
> On Resumption: Returns `OS_UNDEFINED`.

link   */* static */ void link(const string& to, const string& from)*
Create a hard link (duplicate entry to the same `inode`) from `from` to `to`.

> Events: `syscall`

readable   */* static */ bool readable(const string& path)*
Return `true` if the permissions for `path` indicate readability based on the real (as opposed to the effective) user ID and group.

remove   */* static */ void remove(const string& path)*
Remove `path` from the file system. This operates on regular files, directories and some special files. For symbolic links, it removes the link itself, not the file the link refers to.

This function causes the named file (or directory) to be unlinked from the file system. If the file is in use, it may continue to be used as it is not actually deleted until closed.

> Events: `syscall`

remove_if_exists	*/* static */ void remove_if_exists(const string& path)* If `path` exists, remove it. This checks for the existence of `path` and then conditionally calls `remove`. Unlike `remove()`, this function will not generate errors if `path` does not exist; however, events for other conditions, such as permissions, may still occur. Events: `syscall`
rename	*/* static */ void rename(const string& from, const string& to)* Rename the path from `from` to `to`. Whether or not it allows the destination to be on a different file system is implementation dependent. Note carefully the order of the parameters. This is consistent with ordering of the UNIX `rename()` primitive, though backwards from `link()` and `symbolic_link()` and typical C++ library usage of putting the destination first. Events: `syscall`
resize	*/* static */ void resize(const string& path, os_off_t length)* Resize `path` to `length` bytes long. If the length of the file is less than `length` bytes, the call is an attempt to make the file larger. It is implementation dependent whether or not this is allowed. When allowed, the gap in the resulting file will read as all zeros. This function is only valid for paths to regular files. Events: `syscall`
status	*/* static */ os_io_status status(const string& path)* Return the status associated with `path`. See class `os_io_status` for more information. When `path` refers to a symbolic link, return information on the file referenced by the link. Events: `syscall` On Resumption: Returns an `UNDEFINED` status object.
symbolic_link	*/* static */ string symbolic_link(const string& path)* Return the path associated with the symbolic link named by `path`. A system error is generated if path is not the name of a symbolic link or is not accessible. This function has a hard-coded limit as to the length of the return value. If the limit is insufficient, a system error is generated. To alter the limit, change the value of `max_path_length` in `<ospace/file/filesys.h>` and recompile the library. Events: `syscall` On Resumption: Returns an empty string.

symbolic_link   */* static */ void symbolic_link(const string& to, const string& from)*
Create a symbolic link from `from` to `to`.

> Events: `syscall`

symbolic_link_status   */* static */ os_io_status symbolic_link_status(const string& path)*
This is the same as `status()`, except that when `path` refers to a symbolic link, the status is returned for the link itself.

> Events: `syscall`
> On Resumption: See the constructor for class `os_io_status`.

writeable   */* static */ bool writeable(const string& path)*
Return `true` if the user has permissions to write to `path`, based on the real (as opposed to the effective) user ID and group.

filter

Description:
> `os_filter` is the abstract base class of all filters. Derived filter classes override the pure protected virtual function `accepts()` to define how they pass events. Filters are used in conjunction with handlers. They allow the handlers to be choosy about what kind of events they handle by only passing them events that satisfy a certain criteria.

Declaration:
```
#include <ospace/event/filter.h>
class os_filter
```

Constructor	*os_filter()* Constructor.
Constructor	*os_filter(const os_filter& filter)* Construct myself to be a copy of `filter`.
Destructor	*/* virtual */ ~os_filter()* Destructor.
=	*os_filter& operator=(const os_filter& filter)* Assign myself from `filter`.
passes	*bool passes(const os_event* event)* Return `true` if I pass `event`.

front_insert_iterator, front_inserter

Description:

A `front_insert_iterator` is an iterator that always inserts an item at the front of its associated container.

Declaration:
```
#include <iterator.h>
template< Container >
class front_insert_iterator : public output_iterator
```

Adapter:
```
template< class Container >
front_insert_iterator< Container >
front_inserter( Container& container )
```

Constructor	*front_insert_iterator(Container& container)* Construct myself to be associated with `container`.
=	*front_insert_iterator< Container >& operator=(const value_type value)* Insert a copy of `value` at the front of my associated container.
*	*front_insert_iterator< Container >& operator *()* Return a reference to myself.
++	*front_insert_iterator< Container >& operator++()* Return a reference to myself.
++	*front_insert_iterator< Container > operator++(int)* Return a copy of myself.

Example <ospace/stl/examples/finsert1.cpp>

```
#include <stl.h>
#include <iostream.h>

char* array [] = { "laurie", "jennifer", "leisa" };

int main ()
{
  deque<char*> names; // Can't use a vector.
  copy (array, array + 3,
    front_insert_iterator<deque <char*> > (names));
  deque<char*>::iterator i;
  for (i = names.begin (); i != names.end (); i++)
    cout << *i << endl;
  return 0;
}
```

leisa
jennifer
laurie

Example <ospace/stl/examples/finsert2.cpp>

```
#include <stl.h>
#include <iostream.h>

char* array [] = { "laurie", "jennifer", "leisa" };

int main ()
{
  deque<char*> names;
  copy (array, array + 3, front_inserter (names));
  deque<char*>::iterator i;
  for (i = names.begin (); i != names.end (); i++)
    cout << *i << endl;
  return 0;
}
```

leisa
jennifer
laurie

greater

Description:

greater is a binary function object that returns true if its first operand is greater than its second operand.

Declaration:
```
#include <function.h>
template< class T >
struct greater : binary_function< T, T, bool >
```

()   *bool operator()(const T& x, const T& y) const*
                             Return x > y.

Example <ospace/stl/examples/greater.cpp>

```
#include <stl.h>
#include <iostream.h>

int array [4] = { 3, 1, 4, 2 };

int main ()
{
  sort (array, array + 4, greater<int> ());
  for (int i = 0; i < 4; i++)
    cout << array[i] << endl;
  return 0;
}

4
3
2
1
```

greater_equal

Description:

greater_equal is a binary function object that returns true if its first operand is greater than or equal to its second operand.

Declaration:
```
#include <function.h>
template< class T >
struct greater_equal : binary_function< T, T, bool >
```

()   *bool operator()(const T& x, const T& y) const*
                Return x >= y.

Example <ospace/stl/examples/greateq.cpp>

```
#include <stl.h>
#include <iostream.h>

int array [4] = { 3, 1, 4, 2 };

int main ()
{
  sort (array, array + 4, greater_equal<int> ());
  for (int i = 0; i < 4; i++)
    cout << array[i] << endl;
  return 0;
}

4
3
2
1
```

group

Description:

An os_group represents a group. As well as having an owner (user), most entities such as processes and files have an associated group. An os_group object may be constructed from either a numeric group id or from a symbolic group name. Once constructed, an os_group allows easy access to information about a group, such as its name and associated users. Conversions allows os_groups and os_gid_ts to be used interchangeably.

Declaration:
```
#include <ospace/security/group.h>
class os_group
```

Constructor	*os_group(os_gid_t gid)* Construct myself with group id gid (default OS_UNDEFINED). Events: other On Resumption: Set my group id to OS_UNDEFINED.
Constructor	*os_group(const os_group& group)* Construct myself to be a copy of group.
Constructor	*os_group(const struct group& group)* Construct myself from group.
Constructor	*os_group(const string& name)* Construct myself to represent the group with name name. Events: other On Resumption: Set my group id to OS_UNDEFINED.
<	*bool operator<(const os_group& group) const* Return true if my group id is less than group's.
=	*os_group& operator=(const os_group& group)* Assign myself from group.
=	*os_group& operator=(os_gid_t gid)* Assign myself from gid.
==	*bool operator==(const os_group& group) const* Return true if my group id is the same as group's.
defined	*bool defined() const* Return true if my group id is not OS_UNDEFINED.
gid	*os_gid_t gid() const* Return my group id.

groups	*/* static */ vector< os_gid_t > groups()* Return a vector of all group ids.
name	*string name() const* Return my name.
os_gid_t	*operator os_gid_t() const* Return my group id.
password	*string password() const* Return my encrypted password.
print	*void print(ostream& stream) const* Print my group name and id to `stream`.
users	*vector< os_uid_t > users() const* Return a vector of all my user's ids.

Non-Member Functions:

<<	*ostream& operator<<(ostream& stream, const os_group& group)* Print `group` to `stream`.
<<	*os_bstream& operator<<(os_bstream& stream, const os_group& group)* Write `group` to `stream`.
>>	*os_bstream& operator>>(os_bstream& stream, os_group& group)* Read `group` from `stream`.

handler

Description:

os_handler is the abstract base class of all event handlers.

The handler system manages a single stack of handlers, which is initially empty.[3] When a handler is constructed, it is pushed onto this stack; when it is destroyed, it is popped from the stack.

When an error event is generated and encoded into an os_event object, it is propagated down through the stack of handlers, allowing each handler to process the error event if it wishes. The processing of the error event ends when either one of the following occurs:

- The handlers prevent the error event from propagating further.
- The error event falls off the bottom of the stack. If this occurs, the error event is passed to the global error event handler (described shortly).

If there are no handlers on the stack to handle the error event, it is passed directly to the global error event handler.

By default, the global error event handler displays a diagnostic message to the standard error channel and then terminates the program. If you wish, you may replace the default global error event handler with your own. To do this, call os_set_error_handler() with a pointer to your own error event handler. Your error event handler should take a pointer to an os_event object and return void. See the *Systems<ToolKit> User's Manual* for more details.

When the global error event handler is called by the portable event handling system, the os_event object is on the heap. If your error event handler returns, it should delete the os_event object first to prevent a memory leak.

Declaration:

```
#include <ospace/event/handler.h>
class os_handler
```

Destructor	/* virtual */ ~os_handler() Destroy myself.
filter	void filter(os_filter* filter) Set my current filter to filter.
filter	os_filter* filter() const Return my filter.

---

[3] In a multi-threaded environment, there is one stack of handlers for each thread.

print   /* virtual */ void print(ostream& stream) const
Print myself to stream.

host

Description:

A host is a computer that is connected to zero or more networks. Every host on the internet has a name, a set of aliases and a set of IP addresses (since a single host may be connected to more than one network). Information about hosts is usually stored in `/etc/hosts`.

An `os_host` is an object that represents a single host computer. It may be constructed from the TCP hostname or an IP address.

Declaration:
```
#include <ospace/socket/host.h>
class os_host
```

Constructor	*os_host()* Construct myself to have an empty name.
Constructor	*os_host(const hostent& host)* Construct myself from the `hostent` structure `host`.
Constructor	*os_host(const os_host& host)* Construct myself to be a copy of `host`.
Constructor	*os_host(const string& name)* Construct myself to be the host with name name. Events: `other` On Resumption: I will be in an unusable state.
Constructor	*os_host(const os_ip_address& address)* Construct myself to be the host with IP address `address`. Events: `other` On Resumption: I will be in an unusable state.
<	*bool operator<(const os_host& host) const* Return `true` if my name is less than `host`'s.
=	*os_host& operator=(const os_host& host)* Assign myself from `host`.
==	*bool operator==(const os_host& host) const* Return `true` if my name is the same as `host`'s.
aliases	*const vector< string >& aliases() const* Return a vector of my aliases.

defined   *bool defined() const*
Return `true` if my name is not empty.

hosts   */* static */ vector< os_host* > hosts()*
Return a vector of pointers to objects on the heap representing all of the hosts in the host database. It is the caller's responsibility to properly delete the objects in the vector.

ip_addresses   *const vector< os_ip_address >& ip_addresses() const*
Return a vector of my IP addresses.

my_host   */* static */ const os_host& my_host()*
Return a reference to an `os_host` that represents the local host.

> Events: `other`
> On Resumption: Return value for this and subsequent calls may be invalid.

name   *string name() const*
Return my name.

print   *void print(ostream& stream) const*
Print myself to `stream`.

Non-Member Functions:

<<   *ostream& operator<<(ostream& stream, const os_host& host)*
Print `host` to `stream`.

<<   *os_bstream& operator<<(os_bstream& stream, const os_host& host)*
Write `host` to `stream`.

>>   *os_bstream& operator>>(os_bstream& stream, os_host& host)*
Read `host` from `stream`.

insert_iterator, inserter

Description:

    An `insert_iterator` is an iterator that inserts items using an auxiliary iterator.

Declaration:

```
#include <iterator.h>
template< Container >
class insert_iterator : public output_iterator
```

Adapter:

```
template< class Container, class Iterator >
insert_iterator< Container >
inserter( Container& c, Iterator iter )
```

Constructor	*insert_iterator(Container& container, Container::iterator iter) :*
=	*insert_iterator<Container>& operator=(const value_type& value)* Insert a copy of `value` using the iterator `iter` that I was constructed with.
*	*insert_iterator<Container>& operator *()* Return a reference to myself.
++	*insert_iterator<Container>& operator ++()* Return a reference to myself.
++	*insert_iterator<Container> operator++(int)* Return a copy of myself.

Example <ospace/stl/examples/insert1.cpp>

```
#include <stl.h>
#include <iostream.h>

char* array1 [] = { "laurie", "jennifer", "leisa" };
char* array2 [] = { "amanda", "saskia", "carrie" };

int main ()
{
  deque<char*> names (array1, array1 + 3);
  deque<char*>::iterator i = names.begin () + 2;
  copy (array2, array2 + 3,
    insert_iterator<deque <char*> > (names, i));
  deque<char*>::iterator j;
  for (j = names.begin (); j != names.end (); j++)
  cout << *j << endl;
  return 0;
}
```

laurie
jennifer
amanda
saskia
carrie
leisa

Example <ospace/stl/examples/insert2.cpp>

```
#include <stl.h>
#include <iostream.h>

char* array1 [] = { "laurie", "jennifer", "leisa" };
char* array2 [] = { "amanda", "saskia", "carrie" };

int main ()
{
  deque<char*> names (array1, array1 + 3);
  deque<char*>::iterator i = names.begin () + 2;
  copy (array2, array2 + 3, inserter (names, i));
  deque<char*>::iterator j;
  for (j = names.begin (); j != names.end (); j++)
    cout << *j << endl;
  return 0;
}
```

laurie
jennifer
amanda
saskia
carrie
leisa

interval_timer

Description:

An os_interval_timer may be programmed to deliver a signal to the current process after a specified time. The signal may be delivered just once, or on a periodic basis. Three kinds of timing are supported:

- 1. *Real time*, in which the timer decrements in wall-clock time and sends a SIGALRM signal upon expiration. This timer is associated with the type ITIMER_REAL.

- 2. *Virtual time*, in which the timer only decrements when the current process is running and sends a SIGVTALRM upon expiration. This timer is associated with the type ITIMER_VIRTUAL.

- 3. *Profile time*, in which the timer only decrements when the current process is running or the kernel is executing on its behalf and sends SIGPROF upon expiration. This timer is associated with the type ITIMER_PROF.

All timers are disabled by default. To access these timers, you must use the interval timer interface of os_this_process; they may not be constructed directly.

Declaration:
```
#include <ospace/process/inttimer.h>
class os_interval_timer
```

Constructor	*os_interval_timer()* Construct myself to be an undefined kind of timer.
Constructor	*os_interval_timer(const os_interval_timer& timer)* Construct myself to be a copy of timer.
<	*bool operator<(const os_interval_timer& timer) const* Return true if I'm considered to be less than timer.
=	*os_interval_timer& operator=(const os_interval_timer& timer)* Assign myself from timer.
==	*bool operator==(const os_interval_timer& timer) const* Return true if I'm the same kind of timer as timer.
active	*bool active() const* Return true if I'm currently active. Events: syscall On Resumption: Returns false.

cancel *void cancel()*
Cancel my timer immediately.

> Events: `syscall`

cancel_after expiration

void cancel_after_expiration()

Cancel my timer after the next expiration.

> Events: `syscall`

defined *bool defined() const*
Return `true` if my type is not `OS_UNDEFINED`.

print *void print(ostream& stream) const*
Print my type to `stream`.

> Events: `syscall`

repeat_interval *os_time_period repeat_interval() const*
If I'm a repeating timer, return the interval between timer expiration. If I'm not a repeating timer, return 0.

> Events: `syscall`
> On Resumption: Returns `os_time_period( 0 )`.

repeat_timer *void repeat_timer(const os_time_period& period)*
Set me to be a repeating timer that will expire every `period`.

> Events: `syscall`
> On Resumption: The timer is not set.

time_left *os_time_period time_left() const*
Return the time left until I expire.

> Events: `syscall`
> On Resumption: Returns `os_time_period( 0 )`.

timer *void timer(const os_time_period& period)*
Expire exactly once after `period` has passed.

> Events: `syscall`
> On Resumption: The timer is not set.

type *int type() const*
Return my type.

Non-Member Functions:

<< *ostream& operator<<(ostream& stream,*
const os_interval_timer& timer)
Print `timer` to `stream`.

io_control

Description:

`os_io_control` contains attributes commonly used in the creation and use of I/O objects. The valid attributes for each type of I/O object vary. See the *Options* section of the catalog entry for a specific I/O object for a list of its valid I/O control attributes.

You can specify special I/O characteristics for any object with a constructor that takes an `os_ioctl_t`. A parameter of this type accepts either an `os_io_control` object or a bitwise or-ing of the following flags:

- `O_APPEND`   Appends all writes to the end of the file.
- `O_CLOSE_ON_EXEC`   Closes the I/O object when its process exec's.
- `O_NOERROR`   By default, an event is generated if you try to read a message longer than the receive buffer. This flag silently truncates messages longer than the receive buffer and generates no event.
- `O_NONBLOCK`   By default, any I/O operation is blocked until it is satisfied. This flag immediately returns any I/O operations that would normally be blocked and generates an event.
- `O_RDONLY`   Opens the I/O object for reading only. Any attempt to write to it generates an event. This is the default.
- `O_RDWR`   Opens the I/O object for reading and writing.
- `O_WRONLY`   Opens the I/O object for writing only. Any attempt to read from it generates an event.
- `O_UNDO`   Automatically undoes semaphore operations, if the process terminates abnormally.

Declaration:
```
#include <ospace/iocontrl.h>
class os_io_control
```

Constructor   *os_io_control(os_ioctl_t control)*
Construct myself to have encoded bits `control` (default 0).

Constructor   *os_io_control(const os_io_control& control)*
Construct myself to be a copy of `control`.

=   *os_io_control& operator=(os_ioctl_t control)*
Assign myself from `control`.

=   *os_io_control& operator=(const os_io_control& control)*
Assign myself from `control`.

==	*bool operator==(const os_io_control& control) const* Return `true` if my value is the same as `controls`.
append	*bool append() const* Return `true` if append on write.
append	*void append(bool flag)* Set write on append to `flag`.
async	*void async(bool flag)* Set asynchronous reading to `flag`.
async	*bool async() const* Return `true` if asynchronous signaling on data ready.
close_on_exec	*void close_on_exec(bool flag)* Set close on exec to `flag`.
close_on_exec	*bool close_on_exec() const* Return `true` if close on process exec.
no_error	*bool no_error() const* Return `true` if error inhibition on truncate.
no_error	*void no_error(bool flag)* Set error inhibition on truncation to `flag`.
non_blocking	*void non_blocking(bool flag)* Set non-blocking to `flag`.
non_blocking	*bool non_blocking() const* Return `true` if non-blocking.
os_ioctl_t	*operator os_ioctl_t() const* Return my encoded control bits.
print	*void print(ostream& stream) const* Print myself to `stream`.
read_only	*bool read_only() const* Return `true` if read only.
read_write	*bool read_write() const* Return `true` if read and write.
readable	*bool readable() const* Return `true` if readable.
set_read_only	*void set_read_only()* Change my flow setting to read only.
set_read_write	*void set_read_write()* Change my flow setting to read and write.

set_write_only	*void set_write_only()* Change my flow setting to write only.
sync	*bool sync() const* Return `true` if synchronous writes.
sync	*void sync(bool flag)* Set synchronous writing to `flag`.
undo	*bool undo() const* Return `true` if undo.
undo	*void undo(bool flag)* Set undo to `flag`.
value	*os_ioctl_t value() const* Return my encoded control bits.
value	*void value(os_ioctl_t control)* Set my encoded control bits to `control`.
write_only	*bool write_only() const* Return `true` if write only.
writeable	*bool writeable() const* Return `true` if writeable.

Non-Member Functions:

<<	*ostream& operator<<(ostream& stream, const os_io_control& control)* Print `control` to `stream`.
<<	*os_bstream& operator<<(os_bstream& stream, const os_io_control& control)* Write `control` to `stream`.
>>	*os_bstream& operator>>(os_bstream& stream, os_io_control& control)* Read `control` from `stream`.

io_multiplexer

Description:

A server must often serve more than one I/O object. For example, the Internet daemon, `inetd`, accepts connections on one of many known sockets and creates a child process of the appropriate type to handle an incoming connection on a particular socket. To wait until an interesting condition occurs on one or more I/O objects, use an I/O multiplexer.

Systems<ToolKit> includes a class called `os_io_multiplexer` for multiplexing I/O. The three possible types of interesting condition that it can wait for are listed below.

- **Readable**—Input is available to read or a socket connection request is received.
- **Writeable**—Output is possible.
- **Exception**—Out-of-band data is available to read.

An `os_io_multiplexer` contains a set of descriptors that are considered for each kind of condition. To set or access the descriptors that are scanned for read, write and exception conditions, use `read_scan()`, `write_scan()` and `exception_scan()`.

When you send execute `select()` with an optional time-out parameter, it blocks the process until at least one interesting condition is detected or a time-out occurs, at which point it returns the number of descriptors with a pending condition. Then, to find out which descriptors are associated with the detected conditions, use `readable()`, `writeable()` and `exceptional()`.

Declaration:
```
#include <ospace/io/iomux.h>
class os_io_multiplexer
```

Constructor	*os_io_multiplexer()* Construct myself with no associated descriptors.
==	*bool operator==(const os_io_multiplexer& io_multiplexer) const* Return `true` if my read, write and exception vectors are the same as `io_multiplexer`'s.
exception_scan	*void exception_scan(const vector< os_desc_t >& descriptors)* Set the descriptors that should be considered for pending exceptions to `descriptors`.
exception_scan	*vector< os_desc_t > exception_scan() const* Return the vector of descriptors that are scanned for pending exceptional conditions.
exceptional	*vector< os_desc_t > exceptional() const* Return the vector of descriptors that have pending exceptional conditions.

max_descriptor	*int max_descriptor() const* Return the maximum descriptor in any of my descriptor sets.
print	*void print(ostream& stream) const* Print myself to `stream`.
read_scan	*vector< os_desc_t > read_scan() const* Return the vector of descriptors that are scanned for read-readiness.
read_scan	*void read_scan(const vector< os_desc_t>& descriptors)* Set the descriptors that should be scanned for read-readiness to `descriptors`.
readable	*vector< os_desc_t > readable() const* Return the vector of descriptors that are ready to read.

select	*int select(const os_time_period& time_out)*
	Block until at least one of my descriptors has a pending action or until `time_out` time passes. Return the number of descriptors that are ready for some action. Returns 0 on timeout.
	
	    ' Events: `syscall`
	    On Resumption: Returns 0. The descriptor sets returned by `readable()`, `writeable()` and `exceptional()` are not modified.

select	*int select()*
	Block until at least one of my descriptors has a pending action. Return the number of descriptors that are ready for some action.
	
	    Events: `syscall`
	    On Resumption: Returns 0. The descriptor sets returned by `readable()`, `writeable()` and `exceptional()` are not modified.

write_scan	*vector< os_desc_t > write_scan() const* Return the vector of descriptors that are scanned for write-readiness.
write_scan	*void write_scan(const vector< os_desc_t >& descriptors)* Set the descriptors that should be scanned for write-readiness to `descriptors`.
writeable	*vector< os_desc_t > writeable() const* Return the vector of descriptors that are ready to write.

Non-Member Functions:

<<	*ostream& operator<<(ostream& stream, const os_io_multiplexer& mux)* Print `mux` to `stream`.

io_status

Description:
You can use an I/O object's `os_io_status` to obtain and modify many of its characteristics, such as its mode, user and group.

There are two ways to obtain an `os_io_status` object:

— Construct the `os_io_status` object on the file system path of an I/O object. This only works for `os_file`, `os_named_pipe` and UNIX file system based sockets.

— Ask the I/O object for its status by sending it `status()`. The I/O object must be open for this function to succeed.

Declaration:
```
#include <ospace/io/iostat.h>
class os_io_status
```

Constructor	*os_io_status(os_desc_t descriptor)* Construct myself with the status information of the open I/O object whose descriptor is `descriptor`. Events: `syscall` On Resumption: I may be in an unusable state.
Constructor	*os_io_status()* Construct myself to be uninitialized.
Constructor	*os_io_status(const os_io_status& io_status)* Construct myself to be a copy of `io_status`.
Constructor	*os_io_status(const string& path, int type)* If `type` is `for_file`, construct myself with the status of the file called `path`. If `type` is `for_link`, construct myself with the status of the symbolic link called `path`. Events: `syscall` On Resumption: I may be in an unusable state.
=	*os_io_status& operator=(const os_io_status& io_status)* Assign myself from `io_status`.
==	*bool operator==(const os_io_status& io_status) const* Return `true` if I contain the same status information as `io_status`.

access_time	*os_time_and_date access_time() const*
	 Return the last time that the I/O object was accessed.
	
	      Events: `other`
	      On Resumption: Returned value may be invalid.

block_count	*long block_count() const* Return the number of blocks allocated to the I/O object.
block_size	*long block_size() const* Return the preferred block size (in bytes) for I/O.
device	*os_dev_t device() const* Return the device identifier associated with the I/O object.
get_major	*int get_major() const* Return the major device identifier associated with the I/O object.
get_minor	*int get_minor() const* Return the minor device identifier associated with the I/O object.
group	*os_gid_t group() const* Return the group of the I/O object.

group	*void group(os_gid_t group)*
	 Set my group to `group`.
	
	      Events: `syscall`
	      On Resumption: My group may be unchanged.

inode	*ino_t inode() const* Return the serial number of the I/O object. In most architectures this is called the `inode` number and identifies a physical location on some storage media associated with the descriptor or file. A file can be uniquely identified by its device identifier and its serial number.
link_count	*nlink_t link_count() const* Return the number of links made to this I/O object.
mode	*os_mode_t mode() const* Return the mode (permissions) of the I/O object.

mode	*void mode(os_mode_t mode)*
	 Set my mode to `mode`.
	
	      Events: `syscall`
	      On Resumption: My mode may be unchanged.

modify_time	*os_time_and_date modify_time() const*
	 Return the last time that the I/O object was modified.
	
	      Events: `other`
	      On Resumption: Returned value may be invalid.

os_stat_t	*operator os_stat_t( ) const* Return me as a `os_stat_t` structure.
print	*void print(ostream& stream) const* Print myself to `stream`.
raw_device	*os_dev_t raw_device() const* Return the device identifier associated with the I/O object.
raw_major	*int raw_major() const* Return the major device identifier associated with the I/O object.
raw_minor	*int raw_minor() const* Return the minor device identifier associated with the I/O object.
size	*os_off_t size( ) const* Return the size of the I/O object in bytes.
status_time	*os_time_and_date status_time() const* Return the last time that the status of the I/O object was modified. Status information includes user and group of owner, mode and link counts. Events: `other` On Resumption: Returned value may be invalid.
user	*os_uid_t user( ) const* Return the user of the I/O object.
user	*void user(os_uid_t user)* Set my user to `user`. Events: `syscall` On Resumption: My user may be unchanged.

Non-Member Functions:

<<	*ostream& operator<<(ostream& stream, const os_io_status& status)* Print `status` to `stream`.
<<	*os_bstream& operator<<(os_bstream& stream, const os_io_status& status)* Write `status` to `stream`.
>>	*os_bstream& operator>>(os_bstream& stream, os_io_status& status)* Read `status` from `stream`.

ip_address

Description:

A TCP/IP host has one IP address for every network that it is connected to. If a host is connected to more than one network, it is called a multihomed host. An IP address is stored as a 32 bit number and is often displayed as four one-byte numbers. When displayed in text form, IP addresses are usually displayed as four numbers separated by periods.

An `os_ip_address` may be constructed from either a text name or from its numeric equivalent. `operator in_addr()` allows an `os_ip_address` to be used whenever an `in_addr` is expected.

Declaration:

```
#include <ospace/socket/ipaddr.h>
class os_ip_address
```

Constructor	*os_ip_address(unsigned long code)* Construct myself to have the encoded IP address `code` (default `INADDR_ANY`).
Constructor	*os_ip_address(const in_addr& address)* Construct myself to have the encoded IP address `address`.
Constructor	*os_ip_address(const os_ip_address& address)* Construct myself to be a copy of `address`.
Constructor	*os_ip_address(const string& address)* Construct myself to have the IP address described by `address`. If `address` begins with a digit, it is assumed to be an IP address in the format "`ddd.ddd.ddd.ddd`", where `ddd` is the text form of a one byte number. If address starts with a non-numeric character it is assumed to be the name of a host. See `os_host` for more information. Events: `other` On Resumption: I will be in an unusable state.
<	*bool operator<(const os_ip_address& address) const* Return `true` if my address is considered to be less than `address`'s.
=	*os_ip_address& operator=(const in_addr& address)* Assign myself from `address`.
=	*os_ip_address& operator=(const os_ip_address& address)* Assign myself from `address`.

==	*bool operator==(const os_ip_address& address) const* Return `true` if I am the same address as `address`.
in_addr	*operator in_addr() const* Return myself as an `in_addr` structure.
as_long	*unsigned long as_long() const* Return my encoded IP address.
class_type	*char class_type() const* If I am an A, B, C or D class address, return the corresponding uppercase letter, else return a space character.
defined	*bool defined() const* Return `true` if my encoded value is not zero.
local	*bool local() const* Return `true` if I am my host's IP address.
my_address	*/* static */ const os_ip_address& my_address()* Return the IP address of my host. Events: `other` On Resumption: The return value may be invalid.
print	*void print(ostream& stream) const* Print my IP address to `stream`.
set from_long	*void set_from_long(unsigned long code)* Set my address from the encoded IP address `code`.
set_from_numeric	*void set_from_numeric(const string& str)* Set my IP address from `str`, which should be in the format "ddd.ddd.ddd.ddd", where ddd is the text form of a one byte number. Events: `other` On Resumption: I will be in an unusable state.
set_from_symbolic	*void set_from_symbolic(const string& host_name)* Set my IP address to be that of the host whose name is `host_name`. Events: `other` On Resumption: I will be in an unusable state.

Non-Member Functions:

<<   *ostream& operator<<(ostream& stream, const os_ip_address& address)*
                     Print `address` to `stream`.

<<   *os_bstream& operator<<(os_bstream& stream, const os_ip_address& address)*
                     Write `address` to `stream`.

>>   *os_bstream& operator>>(os_bstream& stream, os_ip_address& address)*
                     Read `address` from `stream`.

istream_iterator

Description:

An `istream_iterator` is an iterator that reads items in a typesafe manner from a standard input stream.

Declaration:
```
#include <iterator.h>
template< class T, class Distance >
class istream_iterator : public input_iterator< T, Distance >
```

Constructor	*istream_iterator()* Construct myself to serve as a past-the-end value.
Constructor	*istream_iterator(istream& stream)* Construct myself to be associated with the input stream `stream` and cache my first element.
*	*const T& operator*() const* Return a reference to my currently cached input item.
++	*istream_iterator< T, Distance >& operator++()* Read and cache the next item in my input stream. Return a reference to myself.
++	*istream_iterator< T, Distance > operator++(int)* Read and cache the next item in my input stream. Return a copy of my previous value.
==	*bool operator==(const istream_iterator< T, Distance >& iter) const* Return `true` if I have the same stream and state as `iter`.
!=	*bool operator!=(const istream_iterator< T, Distance >& iter) const* Return `true` if I don't have the same stream or state as `iter`.

Example <ospace/stl/examples/istmit1.cpp>

```
#include <stl.h>
#include <iostream.h>

int main ()
{
  char buffer [100];
  int i = 0;
  cin.unsetf(ios::skipws); // Disable white-space skipping.
  cout << "Please enter a string: ";
  istream_iterator<char, ptrdiff_t> s (cin);
  while (*s != '\n')
    buffer[i++] = *s++;
  buffer[i] = '\0'; // Null terminate buffer.
  cout << "read " << buffer << endl;      char buffer [100];
  return 0;
}
```

Please enter a string: truth
read truth

Example <ospace/stl/examples/istmit2.cpp>

```
#include <iostream.h>
#include <fstream.h>
#include <stl.h>

typedef vector<char> Line;

void printLine (const Line* line_)
{
  vector<char>::const_iterator i;
  for (i = line_->begin (); i != line_->end (); i++)
   cout << *i;
  cout << endl;
}

int main ()
{
  Line buffer;
  vector<Line*> lines;
  ifstream s ("data.txt");
  s.unsetf (ios::skipws); // Disable white-space skipping.
  istream_iterator<char, ptrdiff_t> it1 (s); // Position at start.
  istream_iterator<char, ptrdiff_t> it2; // Past-the-end marker
  copy (it1, it2, back_inserter (buffer));
  Line::iterator i = buffer.begin ();
  Line::iterator p;
```

```
      while (i != buffer.end ())
      {
        p = find (i, buffer.end (), '\n');
        lines.push_back (new Line (i, p));
        i = ++p;
      }
      sort (lines.begin (), lines.end (), less_p<Line*> ());
      cout << "Read " << lines.size () << " lines" << endl;
      vector<Line*>::iterator j;
      for (j = lines.begin (); j != lines.end (); j++)
        printLine (*j);
      release (lines.begin (), lines.end ()); // Release memory.
      return 0;
    }
```

data.txt:

cat
dog
ape

read 3 lines
ape
cat
dog

key

Description:
os_key represents a System V Interprocess Communication (IPC) key. It allows you to construct keys from either an integer value or from a filename/value pair.

Declaration:
```
#include <ospace/io/key.h>
class os_key
```

Constructor *os_key(os_key_t value)*
Construct myself with value value (default OS_UNDEFINED).

Constructor *os_key(const os_key& key)*
Construct myself to be a copy of key.

Constructor *os_key(const string& filename, char project_code)*
Construct myself using filename and project_code as a seed. If filename does not exist or is inaccessible, set my value to OS_UNDEFINED.
> Events: other
> On Resumption: My value will be OS_UNDEFINED.

< *bool operator<(const os_key& key) const*
Return true if my value is less than key's.

= *os_key& operator=(const os_key& key)*
Assign myself from key.

== *bool operator==(const os_key& key) const*
Return true if my value is the same as key's.

defined *bool defined() const*
Return true if I my value is not OS_UNDEFINED.

print *void print(ostream& stream) const*
Print my value to stream.

value *void value(os_key_t value)*
Set my value to value.

value *os_key_t value() const*
Return my value.

key

Non-Member Functions:

<<
        ostream& operator<<(ostream& stream, const os_key& key)
Print `key` to `stream`.

<<
        os_bstream& operator<<(os_bstream& stream, const os_key& key)
Write `key` to `stream`.

>>
        os_bstream& operator>>(os_bstream& stream, os_key& key)
Read `key` from `stream`.

less

Description:

less is a binary function object that returns `true` if its first operand is less than its second operand.

Declaration:
```
#include <function.h>
template< class T >
struct less : binary_function< T, T, bool >
```

() *bool operator()(const T& x, const T& y) const*
Return `x < y`.

Example <ospace/stl/examples/less.cpp>

```
#include <stl.h>
#include <iostream.h>

int array [4] = { 3, 1, 4, 2 };

int main ()
{
  sort (array, array + 4, less<int> ());
  for (int i = 0; i < 4; i++)
    cout << array[i] << endl;
  return 0;
}

1
2
3
4
```

less_equal

Description:

less_equal is a binary function object that returns true if its first operand is less than or equal to its second operand.

Declaration:
```
#include <function.h>
template< class T >
struct less_equal : binary_function< T, T, bool >
```

()   *bool operator()(const T& x, const T& y) const*
                            Return x <= y.

Example <ospace/stl/examples/lesseq.cpp>

```
#include <stl.h>
#include <iostream.h>

int array [4] = { 3, 1, 4, 2 };

int main ()
{
  sort (array, array + 4, less_equal<int> ());
  for (int i = 0; i < 4; i++)
    cout << array[i] << endl;
  return 0;
}

1
2
3
4
```

list

Description:

A list is a sequential container that is optimized for insertion and erasure at arbitrary points in its structure at the expense of giving up indexed-based access.

Declaration:

```
#include <list.h>
template< class T >
class list
```

Constructor	*list( )* Construct myself to be empty.
Constructor	*list(alloc_type& alloc)* Construct myself to be empty. Use alloc to allocate storage.
Constructor	*list(size_type n)* Construct me to contain n elements set to their default value.
Constructor	*list(alloc_type& alloc, size_type n)* Construct me to contain n elements set to their default value. Use alloc to allocate storage.
Constructor	*list(size_type n, const T& value)* Construct me to contain n copies of value.
Constructor	*list(alloc_type& alloc, size_type n, const T& value)* Construct me to contain n copies of value. Use alloc to allocate storage.
Constructor	*list(const T* first, const T* last)* Construct me to contain copies of all of the elements in the range [first, last).
Constructor	*list(alloc_type& alloc, const T* first, const T* last)* Construct me to contain copies of all of the elements in the range [first, last). Use alloc to allocate storage.
Constructor	*list(const list< T >& x)* Construct myself to be a copy of x.
Constructor	*list(alloc_type& alloc, const list< T >& x)* Construct myself to be a copy of x. Use alloc to allocate storage.
Destructor	*~list( )* Destroy myself, erasing all of my items.

list

=	*list< T >& operator=(const list< T >& x)* Replace my contents by a copy of x's.
==	*bool operator==(const list< T >& x) const* Return `true` if I contain the same items in the same order as x.
<	*bool operator<(const list< T >& x) const* Return `true` if I'm lexigraphically less than x.
back	*T& back()* Return a reference to my last element. <blockquote>Events: `other (os_empty_error)`</blockquote>
back	*const T& back() const* Return a reference to my last element. <blockquote>Events: `other (os_empty_error)`</blockquote>
begin	*iterator begin()* Return an iterator positioned at my first item.
begin	*const_iterator begin() const* Return an iterator positioned at my first item.
empty	*bool empty() const* Return `true` if I contain no entries.
end	*iterator end()* Return an iterator positioned immediately after my last item.
end	*const_iterator end() const* Return an iterator positioned immediately after my last item.
erase[4]	*void erase()* Erase all of my elements.
erase	*void erase(iterator pos)* Erase the element at `pos`.
erase	*void erase(iterator first, iterator last)* Erase the elements in range `[first, last)`.
front	*T& front()* Return a reference to my first element. <blockquote>Events: `other (os_empty_error)`</blockquote>

---

[4] Non-standard, unique to Systems<ToolKit>

front *const T& front() const*
Return a reference to my first element.

> Events: `other (os_empty_error)`

insert *iterator insert(iterator pos, const T& value)*
Insert a copy of `value` at `pos` and return an iterator pointing to the new element's position.

insert *void insert(iterator pos, size_type n, const T& value)*
Insert `n` copies of `value` at `pos`.

insert *void insert(iterator pos, const T* first, const T* last)*
Insert copies of the elements in the range `[first, last)` at `pos`.

max_size *size_type max_size() const*
Return the maximum number of entries that I can contain.

merge *void merge(const list< T >& x)*
Move the elements of `x` into myself and place them so that all of my elements are sorted using the < operator. This operation assumes that both myself and `x` were already sorted using `operator<`.

push_back *void push_back(const T& value)*
Add `value` at my end.

push_front *void push_front(const T& value)*
Insert a copy of `value` in front of my first element.

pop_back *void pop_back()*
Erase my last element.

> Events: `other (os_empty_error)`

pop_front *void pop_front()*
Erase my first element.

> Events: `other (os_empty_error)`

rbegin *reverse_iterator rbegin()*
Return a reverse iterator positioned at my last item.

rbegin *const_reverse_iterator rbegin() const*
Return a reverse iterator positioned at my last item.

remove *void remove(const T& value)*
Erase all elements that match `value`, using `operator==` to perform the comparison.

rend *reverse_iterator rend()*
Return a reverse_iterator positioned immediately before my first item.

rend

const_reverse_iterator rend() const
Return a reverse_iterator positioned immediately before my first item.

reverse

void reverse()
Reverse the order of my elements. The time complexity is O(N).

size

size_type size() const
Return the number of entries that I contain.

sort

void sort()
Sort my elements using operator<. The time complexity is O(NlogN).

splice

void splice(iterator pos, list< T >& x)
Remove all of the elements in x and insert them at position pos.

splice

void splice(iterator to, list< T >& x, iterator from)
Remove the element in x at position from and insert it at position to.

splice

void splice(iterator pos, list< T >& x, iterator first, iterator last)
Remove the elements from x in the range [first, last) and insert them at position pos.

swap

void swap(list< T >& x)
Swap my contents with x's.

unique

void unique()
Replace all repeating sequences of a single element by a single occurrence of that element.

logical_and

Description:
logical_and is a binary function object that returns true if both of its operands are true.

Declaration:
```
#include <function.h>
template< class T >
struct logical_and : binary_function< T, T, bool >
```

()   *bool operator()(const T& x, const T& y) const*
                      Return (x && y).

Example <ospace/stl/examples/logicand.cpp>

```
#include <stl.h>
#include <iostream.h>

int input1 [4] = { 1, 1, 0, 1 };
int input2 [4] = { 0, 1, 0, 0 };

int main ()
{
  int output [4];
  transform (input1, input1 + 4, input2, output,
    logical_and<bool> ());
  for (int i = 0; i < 4; i++)
    cout << output[i] << endl;
  return 0;
}

0
1
0
0
```

logical_not

Description:
> `logical_not` is a unary function object that returns `true` if its operand is zero (`false`).

Declaration:
```
#include <function.h>
template< class T >
struct logical_not : unary_function< T, bool >
```

() *bool operator()(const T& x) const*
Return `!x`.

Example <ospace/stl/examples/logicnot.cpp>

```
#include <stl.h>
#include <iostream.h>

int array [7] = { 1, 0, 0, 1, 1, 1, 1 };

int main ()
{
  int n = 0;
  count_if (array, array + 7, logical_not<int> (), n);
  cout << "count = " << n << endl;
  return 0;
}
```

count = 2

logical_or

Description:

`logical_or` is a binary function object that returns `true` if either of its operands are `true`.

Declaration:
```
#include <function.h>
template< class T >
struct logical_or : binary_function< T, T, bool >
```

()   *bool operator()(const T& x, const T& y) const*
                            Return `(x || y)`.

Example <ospace/stl/examples/logicor.cpp>

```
#include <stl.h>
#include <iostream.h>

int input1 [4] = { 1, 0, 0, 1 };
int input2 [4] = { 0, 1, 0, 0 };

int main ()
{
  int output [4];
  transform (input1, input1 + 4, input2, output,
    logical_or<bool> ());
  for (int i = 0; i < 4; i++)
    cout << output[i] << endl;
  return 0;
}

1
1
0
1
```

map

Description:

A map is an associative container that manages a set of ordered key/value pairs. The pairs are ordered by key, based on a user-supplied comparitor function. Only one value may be associated with a particular key. A map's underlying data structure allows you to very efficiently find the value associated with a particular key.

Declaration:
```
#include <map.h>
template< class Key, class Value, class Compare >
class map
```

Constructor	*map( )* Construct myself to be an empty map that orders its keys using the compare function specified when my template was instantiated.
Constructor	*map(alloc_type& alloc)* Construct myself to be an empty map that orders its keys using the compare function specified when my template was instantiated. Use alloc to allocate storage.
Constructor	*map(const Compare& compare)* Construct myself to be an empty map that orders its keys using the compare function compare.
Constructor	*map(alloc_type& alloc, const Compare& compare)* Construct myself to be an empty map that orders its keys using the compare function compare. Use alloc to allocate storage.
Constructor	*map(const value_type* first, const value_type* last)* Construct myself to contain copies of the key/value pairs in the range [first, last), using the compare function specified when my template was instantiated to order my keys.
Constructor	*map(alloc_type& alloc, const value_type* first, const value_type* last)* Construct myself to contain copies of the key/value pairs in the range [first, last), using the compare function specified when my template was instantiated to order my keys. Use alloc to allocate storage.
Constructor	*map(const value_type* first, const value_type* last,* *const Compare& compare)* Construct myself to contain copies of the key/value pairs in the range [first, last), using compare to order my keys.

Constructor	*map(alloc_type& alloc, const value_type* first,* *const value_type* last, const Compare& compare)* Construct myself to contain copies of the key/value pairs in the range `[first, last)`, using `compare` to order my keys. Use `alloc` to allocate storage.
Constructor	*map(const map< Key,Value,Compare >& x)* Construct myself to be a copy of `x`.
Constructor	*map(alloc_type& alloc, const map< Key,Value,Compare >& x)* Construct myself to be a copy of `x`. Use `alloc` to allocate storage.
Destructor	*~map()* Destroy myself, erasing all of my key/value pairs.
=	*map< Key,Value,Compare >& operator=(const map<* *Key,Value,Compare >& x)* Replace my contents by a copy of `x`'s.
==	*bool operator==(const map< Key,Value,Compare >& x) const* Return `true` if I contain the same items in the same order as `x`.
<	*bool operator<(const map< Key,Value,Compare >& x) const* Return `true` if I'm lexigraphically less than `x`.
[]	*Value& operator [](const Key& key)* If no value is associated with `key`, associate `key` with a default-constructed value and return a reference to this new value, otherwise return a reference to the value already associated with `key`.
begin	*iterator begin()* Return an iterator positioned at my first key/value pair.
begin	*const_iterator begin() const* Return an iterator positioned at my first key/value pair.
count	*size_type count(const Key& key) const* Return the number of key/value pairs that I contain whose key matches `key`.
empty	*bool empty() const* Return `true` if I contain no entries.
end	*iterator end()* Return an iterator positioned immediately after my last key/value pair.
end	*const_iterator end() const* Return an iterator positioned immediately after my last key/value pair.

equal_range	*pair< iterator, iterator > equal_range(const Key& key)* Return a pair of iterators whose first element is equal to lower_bound() and whose second element is equal to upper_bound().
equal_range	*pair< const_iterator, const_iterator > equal_range(const Key& key) const* Return a pair of iterators whose first element is equal to `lower_bound()` and whose second element is equal to `upper_bound()`.
erase[5]	*void erase()* Erase all of my key/value pairs.
erase	*void erase(iterator pos)* Erase the key/value pair at `pos`.
erase	*void erase(iterator first, iterator last)* Erase the key/value pairs in range `[first, last)`.
erase	*size_type erase(const Key& key)* Erase all key/value pairs whose key matches `key` and return the number of elements that were erased.
find	*iterator find(const Key& key)* If I contain a key/value pair whose key matches `key`, return an iterator positioned at the matching pair, otherwise return an iterator positioned at end().
find	*iterator find(const Key& key) const* If I contain a key/value pair whose key matches `key`, return a constant iterator positioned at the matching pair, otherwise return a constant iterator positioned at end().
insert	*pair< iterator, bool > insert(const value_type& pair)* If I don't contain a key/value pair whose key matches that of `pair`, insert a copy of `pair` and return a pair whose first element is an iterator positioned at the new key/value pair and whose second element is `true`. If I already contain a key/value pair whose key matches that of `pair`, return a pair whose first element is an iterator positioned at the existing key/value pair and whose second element is `false`.
insert	*void insert(const value_type* first, const value_type* last)* Insert copies of the key/value pairs in the range `[first, last)`.

---

[5] Non-standard, unique to Systems<ToolKit>

insert	*iterator insert(iterator pos, const value_type& pair)* Insert a copy of `pair` if I don't already contain an key/value pair whose key that matches its key, using `pos` as a hint on where to start searching for the correct place to insert.
insert[6]	*pair< iterator, bool > insert(const Key& key, const Value& value)* If I don't contain a key which matches `key`, insert the new key/value pair and return a pair whose first element is an iterator positioned at the new key/value pair and whose second element is `true`. If I already contain a key which matches `key`, return a pair whose first element is an iterator positioned at the existing key/value pair and whose second element is `false`.
key_comp	*Compare key_comp() const* Return the comparison object used to compare my keys.
lower_bound	*iterator lower_bound(const Key& key)* Return an iterator positioned at the first location where a pair with key `key` could be inserted without violating the ordering criteria. If no such location is found, return an iterator positioned at end().
lower_bound	*const_iterator lower_bound(const Key& key) const* Return an iterator positioned at the first location where a pair with key `key` could be inserted without violating the ordering criteria. If no such location is found, return an iterator positioned at end().
max_size	*size_type max_size() const* Return the maximum number of key/value pairs that I can contain.
rbegin	*reverse_iterator rbegin()* Return a reverse iterator positioned at my last key/value pair.
rbegin	*const_reverse_iterator rbegin() const* Return a reverse iterator positioned at my last key/value pair.
rend	*reverse_iterator rend()* Return a reverse_iterator positioned immediately before my first key/value pair.
rend	*const_reverse_iterator rend() const* Return a reverse_iterator positioned immediately before my first key/value pair.
size	*size_type size() const* Return the number of key/value pairs that I contain.

---

[6] Non-standard, unique to Systems<ToolKit>

map

swap
void swap(map< Key,Value,Compare >& x)
Swap my contents with x's.

upper_bound
iterator upper_bound(const Key& key)
Return an iterator positioned at the last location where a pair with key key
could be inserted without violating the ordering criteria. If no such
location is found, return an iterator positioned at end().

upper_bound
const_iterator upper_bound(const Key& key) const
Return an iterator positioned at the last location where a pair with key key
could be inserted without violating the ordering criteria. If no such
location is found, return an iterator positioned at end().

value_comp
map_compare< Key,Value,Compare > value_comp() const
Return the comparison object using for comparing my key/value pairs.

message_queue

Description:

Message queues are an interprocess facility that allow you to send raw data between processes on the same machine. This class is a thin wrapper around System V message queues. It supports a raw interface for reading and writing messages. When a buffer is written, the first `long` of the buffer should hold the message type. When a message is read, the first `long` of the buffer is filled with the message type.

When a message is received, the received type is cached internally and can be obtained using the `last_type()` message. By default, reading a message queue will return you the first message in its input queue. You may request that only messages with a specific type are read by using `read_type()`, or that only messages with a type less than or equal to a specific type are read by using `read_type_equal_or_less_than()`. If an attempt is made to read a message that is longer than the buffer you supply and the queue's I/O control includes the `O_NOERROR` flag, the message is silently truncated; otherwise, an `E2BIG` error is generated and the message remains on the queue.

Conversions allow `os_message_queue` and `os_vid_t` (the System V IPC id) to be used interchangeably.

Declaration:
```
#include <ospace/mqueue/mqueue.h>
class os_message_queue
```

Options:

Legal open control:	`O_OPEN, O_CREAT, O_EXCL`
Legal I/O control:	`O_NONBLOCK, O_NOERROR`
Default I/O control:	0 (blocking, error on read buffer overflow)

Constructor
    os_message_queue(os_vid_t id)
Construct myself to reference the existing message queue with id `id`. Initialize me to receive any message type using default I/O control (blocking and error on truncate).

Constructor
    os_message_queue(const os_key& key, os_ioctl_t control)
Construct myself to reference the existing message queue with key `key` and set my I/O control to `control` (default is blocking and error on truncate).

        Events: `syscall`
        On Resumption: My id is set to `OS_UNDEFINED`.

Constructor   *os_message_queue(os_mode_t mode, os_ioctl_t control)*
Construct myself to reference a new message queue with a private key, mode `mode` and I/O control `control` (default blocking and error on truncate).

> Events: `syscall`
> On Resumption: My id is set to `OS_UNDEFINED`.

Constructor   *os_message_queue(const os_key& key, os_open_t open, os_mode_t mode, os_ioctl_t control)*
Construct myself to reference a new message queue with key `key`, open control flags `open`, mode `mode` and I/O control `control` (default blocking and error on truncate). If a message queue with key `key` already exists, reference the existing message queue and ignore the `mode` parameter.

> Events: `syscall`
> On Resumption: My id is set to `OS_UNDEFINED`.

<   *bool operator<(const os_message_queue& queue) const*
Return `true` if my id is less than `queue`'s.

==   *bool operator==(const os_message_queue& queue) const*
Return `true` if my id is the same as `queue`'s.

bytes_on_queue   *int bytes_on_queue() const*
Return the number of bytes of data waiting in my queue.

> Events: `syscall`
> On Resumption: Returns 0.

clear   *void clear()*
Reset my state to good.

creator_group   *os_gid_t creator_group() const*
Return my creator's group id.

> Events: `syscall`
> On Resumption: Returns 0.

creator_user   *os_uid_t creator_user() const*
Return my creator's user id.

> Events: `syscall`
> On Resumption: Returns 0.

defined   *bool defined() const*
Return `true` if my id is not `OS_UNDEFINED`.

good   *bool good() const*
Return `true` if I'm not in a failed state.

id
void id(os_vid_t id)
Set my id to `id`.

id
os_vid_t id() const
Return my id.

io_control
void io_control(os_ioctl_t control)
Set my I/O control setting to `control`.

io_control
os_ioctl_t io_control() const
Return my I/O control setting.

last_change_time
os_time_and_date last_change_time() const
Return the last time that my queue state changed.

> Events: `syscall`
> On Resumption: Returns `os_time_and_date( 0 )`.

last_receive_process
os_pid_t last_receive_process() const
Return the last process that received a message from my queue.

> Events: `syscall`
> On Resumption: Returns 0.

last_receive_time
os_time_and_date last_receive_time() const
Return the time that the last message was read from my queue.

> Events: `syscall`
> On Resumption: Returns `os_time_and_date( 0 )`.

last_send_process
os_pid_t last_send_process() const
Return the last process to send a message to my queue.

> Events: `syscall`
> On Resumption: Return 0.

last_send_time
os_time_and_date last_send_time() const
Return the time that the last message was written to my queue.

> Events: `syscall`
> On Resumption: Returns `os_time_and_date( 0 )`.

last_type
long last_type() const
Return the type of the last message received. If no messages have yet been received, return `OS_UNDEFINED`.

max_bytes_on_queue
int max_bytes_on_queue() const
Return the maximum number of bytes that can be waiting on my queue.

> Events: `syscall`
> On Resumption: Returns 0.

messages_on_queue	*int messages_on_queue() const*
	Return the number of messages waiting in my queue.
	
	    Events: `syscall`
	    On Resumption: Returns 0.

mode	*os_mode_t mode() const*
	Return my mode.
	
	    Events: `syscall`
	    On Resumption: Returns 0.

mode	*void mode(os_mode_t mode)* Set my mode to `mode`. Events: `syscall`
ok	*bool ok() const* Return `true` if I'm not failed.
os_vid_t	*operator os_vid_t() const* Return my id.

owner_group	*os_gid_t owner_group() const*
	Return my owner's group id.
	
	    Events: `syscall`
	    On Resumption: Returns 0.

owner group	*void owner_group(os_gid_t group)* Set my owner's group to `group`. Events: `syscall`

owner_user	*os_uid_t owner_user() const*
	Return my owner's user id.
	
	    Events: `syscall`
	    On Resumption: Returns 0.

owner_user	*void owner_user(os_uid_t user)* Set my owner's user to `user`. Events: `syscall`
print	*void print(ostream& stream) const* Print my id to `stream`.

read
                    int read(void buffer, int bytes)*

Read a raw message into `buffer` based on my current type filtering. See the `read...()` family of type filtering members to select the message filtering you want. The first `long` of the buffer is filled with the message type. The remainder of the buffer is filled with up to `bytes` bytes of data. Return the number of bytes of data placed in `buffer`, not including the type.

    Events: `syscall`
    On Resumption: Returns `-1`.

read_any_type
    void read_any_type()

Read the next available message regardless of its type.

read_type
    void read_type(long type)

Only read messages of type `type`. The value of `type` must be positive.

read_type_equal to_or_less_than

    void read_type_equal_to_or_less_than(long type)

Only read messages of type equal to or less than `type`. The value of `type` must be positive.

remove
    void remove()

Immediately remove the message queue from the operating system. Any remaining data in the queue is lost. Any process still trying to access the queue will get errors.

    Events: `syscall`

slot_sequence number

    int slot_sequence_number() const

Return my slot usage sequence number.

    Events: `syscall`
    On Resumption: Returns 0.

write
    int write(const void buffer, int bytes)*

Write a raw message from `buffer`. The first long in `buffer` is the message type. `bytes` is the number of bytes in `buffer`, not including the message type. Return `bytes` on success.

    Events: `syscall`
    On Resumption: Returns `-1`.

Non-Member Functions:

<<
         ostream& operator<<(ostream& stream, const os_message_queue& queue)

Print `queue` to `stream`.

minus

Description:

minus is a binary function object that returns the result of subtracting its second operand from its first operand.

Declaration:
```
#include <function.h>
template< class T >
struct minus : binary_function< T, T, T >
```

()   *T operator()(const T& x, const T& y) const*
                                Return `x - y`.

Example <ospace/stl/examples/minus.cpp>

```cpp
#include <stl.h>
#include <iostream.h>

int input1 [4] = { 1, 5, 7, 8 };
int input2 [4] = { 1, 4, 8, 3 };

int main ()
{
  int output [4];
  transform (input1, input1 + 4, input2, output, minus<int> ());
  for (int i = 0; i < 4; i++)
    cout << output[i] << endl;
  return 0;
}

0
1
-1
5
```

mode

Description:

The os_mode class is an encapsulation of POSIX permission characteristics. It allows you to set these characteristics without having to remember the names of the POSIX flags (S_IRWXU, S_IRWXG, etc., defined in /usr/include/sys/stat.h) or their numeric representation. It is also useful for converting these permission characteristics into a text string as displayed by the UNIX ls command.

Conversions allow os_mode and os_mode_t to be used interchangeably.

Any constructor which takes a os_mode_t parameter allows you to specify the permissions flags that an I/O object is created with. A parameter of this type accepts either an os_mode object or an octal representation of the permissions. The default os_mode_t value for all I/O objects except directories is 0660, which means that the I/O object is readable and writeable by processes with the same user or group. The default os_mode_t value for directories is 0770, which means that they're also searchable by processes with the same user or group.

Declaration:
```
#include <ospace/io/mode.h>
class os_mode
```

Constructor	*os_mode(os_mode_t mode)* Construct myself with POSIX.1 encoded mode mode (default 0).
Constructor	*os_mode(const os_mode& mode)* Construct myself to be a copy of mode.
<	*bool operator<(const os_mode& mode) const* Return true if my value is less than mode's.
=	*os_mode& operator=(const os_mode& mode)* Assign myself from mode.
=	*os_mode& operator=(os_mode_t mode)* Assign myself from mode.
==	*bool operator==(const os_mode& mode) const* Return true if my value is the same as mode's.
block_special	*bool block_special() const* Return true if I'm a block special mode.
char_special	*bool char_special() const* Return true if I'm a character special mode.

directory	*bool directory() const* Return `true` if I'm a directory mode.
fifo	*bool fifo() const* Return `true` if I'm a FIFO mode.
group_execute	*bool group_execute() const* Return my group execute/directory search permission.
group_execute	*void group_execute(bool flag)* Set my group execute/directory search permission to `flag`.
group_read	*bool group_read() const* Return my group read permission.
group_read	*void group_read(bool flag)* Set my group read permission to `flag`.
group_write	*bool group_write() const* Return my group write permission.
group_write	*void group_write(bool flag)* Set my group write permission to `flag`.
mandatory_locking	*void mandatory_locking(bool flag)* Set mandatory record locking to `flag`.
mandatory_locking	*bool mandatory_locking() const* Return `true` if I am set for mandatory record locking.
os_mode_t	*operator os_mode_t() const* Return my POSIX.1 encoded mode bits.
others_execute	*bool others_execute() const* Return my others execute/directory search permission.
others_execute	*void others_execute(bool flag)* Set my others execute/directory search permissions to `flag`.
others_read	*void others_read(bool flag)* Set my others read permission to `flag`.
others_read	*bool others_read() const* Return my others read permission.
others_write	*void others_write(bool flag)* Set my others write permissions to `flag`.
others_write	*bool others_write() const* Return my others write permission.
print	*void print(ostream& stream) const* Print myself to `stream` using the standard POSIX notation.

mode

regular	*bool regular() const* Return `true` if I'm a regular file mode.
set_group_id	*void set_group_id(bool flag)* Set my "set group ID" bit to `flag`.
set_group_id	*bool set_group_id() const* Return my "set group ID" setting.
set_user_id	*void set_user_id(bool flag)* Set my "set user ID" bit to `flag`.
set_user_id	*bool set_user_id() const* Return my "set user ID" setting.
socket	*bool socket() const* Return `true` if I'm a socket mode.
sticky	*bool sticky() const* Return my "sticky" bit setting (not POSIX.1).
sticky	*void sticky(bool flag)* Set my "sticky" bit to `flag`.
symbolic_link	*bool symbolic_link() const* Return `true` if I'm a symbolic link mode.
user_execute	*bool user_execute() const* Return my owner execute/directory search permission.
user_execute	*void user_execute(bool flag)* Set my user execute/directory search permissions to `flag`.
user_read	*void user_read(bool flag)* Set my user read permission to `flag`.
user_read	*bool user_read() const* Return my owner read permission.
user_write	*void user_write(bool flag)* Set my user write permission to `flag`.
user_write	*bool user_write() const* Return my owner write permission.
value	*void value(os_mode_t mode)* Set my POSIX.1 encoded mode bits to `mode`.
value	*os_mode_t value() const* Return my POSIX.1 encoded mode bits.

Non-Member Functions:

<<　　　　　　　　*ostream& operator<<(ostream& stream, const os_mode& mode)*
　　　　　　　　Print mode using `ls -al` style output to `stream`.

<<　　　　　　　　*os_bstream& operator<<(os_bstream& stream, const os_mode& mode)*
　　　　　　　　Write mode to `stream`.

>>　　　　　　　　*os_bstream& operator>>(os_bstream& stream, os_mode& mode)*
　　　　　　　　Read mode from `stream`.

modulus

Description:

modulus is a binary function object that returns its second operand in the modulus of the first operand.

Declaration:
```
#include <function.h>
template< class T >
struct modulus : binary_function< T, T, T >
```

()   *T operator()(const T& x, const T& y) const*
                           Return x % y.

Example <ospace/stl/examples/modulus.cpp>

```
#include <stl.h>
#include <iostream.h>

int input1 [4] = { 6, 8, 10, 2 };
int input2 [4] = { 4, 2, 11, 3 };

int main ()
{
  int output [4];
  transform (input1, input1 + 4, input2, output, modulus<int> ());
  for (int i = 0; i < 4; i++)
    cout << output[i] << endl;
  return 0;
}

2
0
10
2
```

monitor

Description:

An `os_monitor` is a template class that is derived from `os_read_write_semaphore`. When an `os_monitor` is constructed, it is associated with the object to be locked. Threads that wish to lock and access this object must adopt a cooperative scheme in which `read_lock()` is used to request a read lock, `write_lock()` is used to request a write lock, and `operator*` and `operator->` are used to access the monitor's associated object. `read_unlock()` and `write_unlock()` should be used to unlock the monitor when access to its associated object is no longer required.

In the following function signatures, the character `T` is used to represent the single template argument to `os_monitor`.

Declaration:
```
#include <ospace/sync/monitor.h>
template< class T >
class os_monitor : public os_read_write_semaphore
```

Constructor *os_monitor(T& object)*
Construct myself to monitor `object`.

* *const T& operator*() const*
Return a reference to the object that I monitor.

* *T& operator*()*
Return a reference to the object that I monitor.

-> *const T* operator–>() const*
Return a pointer to the object that I monitor.

-> *T* operator–>()*
Return a pointer to the object that I monitor.

multimap

Description:

A `multimap` is an associative container that manages a set of ordered key/value pairs. The pairs are ordered by key, based on a user-supplied comparitor function. More than one value may be associated with a particular key. A `multimap`'s underlying data structure allows you to very efficiently find all of the values associated with a particular key.

Declaration:
```
#include <map.h>
template< class Key, class Value, class Compare >
class multimap
```

Constructor	*multimap( )* Construct myself to be an empty multimap that orders its keys using the compare function specified when my template was instantiated.
Constructor	*multimap(alloc_type& alloc)* Construct myself to be an empty multimap that orders its keys using the compare function specified when my template was instantiated. Use `alloc` to allocate storage.
Constructor	*multimap(const Compare& compare)* Construct myself to be an empty multimap that orders its keys using the compare function `compare`.
Constructor	*multimap(alloc_type& alloc, const Compare& compare)* Construct myself to be an empty multimap that orders its keys using the compare function `compare`. Use `alloc` to allocate storage.
Constructor	*multimap(const value_type* first, const value_type* last)* Construct myself to contain copies of the key/value pairs in the range `[first, last)`, using the compare function specified when my template was instantiated to order my keys.
Constructor	*multimap(alloc_type& alloc, const value_type* first, const value_type* last)* Construct myself to contain copies of the key/value pairs in the range `[first, last)`, using the compare function specified when my template was instantiated to order my keys. Use `alloc` to allocate storage.
Constructor	*multimap(const value_type* first, const value_type* last, const Compare& compare)* Construct myself to contain copies of the key/value pairs in the range `[first, last)`, using `compare` to order my keys.

Constructor	*multimap(alloc_type& alloc, const value_type* first,* *const value_type* last, const Compare& compare)* Construct myself to contain copies of the key/value pairs in the range `[first, last)`, using `compare` to order my keys. Use `alloc` to allocate storage.
Constructor	*multimap(const multimap< Key,Value,Compare >& x)* Construct myself to be a copy of `x`.
Constructor	*multimap(alloc_type& alloc,* *const multimap< Key,Value,Compare >& x)* Construct myself to be a copy of `x`. Use `alloc` to allocate storage.
Destructor	*~multimap()* Destroy myself, erasing all of my key/value pairs.
=	*multimap< Key,Value,Compare >& operator=* *(const multimap< Key,Value,Compare >& x)* Replace my contents by a copy of `x`'s.
==	*bool operator==* *(const multimap< Key,Value,Compare >& x) const* Return `true` if I contain the same items in the same order as `x`.
<	*bool operator<* *(const multimap< Key,Value,Compar e>& x) const* Return `true` if I'm lexigraphically less than `x`.
begin	*iterator begin()* Return an iterator positioned at my first key/value pair.
begin	*const_iterator begin() const* Return an iterator positioned at my first key/value pair.
count	*size_type count(const Key& key) const* Return the number of key/value pairs that I contain whose key matches `key`.
empty	*bool empty() const* Return `true` if I contain no entries.
end	*iterator end()* Return an iterator positioned immediately after my last key/value pair.
end	*const_iterator end() const* Return an iterator positioned immediately after my last key/value pair.
equal_range	*pair< iterator, iterator > equal_range(const Key& key)* Return a pair of iterators whose first element is equal to lower_bound() and whose second element is equal to upper_bound().

equal_range

pair< const_iterator, const_iterator >
equal_range(const Key& key) const
Return a pair of iterators whose first element is equal to lower_bound()
and whose second element is equal to upper_bound().

erase[7]

void erase()
Erase all of my key/value pairs.

erase

void erase(iterator pos)
Erase the key/value pair at pos.

erase

void erase(iterator first, iterator last)
Erase the key/value pairs in range [first, last).

erase

size_type erase(const Key& key)
Erase all key/value pairs whose key matches key and return the number of
elements that were erased.

find

iterator find(const Key& key) const
If I contain a key/value pair whose key matches key, return an iterator
positioned at the matching pair, otherwise return an iterator positioned at
end().

insert

iterator insert(const value_type& pair)
Insert a copy of the key/value pair pair, and return an iterator to the new
key/value pair.

insert

void insert(const value_type first, const value_type* last)*
Insert copies of the key/value pairs in the range [first, last).

insert

iterator insert(iterator pos, const value_type& pair)
Insert a copy of pair, using pos as a hint on where to start searching for
the correct place to insert.

key_comp

Compare key_comp() const
Return the comparison object used to compare my keys.

lower_bound

iterator lower_bound(const Key& key)
Return an iterator positioned at the first location where a pair with key
key could be inserted without violating the ordering criteria. If no such
location is found, return an iterator positioned at end().

lower_bound

const_iterator lower_bound(const Key& key) const
Return an iterator positioned at the first location where a pair with key
key could be inserted without violating the ordering criteria. If no such
location is found, return an iterator positioned at end().

---

[7] Non-standard, unique to Systems<ToolKit>

max_size	*size_type max_size() const* Return the maximum number of key/value pairs that I can contain.
rbegin	*reverse_iterator rbegin()* Return a reverse iterator positioned at my last key/value pair.
rbegin	*const_reverse_iterator rbegin() const* Return a reverse iterator positioned at my last key/value pair.
rend	*reverse_iterator rend()* Return a reverse_iterator positioned immediately before my first key/value pair.
rend	*const_reverse_iterator rend() const* Return a reverse_iterator positioned immediately before my first key/value pair.
size	*size_type size() const* Return the number of key/value pairs that I contain.
swap	*void swap(multimap< Key,Value,Compare >& x)* Swap my contents with x's.
upper_bound	*iterator upper_bound(const Key& key)* Return an iterator positioned at the last location where a pair with key `key` could be inserted without violating the ordering criteria. If no such location is found, return an iterator positioned at end().
upper_bound	*const_iterator upper_bound(const Key& key) const* Return an iterator positioned at the last location where a pair with key `key` could be inserted without violating the ordering criteria. If no such location is found, return an iterator positioned at end().
value_comp	*map_compare< Key,Value,Compare > value_comp() const* Return the comparison object using for comparing my key/value pairs.

multiset

Description:

A `multiset` is a container that is optimized for fast associative lookup. Items are matched using their == operator. When an item is inserted into a `multiset`, it is stored in a data structure that allows the item to be found very quickly. Within the data structure, the items are ordered according to a user-defined comparitor function object. A typical user-supplied function object is `less`, which causes the items to be ordered in ascending order. Unlike `set`s, a `multiset` can contain multiple copies of the same item.

Declaration:
```
#include <set.h>
template< class Key, class Compare >
class multiset
```

Constructor	*multiset()* Construct myself to be an empty multiset that orders elements using the compare function specified when my template was instantiated.
Constructor	*multiset(alloc_type& alloc)* Construct myself to be an empty multiset that orders elements using the compare function specified when my template was instantiated. Use `alloc` to allocate storage.
Constructor	*multiset(const Compare& compare)* Construct myself to be an empty multiset that orders elements using the compare function `compare`.
Constructor	*multiset(alloc_type& alloc, const Compare& compare)* Construct myself to be an empty multiset that orders elements using the compare function `compare`. Use `alloc` to allocate storage.
Constructor	*multiset(const Key* first, const Key* last)* Construct myself to contain copies of the elements in the range `[first, last)`, using the compare function specified when my template was instantiated.
Constructor	*multiset(alloc_type& alloc, const Key* first, const Key* last)* Construct myself to contain copies of the elements in the range `[first, last)`, using the compare function specified when my template was instantiated. Use `alloc` to allocate storage.

Constructor	*multiset(const Key* first, const Key* last,* *const Compare& compare)* Construct myself to contain copies of the elements in the range `[first, last)`, using `compare` to order the elements.
Constructor	*multiset(alloc_type& alloc, const Key* first, const Key* last,* *const Compare& compare)* Construct myself to contain copies of the elements in the range `[first, last)`, using `compare` to order the elements. Use `alloc` to allocate storage.
Constructor	*multiset(const multiset< Key,Compare >& x)* Construct myself to be a copy of `x`.
Constructor	*multiset(alloc_type& alloc, const multiset< Key,Compare >& x)* Construct myself to be a copy of `x`. Use `alloc` to allocate storage.
Destructor	*~multiset()* Destroy myself, erasing all of my items.
=	*multiset< Key,Compare >&* *operator=(const multiset< Key,Compare >& x)* Replace my contents by a copy of `x`'s.
==	*bool operator==(const multiset< Key,Compare >& x) const* Return `true` if I contain the same items in the same order as `x`.
<	*bool operator<(const multiset< Key,Compare >& x) const* Return `true` if I'm lexigraphically less than `x`.
begin	*iterator begin() const* Return an iterator positioned at my first item.
count	*size_type count(const Key& key) const* Return the number of elements that I contain that match `key`.
empty	*bool empty() const* Return `true` if I contain no entries.
end	*iterator end() const* Return an iterator positioned immediately after my last item.
equal_range	*pair< const_iterator, const_iterator >* *equal_range(const Key& key) const* Return a pair of iterators whose first element is equal to lower_bound() and whose second element is equal to upper_bound().

erase[8]	*void erase()* Erase all of my elements.
erase	*void erase(iterator pos)* Erase the element at `pos`.
erase	*void erase(iterator first, iterator last)* Erase the elements in range `[first, last)`.
erase	*size_type erase(const Key& key)* Erase all elements that match `value` and return the number of elements that were erased.
find	*iterator find(const Key& key) const* If I contain an element that matches `value`, return an iterator positioned at the matching element, otherwise return an iterator positioned at end().
insert	*iterator insert(const Key& key)* Insert a copy of `value` and return an iterator positioned at the new element.
insert	*void insert(const Key* first, const Key* last)* Insert copies of the elements in the range `[first, last)`.
insert	*iterator insert(iterator pos, const Key& key)* Insert a copy of `value` and return an iterator positioned at the new element. Use `pos` as a hint on where to start searching for the correct place to insert.
key_comp	*Compare key_comp() const* Return my comparison object.
lower_bound	*iterator lower_bound(const Key& key) const* Return an iterator positioned at the first location that `key` could be inserted without violating the ordering criteria. If no such location is found, return an iterator positioned at end().
max_size	*size_type max_size() const* Return the maximum number of entries that I can contain.
rbegin	*reverse_iterator rbegin() const* Return a reverse iterator positioned at my last item.
rend	*reverse_iterator rend() const* Return a reverse_iterator positioned immediately before my first item.
size	*size_type size() const* Return the number of entries that I contain.

---

[8] Non-standard, unique to Systems<ToolKit>

swap   *void swap(multiset< Key,Compare >& x)*
                     Swap my contents with x's.

upper_bound   *iterator upper_bound(const Key& key) const*
                     Return an iterator positioned at the last location that `key` could be
                     inserted without violating the ordering criteria. If no such location is
                     found return an iterator positioned at end().

value_comp   *Compare value_comp() const*
                     Return my comparison object.

mutex_semaphore

Description:
> To ensure that a shared resource can only be accessed by one thread at a time, use a mutex semaphore. If a thread tries to lock a mutex semaphore it already owns, the request immediately succeeds. A mutex semaphore must be unlocked as many times as it was locked before another thread can lock it.

Declaration:
```
#include <ospace/sync/mutex.h>
class os_mutex_semaphore
```

Typedefs:
```
typedef os_mutex_semaphore os_mutex
```

Constructor	*os_mutex_semaphore(bool locked)* The `locked` parameter determines whether or not I will be initially created in a locked or unlocked state. Events: `syscall`
Destructor	*~os_mutex_semaphore()* Destroy myself, releasing any associated system resources. Events: `syscall`
lock	*void lock()* Acquire a lock, blocking if necessary. A thread will not block if it tries to obtain a mutex that it already owns. Events: `syscall`
obtain	*void obtain()* Acquire a lock on me, blocking if necessary. Synonym for `lock`.
release	*void release()* Release a lock on me. Synonym for `unlock`.
try_lock	*bool try_lock()* Attempt to lock this mutex, with no blocking. Return `true` if successful. Events: `syscall`
unlock	*void unlock()* Release a lock on myself.

named_pipe

Description:

Named pipes (often referred to as FIFOs; first in, first out) are less restricted than unnamed pipes, and offer the following advantages:

– they have a name that exists in the file system

– they may be used by unrelated processes

– they exist until explicitly deleted

To create and open a named pipe, specify its name, open control flags, I/O control flags and permissions during its construction sequence. Once a named pipe is opened, writes add data to the start of its FIFO queue and reads take data from the end of its FIFO queue. When a process finishes with a named pipe, is should close it. When an `os_named_pipe` is destroyed, it is automatically closed. Once created, a named pipe remains in the file system until it is explicitly removed.

To remove a named pipe, use `os_file_system::remove()`. To create an unopened named pipe, use `os_named_pipe::create()`.

Here are the behaviors of a named pipe:

– If a process tries to open a named pipe for read-only and no process currently has it open for writing, the reader will wait until a process opens it for writing, unless non-blocking I/O has been selected, in which case the open succeeds immediately.

– If a process tries to open a named pipe for write-only and no process currently has it open for reading, the writer will wait until a process opens it for reading, unless non-blocking I/O has been selected, in which case the open fails immediately.

– Named pipes will not work across a network.

– If a named pipe is read when it's empty and is not opened by any writers, its eof flag is set.

– If a process writes to a named pipe whose read end is closed, it is sent a `SIGPIPE` signal.

Conversions allow `os_named_pipe` and `os_desc_t` (UNIX descriptor) to be used interchangeably.

Declaration:
```
#include <ospace/pipe/npipe.h>
class os_named_pipe
```

Options:

Legal open control:	O_OPEN, O_CREAT, O_EXCL
Default open control:	O_OPEN
Legal I/O control:	O_ASYNC, O_CLOSE_ON_EXEC, O_NONBLOCK, O_RDONLY, O_RDWR, O_WRONLY
Default I/O control:	O_RDONLY
Default mode:	0660 (read & write by user and group)

Constructor   *os_named_pipe(os_desc_t descriptor)*
Construct myself to reference the pipe with descriptor descriptor
(default OS_UNDEFINED). By default, close myself on destruction.

Constructor   *os_named_pipe(const string& name, os_open_t open_control,*
os_ioctl_t io_control, os_mode_t mode)
Construct myself to reference a pipe with name name and mode mode
(default 0660), using open flags open (default O_OPEN) and control flags
control (default O_RDONLY). By default, close myself on destruction.

> Events: syscall, other
> On Resumption: I will be in an unknown state.

Destructor   *~os_named_pipe()*
Destroy myself, closing my descriptor if necessary.

<   *bool operator<(const os_named_pipe& pipe) const*
Return true if my descriptor is less than pipe's

==   *bool operator==(const os_named_pipe& pipe) const*
Return true if my descriptor is the same as pipe's.

auto_close   *bool auto_close() const*
Return true if I close my descriptor on destruction.

auto_close   *void auto_close(bool flag)*
If flag is true, close my descriptor on destruction.

clear   *void clear()*
Reset my state to good.

close   *void close()*
Close my descriptor and then set it to OS_UNDEFINED. If it's already
closed, do nothing.

> Events: syscall
> On Resumption: My descriptor may be unchanged.

create
/* static */ void create(const string& filepath, os_mode_t mode)
Create (but don't open) a named pipe in the file system with name `filepath` and mode `mode` (default `0660`).

> Events: `syscall`
> On Resumption: The named pipe may not exist.

descriptor
os_desc_t descriptor() const
Return my descriptor.

descriptor
void descriptor(os_desc_t descriptor)
Set my descriptor to `descriptor`.

eof
bool eof() const
Return `true` if I'm at the end of my input.

event_on_eof
void event_on_eof(bool flag)
If `flag` is `true`, I will generate an event on eof.

event_on_eof
bool event_on_eof() const
Return `true` if I will generate an event on eof.

good
bool good() const
Return `true` if I'm not failed and not at eof.

io_control
os_ioctl_t io_control() const
Return my I/O control setting.

> Events: `syscall`
> On Resumption: Returns `OS_UNDEFINED`.

io_control
void io_control(os_ioctl_t control)
Set my I/O control setting to `control`.

> Events: `syscall`
> On Resumption: My I/O control setting may be unchanged.

is_open
bool is_open() const
Return `true` if I'm open.

ok
bool ok() const
Return `true` if I'm not failed.

os_desc_t
operator os_desc_t() const
Return my descriptor.

read
int read(void* buffer, int bytes)
Read up to `bytes` bytes into `buffer`. Return the number of bytes actually read, or `-1` on error.

> Events: `syscall`
> On Resumption: Returns `-1`.

status   *os_io_status status( ) const*
                              Return my I/O status.

> Events: `syscall`
> On Resumption: Return value may be invalid.

write   *int write(const void* buffer, int bytes)*
                              Write `bytes` bytes from `buffer`. Return the number of bytes actually
                              written, or `-1` on error.

> Events: `syscall`
> On Resumption: Returns `-1`.

Non-Member Functions:

<<   *ostream& operator<<(ostream& stream, const os_named_pipe& pipe)*
                              Print `pipe` to `stream`.

negate

Description:

negate is a unary function object that returns the negation of its operand.

Declaration:
```
#include <function.h>
template< class T >
struct negate : unary_function< T, T >
```

()   *T operator()(const T& x) const*
                                Return -x.

Example <ospace/stl/examples/negate.h>

```
#include <stl.h>
#include <iostream.h>

int input [3] = { 1, 2, 3 };

int main ()
{
  int output[3];
  transform (input, input + 3, output, negate<int> ());
  for (int i = 0; i < 3; i++)
    cout << output[i] << endl;
  return 0;
}

-1
-2
-3
```

network

Description:

A network is a set of computers that intercommunicate using one or more protocols. The Internet is the most famous example, linking computers throughout the world using TCP/IP. Every network has a name, a set of aliases and an IP network address. Information about networks is usually stored in /etc/networks.

An os_network represents a single network and may be constructed from its name or an IP address.

Declaration:
```
#include <ospace/socket/network.h>
class os_network
```

Constructor	*os_network()* Construct myself to have an empty name.
Constructor	*os_network(const netent& network)* Construct myself from the netent structure network.
Constructor	*os_network(const os_network& network)* Construct myself to be a copy of network.
Constructor	*os_network(const string& name)* Construct myself from name. Events: other On Resumption: I will be in an unusable state.
Constructor	*os_network(const os_ip_address& address)* Construct myself from the IP address address. Events: other On Resumption: I will be in an unusable state.
<	*bool operator<(const os_network& network) const* Return true if my name is less than network's.
=	*os_network& operator=(const os_network& network)* Assign myself from network.
==	*bool operator==(const os_network& network) const* Return true if my name is the same as network's.
aliases	*const vector< string >& aliases() const* Return a vector of my aliases.

defined	*bool defined( ) const* Return `true` if my name is not empty.
ip_address	*const os_ip_address& ip_address( ) const* Return my IP address.
name	*string name( ) const* Return my name.
networks	*/* static */ vector< os_network* > networks( )* Return a vector of pointers to objects on the heap representing all of the networks in the network database. It is the caller's responsibility to properly delete the objects in the vector.
print	*void print(ostream& stream) const* Print my name and IP address to `stream`.

Non-Member Functions:

<<	*ostream& operator<<(ostream& stream, const os_network& network)* Print `network` to `stream`.
<<	*os_bstream& operator<<(os_bstream& stream, const os_network& network)* Write `network` to `stream`.
>>	*os_bstream& operator>>(os_bstream& stream, os_network& network)* Read `network` from `stream`.

.

not_equal_to

Description:

not_equal_to is a binary function object that returns `true` if its first operand is not equal to its second operand.

Declaration:
```
#include <function.h>
template< class T >
struct not_equal_to : binary_function< T, T, bool >
```

()
bool operator()(const T& x, const T& y) const
Return `x != y`.

Example <ospace/stl/examples/nequal.cpp>

```
#include <stl.h>
#include <iostream.h>

int input1 [4] = { 1, 7, 2, 2 };
int input2 [4] = { 1, 6, 2, 3 };

int main ()
{
  int output [4];
  transform (input1, input1 + 4, input2, output,
    not_equal_to<int> ());
  for (int i = 0; i < 4; i++)
    cout << output[i] << endl;
  return 0;
}

0
1
0
1
```

open_control

Description:

Any I/O class with a constructor that takes an `os_open_t` parameter can be constructed to either access an existing object in the system or create a new object. A parameter of this type accepts either an `os_open_control` object or a bitwise or-ing of the following POSIX flags:

- `O_CREAT` Create the object if it doesn't already exist and then open it.

- `O_EXCL` If `O_CREAT` is specified and the object already exists, generate an event.

- `O_OPEN` Open the object if it already exists, otherwise generate an event. This cannot be specified in addition to `O_CREAT`.

- `O_TRUNC` If the file already exists, truncate it to zero length (for files only).

You can use the `os_open_control` class to set these flags without having to remember the names of the POSIX flags; however, this causes a slight overhead incurred when an `os_open_control` object is converted into an `os_open_t`.

Declaration:
```
#include <ospace/io/openctrl.h>
class os_open_control
```

Constructor	*os_open_control(os_open_t control)* Construct myself to have encoded bits `control` (default 0).
Constructor	*os_open_control(const os_open_control& control)* Construct myself to be a copy of `control`.
<	*bool operator<(const os_open_control& control) const* Return `true` if my value is less than `control`'s.
=	*os_open_control& operator=(const os_open_control& control)* Assign myself from `control`.
=	*os_open_control& operator=(os_open_t control)* Assign myself from `control`.
==	*bool operator==(const os_open_control& control) const* Return `true` if my value is the same as `control`'s.
create	*void create(bool flag)* Set creation to `flag`.
create	*bool create() const* Return `true` if creation is enabled. The I/O object will be created if it doesn't already exist.

exclusive   *void exclusive(bool flag)*
                           Set exclusive creation to `flag`.

exclusive   *bool exclusive() const*
                           Return `true` if exclusive creation is enabled. If creation and exclusive
                           creation is enabled and the I/O object already exists, the creation will fail.

os_open_t   *operator os_open_t() const*
                           Return my encoded control bits.

print   *void print(ostream& stream) const*
                           Print my attributes to `stream`.

truncate   *bool truncate() const*
                           Return `true` if truncation is enabled. If truncation is enabled and the I/O
                           object already exists and is writeable, all of its previous data is deleted
                           when it is opened.

truncate   *void truncate(bool flag)*
                           Set truncation to `flag`. This flag has no meaning or effect for FIFO's and
                           special files.

value   *os_open_t value() const*
                           Return my encoded control bits.

value   *void value(os_open_t control)*
                           Set my encoded control bits to `control`.

Non-Member Functions:

<<   *ostream& operator<<(ostream& stream, const os_open_control&*
                           control)
                           Print `control` to `stream`.

<<   *os_bstream& operator<<(os_bstream& stream, const os_open_control&*
                           control)
                           Write `control` to `stream`.

>>   *os_bstream& operator>>(os_bstream& stream, os_open_control&*
                           control)
                           Read `control` from `stream`.

ostream_iterator

Description:

An `ostream_iterator` is an iterator that outputs items (with an optional trailer) in a typesafe manner to an output stream.

Declaration:
```
#include <iterator.h>
template< class T >
class ostream_iterator : public output_iterator
```

Constructor	*ostream_iterator(ostream& stream)* Construct myself to be associated with `stream`. Set my trailer to an empty string.
Constructor	*ostream_iterator(ostream& stream, char* trailer)* Construct myself to be associated with `stream`. Set my trailer to `trailer`.
=	*ostream_iterator< T >& operator=(const T& value)* Write `value` together with my trailer to my associated stream.
*	*ostream_iterator< T >& operator *()* Return a reference to myself.
++	*ostream_iterator< T >& operator++()* Return a reference to myself.
++	*ostream_iterator< T > operator++(int)* Return a copy of myself.

Example <ospace/stl/examples/ostmit.cpp>

```
#include <stl.h>
#include <iostream.h>

int array [] = { 1, 5, 2, 4 };

int main ()
{
  char* string = "hello";
  ostream_iterator<char> it1 (cout);
  copy (string, string + 5, it1);
  cout << endl;
  ostream_iterator<int> it2 (cout);
  copy (array, array + 4, it2);
  cout << endl;
  return 0;
}

hello
1524
```

pair
___

Description:

A `pair` is an object that contains two other objects. It is most commonly used for conveniently storing and passing pairs of objects.

Declaration:
```
#include <pair.h>
template< class T1, class T2 >
class pair
```

Adapter:
```
template< class T1, class T2 >
pair< T1, T2 >
make_pair( const T1& x, const T2& y )
```

Constructor	*pair()* Construct myself to contain default instances of T1 and T2.
Constructor	*pair(const T1& a, const T2& b)* Construct myself to contain a copy of a as my first item and a copy of b as my second item.
first	*first* My first item. This is a public data member, not a function.
second	*second* My second item. This is a public data member, not a function.

Non-Member Functions:

==	*bool operator==(const pair< T1, T2 >& x, const pair< T1, T2 >& y)* Return `true` if (`x.first == y.first`) and (`x.second == y.second`). This is a templatized non-member function.
<	*bool operator<(const pair< T1, T2 >& x, const pair< T1, T2 >& y)* Return `true` if x is lexographically less than y. That is, (`x.first < y.first`) or (`x.first == y.first && x.second < y.second`). This is a templatized non-member function.

path

Description:

The class `os_path` allows file system paths to be manipulated. Conversions allow `os_paths` to be used interchangeably with `const char`'s and `string`.

Declaration:
```
#include <ospace/file/path.h>
class os_path
```

Constructor	*os_path()* Construct myself to be an empty path.
Constructor	*os_path(const string& filepath)* Construct myself to represent the path `filepath`. If the parameter contains a trailing slash, it will be taken as a directory name only with no file name component. Events: `memory` On Resumption: Constructs an empty path.
Constructor	*os_path(const os_path& path)* Construct myself to be a copy of `path`. Events: `memory` On Resumption: Constructs an empty path.

Constructor	*os_path(const string& dirpath, const string& filename)*
	Construct myself with `dirpath` and `filename`. For a path to a directory use this constructor with an empty string for `filename`.
	
	The `dirpath` parameter will be taken as the path, regardless of whether or not it ends in a slash. That is,
	<pre>os_path x("/foo", "bar");
	os_path y("/foo/", "bar");</pre>will both construct the identical name, `/foo/bar`.
	
	Note however that there is a significant difference between a `dirpath` of `""` and of `"/"` (the former will create a relative path and the latter an absolute path, because a *leading* slash is significant).

Constructor *os_path(const string& dirpath, const string& base,*
const string& extension)
Construct myself with directory path `dirpath` and a file name made using
the specified `base` and `extension`.

This form is similar to the two-argument form with respect to `dirpath`
and `base`. In addition, the `extension` is concatenated to the `base` with a
separator character in between. However, the `base` may itself contain
additional dots without error, so no "sloppiness" is allowed. If there is a
trailing dot in `base` and/or a leading dot in `extension`, they will be kept.
For example,
     os_path z ("/foo/", "bar.", ".baz");
will construct a path named `/foo/bar...baz` (note 3 dots).

!=   *bool operator!=(const string& str) const*
Return `true` if I'm not equal to `str`. This simply compares the string
representation of the paths and does not consider such issues as
simplification.

<   *bool operator<(const os_path& path) const*
Return `true` if I'm less than `path`. This simply compares the string
representation of the paths and does not consider such issues as
simplification.

=   *os_path& operator=(const os_path& path)*
Assign myself to be `path`.

=   *os_path& operator=(const string& filepath)*
Assign myself to be `filepath`. If the parameter contains a trailing slash,
it will be taken as a directory name only with no file name component.

> Events: `memory`
> On Resumption: No change to the object takes place.

==   *bool operator==(const os_path& path) const*
Return `true` if I'm the same as `path`. This simply compares the string
representation of the paths and does not consider such issues as
simplification.

==   *bool operator==(const string& str) const*
Return `true` if I'm the same as `str`. This simply compares the string
representation of the paths and does not consider such issues as
simplification.

[]   *os_path::substring operator[ ](int index)*
This is a synonym for `section()`.

[]   *string operator[ ](int index) const*
This is a synonym for `section()`.

absolute   *bool absolute() const*
Return `true` is I'm an absolute path. An absolute path is one that begins with a leading slash. This is the opposite of `relative()`.

base   *os_path& base(const string& str)*
Set the base portion of my file name to `str` and return a reference to myself.

> Events: `memory`
> On Resumption: `*this` is not updated.

base   *string base() const*
Return the base portion of my file name. The base portion is the part of the file name that is not the extension, as defined by `extension()`. If I have no file name component, return an empty string.

> Events: `memory`
> On Resumption: Returns an empty string.

become_relative_to   *void become_relative_to(const string& dirpath)*
Change myself to become relative to `dirpath`. Both `dirpath` and myself must be absolute paths.

For example, making `/usr/bin/foo/bar` relative to `/usr/bin` produces `foo/bar`. Making `/a/b/file.txt` relative to `/a/b/c` produces `../file.txt`.

> Events: `other`, `memory`
> On Resumption: `*this` is unchanged.

become_simplified   *void become_simplified()*
If possible, simplify myself by removing path levels that are not required. The following actions are performed:
- Consecutive slashes are removed: `foo//bar` becomes `foo/bar`.
- Directories consisting of a single dot are removed.
- Directories consisting of ".." are removed, along with the previous directory.

In normal conditions, `foo/bar/../bas` becomes `foo/bas`. However, exceptional conditions apply. If the path begins with a leading `..`, it is preserved unchanged. `../foo/bar` stays the same. However, an (incorrect) absolute path beginning with a `/..` has the `..` silently removed: `/../foo/bar` becomes `/foo/bar`.
See also `simplified()`.

> Events: `memory`
> On Resumption: Object will hold an unspecified value.

cd

os_path cd(string dirpath) const
This returns the same result as applying cd() (non-const form), but does not alter *this.

Be careful not to use this form by accident. For example, if you have a statement such as P1.cd("xyz"); and P1 is const, there will no compiler error, but neither will there be any lasting effect from this statement.

> Events: memory
> On Resumption: Returns an unspecified value.

cd

os_path& cd(string dirpath)
Change my directory. The behavior is analogous to the shell's cd command. The path component is replaced or appended to, and the file name component is unchanged.

If the dirpath parameter begins with a /, the entire path is replaced by dirpath. Otherwise, the contents of dirpath is appended to the existing path. For example, Given a/b.c,
- cd("/foo") produces /foo/b.c
- cd("foo") produces a/foo/b.c

The presence of a trailing slash in the parameter is not significant. This function will also call become_simplified(), so any cd() will also result in simplification. Returns a reference to myself.

> Events: memory
> On Resumption: *this may be modified and will contain an unspecified value.

const char*

operator const char() const*
Return myself as a const char*. This pointer is no longer valid after I have been modified.

> Events: memory
> On Resumption: Returns 0.

directory

void directory(string str)
Set my directory component to str. See also filename().

> Events: memory
> On Resumption: Object contains an unspecified value

directory	*string directory() const*

Return my directory path. This returns a string containing just the directory component of this path, including a trailing backslash. Note that `directory()` and `filename()` are complementary; if you call both and simply concatenate the results together you will regain the original full name.

> Events: `memory`
> On Resumption: Returns an empty string.

directory_path	*bool directory_path() const*

Return `true` if I do not have a file name component. Such path objects always end with a slash. This is the antonym of `file_path()`.

extension	*string extension() const*

Return my filename extension. The extension is everything that follows the last dot in the file name component. For example, the extension of `foo/bar/jokes.tar.gz` is `gz`, not including the dot. The path `foo/prog_3.01/bin/` has no extension, since this function only looks at the file name component. The file `foo/.bashrc` has no extension, since this class treats a dot as the first character of a file name as part of the name, not an extension.

If I have no extension, return an empty string.

> Events: `memory`
> On Resumption: Returns an empty string.

extension	*os_path& extension(const string& str)*

This replaces the contents of the extension, as described by `extension()`, with `str`. Calling with an empty string will remove the extension but not the dot. Use `no_extension()` to remove an extension. If there was no previous extension, `str` is appended along with a dot. Given `./bar`, calling `extension("bak")` will produce `./bar.bak`. There is no way to append an extension in addition to an extension that may already exist—manipulate the file name component with other members to produce the desired result. Returns a reference to myself.

> Events: `memory`
> On Resumption: `*this` is not altered.

file_path	*bool file_path() const*

Return `true` if I have a file name component. This is the antonym of `directory_path()`.

filename	*string filename() const* Return my filename. This returns a string containing just the file name component of this path. Note that `directory()` and `filename()` are complementary; if you call both and simply concatenate the results together you will regain the original full name. Events: `memory` On Resumption: Returns an empty string.
filename	*os_path& filename(const string& filename)* Set my file name component to `filename` and return a reference to myself. Events: `memory` On Resumption: Does not alter `*this`.
has_directory	*bool has_directory() const* Return `true` if I have a directory path. That is, the file name is qualified with a path. For example, `notes.txt` has no directory, while `plan9/notes.txt` does. Also, you may have a directory with no file name, such as `plan9/`.
has_extension	*bool has_extension() const* Return `true` if my file name component has an extension. See `extension()`.
head	*string head() const* Return the first section in my directory path, or an empty string if I have no directory path. See `has_directory()` and `section()`. Events: `memory`
head	*void head(const string& str)* Set the first section in my directory component to `str`. If there is a file name only with no directory information, `str` is inserted as a new level. See `section()`. Events: `memory`
is_dot_directory	*/* static */ bool is_dot_directory(const string& str)* Return `true` if `str` is `"."` or `".."`.
legal	*bool legal(int index) const* Return `true` if `index` is a legal directory path level. That is, `index >= 0 && index < levels()`.

levels
        int levels() const
Return the number of levels in my directory path. Each component which is followed by a slash is considered one level. A leading slash does not count, but a trailing slash *does*. For example, `/foo` and `foo` both have one level. `/foo/bar` and `foo/bar` both have two levels. `foo/bar/` has three (you can think of the missing implied file name as being the third). See also `section()`.

no_extension
        os_path& no_extension()
Remove my extension, as defined by the *get* form of `extension()`, including the dot. If there was no extension, this function does nothing without error. Returns a reference to myself.

        Events: `memory`
        On Resumption: `*this` is not altered.

string&
        operator const string&() const
Convert myself to a `const string&`.

print
        void print(ostream& stream) const
Print my path to `stream`.

relative
        bool relative() const
Return `true` if I'm a relative path. A relative path is one that does not begin with a leading slash. Because `relative()` and `absolute()` are strict antonyms, an empty path tests as relative.

relative_to
        os_path relative_to(const string& dirpath) const
This does the same thing as `become_relative_to()`, except it returns the result as the function return value rather than updating `this`.

        Events: `other`, `memory`
        On Resumption: Returns a copy of `*this`.

simplified
        os_path simplified() const
Return the value of simplifying myself. See `become_simplified()`.

        Events: `memory`
        On Resumption: Returns an unspecified value.

tail
        string tail() const
Return the last section of my directory component. If there is just a file name only with no directory information, return an empty string. See `section()`.

tail
        void tail(const string& str)
Set the last section in my directory component to `str`. If there is just a file name only with no directory information, `str` is inserted as a new level. See `section()`.

Non-Member Functions:

!=
> *bool operator!=(const string& str, const os_path& path)*
> Return `true` if `str` is not equal to `path`. This simply compares the string representation of the paths and does not consider such issues as simplification.

==
> *bool operator==(const string& str, const os_path& path)*
> Return `true` if `str` is equal to `path`. This simply compares the string representation of the paths and does not consider such issues as simplification.

<<
> *ostream& operator<<(ostream& stream, const os_path& path)*
> Print `path` to `stream`.

<<
> *os_bstream& operator<<(os_bstream& stream, const os_path& path)*
> Write `path` to `stream`.

>>
> *os_bstream& operator>>(os_bstream& stream, os_path& path)*
> Read `path` from `stream`.

plus

Description:

plus is a binary function object that returns the sum of its two operands.

Declaration:
```
#include <function.h>
template< class T >
struct plus : binary_function< T, T, T >
```

()   *T operator()(const T& x, const T& y) const*
                                  Return x + y.

Example <ospace/stl/examples/plus.cpp>

```
#include <stl.h>
#include <iostream.h>

int input1 [4] = { 1, 6, 11, 8 };
int input2 [4] = { 1, 5, 2, 3 };

int main ()
{
  int total = inner_product (input1, input1 + 4, input2, 0,
    plus<int> (), times<int> ());
  cout << "total = " << total << endl;
  return 0;
}
```

total = 77

pointer_to_binary_function, ptr_fun

Description:

`pointer_to_binary_function` is an object that allows you to use a regular C binary function as a binary function object. When executed, it returns the result of executing the regular C function with two operands. Its associated adapter function `ptr_fun()` allows you to conveniently construct a `pointer_to_binary_function` object directly from a C binary function.

Declaration:
```
#include <function.h>
template< class Arg1, class Arg2, class Result >
class pointer_to_binary_function : public binary_function< Arg1, Arg2,
Result >
```

Adapter:
```
template< class Arg1, class Arg2, class Result >
pointer_to_binary_function< Arg1, Arg2, Result > ptr_fun
  (
  Result (*f_)( Arg1, Arg2 )
  )
```

Constructor	*pointer_to_binary_function(Result(*f(Arg1, Arg2))* Construct myself with an associated function `f`.
()	*Result operator()(const Arg1& x, const Arg2& y) const* Return `f( x, y )`

Example <ospace/stl/examples/ptrbinf1.cpp>

```
#include <stl.h>
#include <iostream.h>

int sum (int x_, int y_)
{
  return x_ + y_;
}

int input1 [4] = { 7, 2, 3, 5 };
int input2 [4] = { 1, 5, 5, 8 };

int main ()
{
  int output [4];
  transform (input1, input1 + 4, input2, output,
    pointer_to_binary_function<int, int, int> (sum));
  for (int i = 0; i < 4; i++)
    cout << output[i] << endl;
  return 0;
}

8
7
8
13
```

Example <ospace/stl/examples/ptrbinf2.cpp>

```
#include <stl.h>
#include <iostream.h>

int input1 [4] = { 7, 2, 3, 5 };
int input2 [4] = { 1, 5, 5, 8 };

int main ()
{
  int output [4];
  transform (input1, input1 + 4, input2, output, ptr_fun (sum));
  for (int i = 0; i < 4; i++)
    cout << output[i] << endl;
  return 0;
}

8
7
8
13
```

pointer_to_unary_function, ptr_fun

Description:

`pointer_to_unary_function` is an object that allows you to use a regular C unary function as a unary function object. When executed, it returns the result of executing the regular C function with an operand. Its associated adapter function `ptr_fun()` allows you to conveniently construct a `pointer_to_unary_function` object directly from a C unary function.

Declaration:
```
#include <function.h>
template< class Arg, class Result >
class pointer_to_unary_function : public unary_function< Arg, Result >
```

Adapter:
```
template< class Arg, class Result >
pointer_to_unary_function< Arg, Result > ptr_fun( Result(*f_)( Arg ) )
```

Constructor	*pointer_to_unary_function(Result(*f)(Arg))* Construct myself with associated unary function `f`.
()	*Result operator()(const Arg& x) const* Return `f( x )`.

Example <ospace/stl/examples/ptrunf1.cpp>

```
#include <stl.h>
#include <iostream.h>

int array [3] = { 1, 2, 3 };

int main ()
{
  int* p = find_if (array, array + 3,
    pointer_to_unary_function<int, bool> (even));
  if (p != array + 3)
    cout << *p << " is even" << endl;
  return 0;
}
```

2 is even

Example <ospace/stl/examples/ptrunf2.cpp>

```
#include <stl.h>
#include <iostream.h>

int array [3] = { 1, 2, 3 };

int main ()
{
  int* p = find_if (array, array + 3, ptr_fun(even));
  if (p != array + 3)
    cout << *p << endl;
  return 0;
}
```

2 is even

priority_queue

Description:

A `priority_queue` is an adapter that allows you to use any sequential container that has a random access iterator to maintain a sorted collection of items. It allows you to specify a comparator that is used to sort the items.

Declaration:
```
#include <queue.h>
template< class Container, class Compare >
class priority_queue
```

Constructor	*priority_queue()* Construct myself to be an empty stack.
Constructor	*priority_queue(Container::alloc_type& alloc)* Construct myself to be an empty stack. Use `alloc` to allocate storage.
Destructor	*~priority_queue()* Destroy myself, erasing all of my items.
=	*priority_queue< Container, Compare >& operator=* *(const priority_queue< Container, Compare >& x)* Replace my contents by a copy of x's.
empty	*bool empty() const* Return `true` if I contain no entries.
max_size	*size_type max_size() const* Return the maximum number of entries that I can contain.
pop	*void pop()* Erase my top element. 　Events: `os_empty_error`
push	*void push(const T& value)* Push a copy of `value`.
size	*size_type size() const* Return the number of entries that I contain.
swap	*void swap(priority_queue< Container, Compare >& x)* Swap my contents with x's.

top   *T& top()*
                           Return a reference to my top element.

                               Events: `other (os_empty_error)`

top   *const T& top() const*
                           Return a reference to my top element.

                               Events: `other (os_empty_error)`

process

Description:

To create, suspend, resume interrupt and terminate a process, use the `os_process` class. When a process object is created, the current process spawns a child and stores the child's PID in the process object.

The current process and the child execute concurrently. If you want the current process to wait until one of its children terminates, use one of the `wait()` family of functions described in the "process_status" section of this chapter.

There are several ways to construct a process object:

- To spawn a child that executes a command in a shell, construct the process using the name of the shell and the name of the command.
- To spawn a child that executes a named program with arguments, construct the process using the program name and an optional null-terminated argument list or array of arguments.
- To spawn a child that executes a function within the current program, construct the process using a pointer to the function and an optional null-terminated argument list or array of arguments.

Each of these approaches has a variation that provides a new environment for the process and performs I/O redirection.

Conversions allow `os_process` and `os_pid_t` to be used interchangeably.

Declaration:
```
#include <ospace/process/process.h>
class os_process
```

Constructor	*os_process(const char* name)* Construct myself to be a process executing the program called `name`. Events: `syscall`, `other` On Resumption: Process id set to `OS_UNDEFINED`.
Constructor	*os_process(const char* name, const char* argv[])* Construct myself to be a process executing the program called `name` using the null-terminated argument list `argv`. Be careful to remember to terminate the argument list `argv` with a zero. Events: `syscall` On Resumption: Process id is set to `OS_UNDEFINED`.

Constructor   *os_process(int (*f)())*
Construct myself to be a process executing the function f.

> Events: syscall
> On Resumption: Process id is set to OS_UNDEFINED.

Constructor   *os_process(int (*f)(int argc, const char* argv[]), const char* argv[])*
Construct myself to be a process executing the function f using the null-terminated argument list argv. Be careful to terminate the argument list argv with a zero.

> Events: syscall
> On Resumption: Process id is set to OS_UNDEFINED.

Constructor   *os_process(const char* shell, const char* command)*
Construct myself to be a process executing the command command using the shell shell.

> Events: syscall
> On Resumption: Process id is set to OS_UNDEFINED.

Constructor   *os_process(const os_environment* env, os_desc_t send,*
os_desc_t receive, os_desc_t error, const char* shell,
const char* command)
Construct myself to be a process executing the command command using the shell shell, environment env, send channel send, receive channel receive and error channel error.

> Events: syscall, memory, other
> On Resumption: Process id is set to OS_UNDEFINED.

Constructor   *os_process(const os_environment* env, os_desc_t send,*
os_desc_t receive, os_desc_t error, const char* name)
Construct myself to be a process executing the program called name using environment env, send channel send, receive channel receive and error channel error.

> Events: syscall, memory
> On Resumption: Process id is set to OS_UNDEFINED.

Constructor   *os_process(const os_environment* env, os_desc_t send,*
os_desc_t receive, os_desc_t error, const char* name,
const char* argv[])
Construct myself to be a process executing the program called name using the null-terminated argument list argv, environment env, send channel send, receive channel receive and error channel error.

> Events: syscall, memory
> On Resumption: Process id is set to OS_UNDEFINED.

Constructor *os_process(const os_environment* env, os_desc_t send,*
*os_desc_t receive, os_desc_t error, int (*f)())*
Construct myself to be a process executing the function f using the
environment env, send channel send, receive channel receive and error
channel error.

> Events: syscall, memory
> On Resumption: Process id is set to OS_UNDEFINED.

Constructor *os_process(const os_environment* env, os_desc_t send,*
*os_desc_t receive, os_desc_t error, int (*f)(int argc,*
const char argv[]), const char* argv[])*
Construct myself to be a process executing the function f using the null-
terminated argument list argv, environment env, send channel send,
receive channel receive and error channel error.

> Events: syscall, memory
> On Resumption: Process id is set to OS_UNDEFINED.

Constructor *os_process(const char* name, const char* arg1, const char* arg2, ...)*
Construct myself to be a process executing the program called name using
the null-terminated variable argument list. Be careful to remember the
zero after the last parameter. The maximum arguments are constrained by
the enum os_process::max_args.

> Events: syscall, other
> On Resumption: Process id is set to OS_UNDEFINED.

Constructor *os_process(int (*f)(int argc, const char* argv[]), const char* arg0,*
const char arg1, ...)*
Construct myself to be a process executing the function f using the null-
terminated variable argument list. Be careful to remember the zero after
the last parameter. The maximum arguments are constrained by the enum
os_process::max_args.

> Events: syscall, other
> On Resumption: Process id is set to OS_UNDEFINED.

Constructor *os_process(const os_environment* env, os_desc_t send,*
os_desc_t receive, os_desc_t error, const char name, const char* arg1,*
const char arg2, ...)*
Construct myself to be a process executing the program called name using
the null-terminated variable argument list, environment env, send channel
send, receive channel receive and error channel error. Be careful to
remember the zero after the last parameter. The maximum arguments are
constrained by the enum os_process::max_args.

> Events: syscall, other
> On Resumption: Process id is set to OS_UNDEFINED.

Constructor *os_process(const os_environment* env, os_desc_t send,*
os_desc_t receive, os_desc_t error, int (*f)(int argc,
const char* argv[]), const char* arg0, const char* arg1, ...)
Construct myself to be a process executing the function `f` using the null-terminated variable argument list, environment `env`, send channel `send`, receive channel `receive` and error channel `error`. Be careful to remember the zero after the last parameter. The maximum arguments are constrained by the `enum os_process::max_args`.

> Events: `syscall, other`
> On Resumption: Process id is set to `OS_UNDEFINED`.

Constructor *os_process(os_pid_t pid)*
Construct myself with process id `pid` (default `OS_UNDEFINED`).

Constructor *os_process(const os_process& process)*
Construct myself to be a copy of `process`.

< *bool operator<(const os_process& process) const*
Return `true` if my process id is less than `process`s.

= *os_process& operator=(const os_process& process)*
Assign myself from `process`. Return a reference to myself.

= *os_process& operator=(os_pid_t process)*
Assign myself from `process`. Return a reference to myself.

== *bool operator==(const os_process& process) const*
Return `true` if I have the same process id as `process`.

become_process group_leader

void become_process_group_leader()

Make me a process group leader.

> Events: `syscall`

defined *bool defined() const*
Return `true` if my process id is not `OS_UNDEFINED`. For process activity testing see `valid()`.

hangup *void hangup()*
Send me a hangup signal.

> Events: `syscall, other`

interrupt *void interrupt()*
Send me an interrupt signal.

> Events: `syscall, other`

is_parent_of this_process

bool is_parent_of_this_process() const

Return `true` if I am the parent of the current process.

keyboard_suspend
void keyboard_suspend()
Send me a keyboard stop signal. This is normally generated by a `Ctrl-Z` and will suspend my execution.

Events: `syscall`, `other`

kill
void kill()
Send me a kill signal.

Events: `syscall`, `other`

os_pid_t
operator os_pid_t() const
Return my process id.

pid
os_pid_t pid() const
Return my process id.

pid
void pid(os_pid_t pid)
Set my process id to `pid`.

print
void print(ostream& stream) const
Print myself to `stream`.

priority
int priority() const
Return my execution priority (nice) value. The range varies some between platforms, but is usually -20 (highest priority) to 20 (lowest priority).

Events: `syscall`
On Resumption: Returns -1. Be careful though, this is a valid priority and therefore cannot be used exclusively as an error indicator.

priority
void priority(int value)
Set my execution priority (nice) value to `value`. The range varies between platforms, but is usually -20 (highest priority) to 20 (lowest priority). Only superuser can lower a priority.

Events: `syscall`

process_group
void process_group(os_pid_t group)
Set my process group to `group`.

Events: `syscall`

process_group
os_pid_t process_group() const
Return my process group.

Events: `syscall`
On Resumption: Returns `OS_UNDEFINED`.

quit
void quit()
Send me a quit signal.

> Events: `syscall`, `other`

resume
void resume()
Send me a continue signal. This signal will resume my execution if I was suspended.

> Events: `syscall`, `other`

signal
void signal(os_sig_t signal)
Send myself the signal `signal`.

> Events: `syscall`, `other`

suspend
void suspend()
Send me a stop signal. This will suspend my execution and is only valid for systems that support job control.

> Events: `syscall`, `other`

terminate
void terminate()
Send me a terminate signal. This is the signal sent by default when the kill(1) UNIX command is executed.

> Events: `syscall`, `other`

user_priority
/ static */ void user_priority(os_uid_t user, int value)*
Set the execution priority (nice) value to `value` for any process owned by `user`. The range of nice values varies some between platforms, but is usually -20 (highest priority) to 20 (lowest priority).

> Events: `syscall`

user_priority
/ static */ int user_priority(os_uid_t user)*
Return the execution priority (nice) value associated with any process owned by `user`. The range of nice values varies some between platforms, but is usually -20 (highest priority) to 20 (lowest priority).

> Events: `syscall`
> On Resumption: Returns -1. Be careful though, this is a valid priority and therefore cannot be used exclusively as an error indicator.

valid
bool valid() const
Return `true` if I'm a valid, registered, UNIX process.

Non-Member Functions:

<< *ostream& operator<<(ostream& stream, const os_process& process)*
Print process to stream.

<< *os_bstream& operator<<(os_bstream& stream, const os_process& process)*
Write process to stream.

>> *os_bstream& operator>>(os_bstream& stream os_process& process)*
Read process from stream.

process_group

Description:

Processes can be conveniently grouped together using the concept of a process group. Every process group has a unique numeric identifier. Every process belongs to a single process group and a child inherits its parents process group.

One process in each process group is called its group leader. In most cases, all additional processes in a process group are descendants of the process group leader. The process id and process group id are the same value for the group leader process.

You can send a signal to every process in a process group using the `signal()` function defined in `os_process_group`. Similarly, the current process can wait for any child in a particular process group using `os_this_process::wait_for_any_child_in()`.

When sending signals to process groups, permissions affect whether the signal is actually received. In order for the signal to actually be received, the caller's user id or effective user id must match the effective or saved user id of the receiving process. The single exception to this rule is `resume()`, which can always be sent to all members of the calling process' session.

If the caller has an effective user id of superuser, all of the processes in the process group receive the signal.

Conversions allow `os_process_group` and `os_pid_t` to be used interchangeably.

Declaration:
```
#include <ospace/process/procgrp.h>
class os_process_group
```

Constructor	*os_process_group(os_pid_t pgid)* Construct myself to represent the process group with process group id `pgid` (default `OS_UNDEFINED`).
Constructor	*os_process_group(const os_process_group& process_group)* Construct myself to be a copy of `process_group`.
<	*bool operator<(const os_process_group& process_group) const* Return `true` if my process group id is less than `process_group`'s.
=	*os_process_group& operator=(os_pid_t process_group)* Assign myself from `process_group`.
=	*os_process_group& operator=(* *const os_process_group& process_group)* Assign myself from `process_group`.

==	*bool operator==(const os_process_group& process_group) const* Return `true` if my process group id is the same as `process_group`'s.
defined	*bool defined() const* Return `true` if my process group id is not `OS_UNDEFINED`.
hangup	*void hangup()* Send a hangup signal to all of the processes in my group. Events: `syscall`
interrupt	*void interrupt()* Send an interrupt signal to all of the processes in my group. Events: `syscall`
keyboard_suspend	*void keyboard_suspend()* Send a stop signal as if it were generated by a keyboard action to all of the processes in my group. Events: `syscall`
kill	*void kill()* Send a kill signal to all of the processes in my group. Events: `syscall`
os_pid_t	*operator os_pid_t() const* Return my process group id.
pgid	*void pgid(os_pid_t pgid)* Set my process group id to `pgid`.
pgid	*os_pid_t pgid() const* Return my process group id.
print	*void print(ostream& stream) const* Print my process group id to `stream`.

priority	*int priority() const*
	Return the lowest nice value associated with any of my processes. Nice values are a measure of execution priority. The range varies some between platforms, but is usually -20 (highest priority) to 20 (lowest priority).
	
	    Events: `syscall`
	    On Resumption: Returns -1. Be careful though, this is a valid priority and therefore cannot be used exclusively as an error indicator.

priority	*void priority(int value)* Set the execution priority (nice) value of all processes in my group to `value`. The range varies between platforms, but is usually -20 (highest priority) to 20 (lowest priority). Only superuser can lower a priority. Events: `syscall`

quit   *void quit()*
                        Send a quit signal to all of the processes in my group.

                          Events: `syscall`

resume   *void resume()*
                        Send a continue signal to all of the processes in my group. This signal will
                        resume execution of all stopped process. When sending a continue signal,
                        all processes, regardless of their effective and saved user ids, will receive
                        the signal. Note that this signal is the exception to normal permissions
                        involving sending signals to process groups.

                          Events: `syscall`

signal   *void signal(os_sig_t code)*
                        Send the signal with code `code` to all of the processes in my group.

                          Events: `syscall`

suspend   *void suspend()*
                        Send a stop signal to all of the processes in my group, suspending their
                        execution. This signal is only valid for systems that support job control.

                          Events: `syscall`

terminate   *void terminate()*
                        Send a terminate signal to all of the processes in my group. This is the
                        signal sent by default when the kill(1) UNIX command is executed.

                          Events: `syscall`

valid   *bool valid() const*
                        Return `true` if I'm a valid, registered, UNIX process.

Non-Member Functions:

<<   *ostream& operator<<(ostream& stream, const os_process_group&
                        process_group)*
                        Print `process_group` to `stream`.

<<   *os_bstream& operator<<(os_bstream& stream, const
                        os_process_group& process_group)*
                        Write `process_group` to `stream`.

>>   *os_bstream& operator>>(os_bstream& stream, os_process_group&
                        process_group)*
                        Read `process_group` from `stream`.

process_status

Description:
An `os_process_status` contains information about the status of a process and is obtained with one of the `wait...()` family of functions in `os_this_process`. An `os_process_status` is usually used to determine the way that a process terminated:

- If a process terminated normally, its status will answer `true` to `terminated_normally()` and return its exit code when sent `exit_code()`.

- If a process was terminated by a signal, its status will answer `true` to `terminated_by_signal()` and return the signal number when sent `signal()`.

Declaration:
```
#include <ospace/process/procstat.h>
class os_process_status
```

Constructor	*os_process_status(const os_process_status& status)* Construct myself to be a copy of `status`.
Constructor	*os_process_status()* Construct myself with an undefined pid and status.
<	*bool operator<(const os_process_status& status) const* Return `true` if I'm considered to be less than `status`.
=	*os_process_status& operator=(const os_process_status& status)* Assign myself from `status`.
==	*bool operator==(const os_process_status& status) const* Return `true` if my process and status are the same as `status`'s.
core_dumped	*bool core_dumped() const* Return `true` if I've dumped my core.
defined	*bool defined() const* Return `true` if my status is not `OS_UNDEFINED`.
exit_code	*int exit_code() const* Return my exit code.
int	*operator int() const* Return my exit code.
pid	*os_pid_t pid() const* Return the process id.

print   *void print(ostream& stream) const*
        Print `myself` to `stream`.

process   *os_pid_t process() const*
        Return the process id.

resumed   *bool resumed() const*
        Return `true` if I was suspended and then resumed.

signal   *os_signal signal() const*
        If I was terminated or am currently suspended, return the signal that was
        used to do this, otherwise return a default signal.

suspended   *bool suspended() const*
        Return `true` if I am suspended.

terminated_by_signal *bool terminated_by_signal() const*
        Return `true` if the process was terminated by a signal.

terminated_normally *bool terminated_normally() const*
        Returns `true` if the process terminated normally.

Non-Member Functions:

<<   *ostream& operator<<(ostream& stream, const os_process_status&*
        status)
        Print `status` to `stream`.

<<   *os_bstream& operator<<(os_bstream& stream, const*
        os_process_status& status)
        Write `status` to `stream`.

>>   *os_bstream& operator>>(os_bstream& stream, os_process_status&*
        status)
        Read `status` from `stream`.

queue

Description:

A `queue` is an adapter that allows you to use any container that supports `push_back()` and `pop_front()` as a first-in, first-out data structure.

Declaration:
```
#include <queue.h>
template< class Container >
class queue
```

Constructor	*queue()* Construct myself to be an empty queue.
Constructor	*queue(Container::alloc_type& alloc)* Construct myself to be an empty queue. Use `alloc` to allocate storage.
Destructor	*~queue()* Destroy myself, erasing all of my items.
=	*queue< Container >& operator=(const queue< Container >& x)* Replace my contents by a copy of x's.
==	*bool operator==(const queue< Container >& x) const* Return `true` if I contain the same items in the same order as x.
<	*bool operator<(const queue< Container >& x) const* Return `true` if I'm lexigraphically less than x.
back	*T& back()* Return a reference to my last element. Events: `other (os_empty_error)`
back	*const T& back() const* Return a reference to my last element. Events: `other (os_empty_error)`
empty	*bool empty() const* Return `true` if I contain no entries.
front	*T& front()* Return a reference to my first element. Events: `other (os_empty_error)`

front
const T& front( ) const
Return a reference to my first element.

      Events: `other (os_empty_error)`

max_size
size_type max_size() const
Return the maximum number of entries that I can contain.

pop
void pop()
Erase my top element.

      Events: `other (os_empty_error)`

push
void push(const T& value)
Push a copy of `value`.

size
size_type size() const
Return the number of entries that I contain.

swap
void swap(queue< Container >& x)
Swap my contents with `x`'s.

raw_storage_iterator

Description:
A `raw_storage_iterator` is an iterator that allows you to directly construct objects in raw storage.

Declaration:
```
#include <iterator.h>
template< class OutputIterator, class T >
class raw_storage_iterator : public output_iterator
```

Constructor	*raw_storage_iterator(OutputIterator iterator)* Construct myself to be associated with `iterator`.
*	*raw_storage_iterator< OutputIterator, T >& operator *()* Return a reference to myself.
=	*raw_storage_iterator< OutputIterator, T >& operator=(const T& x)* Construct a copy of `x` using my associated iterator.
++	*raw_storage_iterator< OutputIterator, T >& operator++()* Advance my associated iterator.
++	*raw_storage_iterator< OutputIterator, T > operator++(int)* Advance my associated iterator.

Example <ospace/stl/examples/rawiter.cpp>

```
#include <stl.h>
#include <iostream.h>

class X
{
  public:
    X (int i_ = 0) : i (i_) {}
    int i;
};

ostream& operator<< (ostream& stream_, const X& x_)
{
  return stream_ << x_.i;
}

int main ()
{
  X* p = (X*) ::new (sizeof (X) * 5); // Allocate raw memory.
  X* q = p;
  raw_storage_iterator<X*, X> r (q);
  for (int i = 0; i < 5; i++)
    *r++ = X (i);
  for (i = 0; i < 5; i++)
    cout << *p++ << endl;
  return 0;
}

0
1
2
3
4
```

read_write_semaphore

Description:

An `os_read_write_semaphore` allows you to ensure that access to an object is limited to a single writer or multiple readers. It will grant a read lock to multiple readers, or a write lock to a single writer.

Declaration:
```
#include <ospace/sync/rwsem.h>
class os_read_write_semaphore
```

Constructor	*os_read_write_semaphore()* Constructor. I am initialized with no locks in place.
print	*void print(ostream& stream) const* Printing.
read_lock	*void read_lock() const* Obtains a read lock. Multiple read locks can exist. If there is an outstanding write lock, this blocks until a read lock can be obtained.
read_unlock	*void read_unlock() const* Releases a read lock held by this thread.
try_read_lock	*bool try_read_lock() const* Attempt to acquire a read lock. Instead of blocking, this function returns `false` if it failed to acquire a lock immediately.
try_write_lock	*bool try_write_lock()* Attempt to acquire a write lock. Instead of blocking, this function returns `false` if it failed to acquire a lock immediately.
write_lock	*void write_lock()* Acquire a write lock. This function blocks until a write lock is acquired. There may only be one write lock at a time, however the same thread may call `write_lock` repeatedly without blocking on subsequent calls. These must be matched by an equal number of `write_unlock` calls. A write lock may only exist when there are no read locks.
write_unlock	*void write_unlock()* This releases the write lock held by this thread.

resource

Description:

The current process has a set of resources restricted by the following two limits:

- **Hard limit**—Maximum amount of resources a process can use before it is forcefully terminated.

- **Soft limit**—Maximum amount of resources a process can use before receiving a signal; the process can continue to execute after receiving the signal.

`os_this_process` has several functions that return the limits associated with a particular resource. To change a resource limit, get it, change it and then set it. Only a superuser can change the hard limit of a resource. Conversions allow `os_resource` and `os_rlimit_t` to be used interchangeably.

Declaration:
```
#include <ospace/process/resource.h>
class os_resource
```

Typedefs:
```
typedef struct rlimit os_rlimit_t
```

Constructor	*os_resource(const os_resource& resource)* Construct myself to be a copy of `resource`.
Constructor	*os_resource(const os_rlimit_t& resource)* Construct myself from `resource`.
Constructor	*os_resource()* Construct myself with zero hard and soft limits.
=	*os_resource& operator=(const os_rlimit_t& resource)* Assign myself from `resource`.
=	*os_resource& operator=(const os_resource& resource)* Assign myself from `resource`.
==	*bool operator==(const os_resource& resource) const* Return `true` if I'm the same as `resource`.
hard_limit	*os_lim_t hard_limit() const* Return my hard limit.
hard_limit	*void hard_limit(os_lim_t limit)* Set my hard limit to `limit`.

os_rlimit_t	*operator os_rlimit_t() const* Return myself as an `os_rlimit_t` structure.
print	*void print(ostream& stream) const* Print myself to `stream`.
soft_limit	*void soft_limit(os_lim_t limit)* Set my soft limit to `limit`.
soft_limit	*os_lim_t soft_limit() const* Return my soft limit.

Non-Member Functions:

<<	*ostream& operator<<(ostream& stream, const os_resource& resource)* Print `resource` to `stream`.
<<	*os_bstream& operator<<(os_bstream& stream, const os_resource& resource)* Write `resource` to `stream`.
>>	*os_bstream& operator>>(os_bstream& stream, os_resource& resource)* Read `resource` from `stream`.

resource_usage

Description:

The kernel tracks the resource usage of every process, including the amount of CPU time used and the number of signals received. A resource usage object is read-only and can be asked for its individual resource values.

To receive a resource object containing its resource statistics, use `os_this_process::usage()`; to obtain resource statistics for the terminated child processes of the current process, use `os_this_process::usage_for_terminated_children()`.

An `operator rusage()` exists so that an `os_resource_usage` may be used whenever a `struct rusage` is expected.

Declaration:
```
#include <ospace/process/rscusage.h>
class os_resource_usage
```

Constructor	*os_resource_usage()* Construct myself to be empty.
Constructor	*os_resource_usage(const rusage& usage)* Construct myself from usage.
Constructor	*os_resource_usage(const os_resource_usage& usage)* Construct myself to be a copy of usage.
=	*os_resource_usage& operator=(const os_resource_usage& usage)* Assign myself from usage.
=	*os_resource_usage& operator=(const rusage& usage)* Assign myself from usage.
==	*bool operator== (const os_resource_usage& usage) const* Return true if I'm the same as resource_usage.

average_resident set_bytes

> *int average_resident_set_bytes() const*
>
> Return the average resident set size in bytes. This is the average physical memory use and does not take sharing into account. Note that on SUN platforms this is an approximation and may misrepresent the true resident set size.

average_resident set_pages

> *int average_resident_set_pages() const*
>
> Return the average resident set size in pages. This is the average physical memory use and does not take sharing into account. Note that on SUN platforms this is an approximation and may misrepresent the true resident set size.

forced_context switches

> *int forced_context_switches() const*
>
> Return the number of times a context switch occurred as a result of a higher priority process entering a run state or because the processes time slice was completed.

input_blocks
> *int input_blocks() const*
> Return the number of times the program blocked (waited on the system) for input servicing of a read request.

io_page_faults
> *int io_page_faults() const*
> Return the number of page faults that required physical I/O activity. This type of page fault is the most widely understood. It occurs most commonly when a program references a page that is not in memory. These type of page faults are also associated with many user I/O requests.

max_resident set_bytes

> *int max_resident_set_bytes() const*
>
> Return the maximum byte count in the resident set. This is the maximum amount of physical memory consumed. Note that on SUN platforms this is an approximation and may misrepresent the true resident set size.

max_resident set_pages

> *int max_resident_set_pages() const*
>
> Return the maximum pages in the resident set. This is the maximum amount of physical memory consumed. Note that on SUN platforms this is an approximation and may misrepresent the true resident set size.

| **non_io_page_faults** | *int non_io_page_faults() const* |
| | Return the number of page faults serviced that did not require physical I/O activity. These minor page faults can occur when reclaiming memory from the heap, during startup when first referencing a shared library, etc. |

| **output_blocks** | *int output_blocks() const* |
| | Return the number of times the program blocked (waited on the system) for output servicing of a write request. |

| **print** | *void print(ostream& stream) const* |
| | Print my attributes to `stream`. |

| **received_messages** | *int received_messages() const* |
| | Return the number of messages received from sockets. |

| **received_signals** | *int received_signals() const* |
| | Return the number of signals received by the process. On current SUN implementations this does not include `SIGSTOP` (suspend) and `SIGCONT` (resume) signals. |

| **rusage** | *operator rusage() const* |
| | Return myself as an `rusage` structure. |

| **sent_messages** | *int sent_messages() const* |
| | Return the number of messages sent over sockets. |

| **swaps** | *int swaps() const* |
| | Return the number of times the process was swapped out of main memory. |

| **system_time** | *os_time_period system_time() const* |
| | Return the total time spent executing in system mode. At this time, the time returned for system usage is only accurate to the second. |

| **user_time** | *os_time_period user_time() const* |
| | Return the total time spent executing in user mode. At this time, the time returned for user usage is only accurate to the second. |

voluntary_context switches

> *int voluntary_context_switches() const*
>
> Return the number of times a context switch occurred as a result of the process voluntarily giving up it's time slice prior to completion. A context switch is the transfer of CPU control from one user's program to another. This type of context switch usually results when the user is waiting on a resource (like during I/O requests). A large portion of UNIX systems calls result in voluntary context switching.

Non-Member Functions:

<<   *ostream& operator<<(ostream& stream, const os_resource_usage& usage)*
             Print usage to stream.

<<   *os_bstream& operator<<(os_bstream& stream, const os_resource_usage& usage)*
             Write usage to stream.

>>   *os_bstream& operator>>(os_bstream& stream, os_resource_usage& usage)*
             Read usage from stream.

reverse_bidirectional_iterator

Description:

A `reverse_bidirectional_iterator` allows a bidirectional iterator to be used as a reverse iterator.

Declaration:

```
#include <iterator.h>
template< class BidirectionalIterator, class T, class Reference,
   class Distance >
class reverse_bidirectional_iterator :
   public bidirectional_iterator< T, Distance >
```

Constructor	*reverse_bidirectional_iterator()* Construct myself to serve as a past-the-end marker.
Constructor	*reverse_bidirectional_iterator(BidirectionalIterator iterator)* Construct myself to be associated with `iterator`.
base	*BidirectionalIterator base()* Return a copy of my associated iterator.
*	*Reference operator*()* Return a reference to the item referenced by my associated iterator.
++	*reverse_bidirectional_iterator* *< BidirectionalIterator, T, Reference, Distance >& operator++()* Retreat my associated iterator by one and return a reference to my new value.
++	*reverse_bidirectional_iterator* *< BidirectionalIterator, T, Reference, Distance > operator++(int)* Retreat my associated iterator by one and return a copy of my previous value.
--	*reverse_bidirectional_iterator* *< BidirectionalIterator, T, Reference, Distance >& operator--()* Advance my associated iterator and return a reference to my new value.
--	*reverse_bidirectional_iterator* *< BidirectionalIterator, T, Reference, Distance > operator--(int)* Advance my associated iterator and return a copy of my previous value.

==   *bool operator==*
(const reverse_bidirectional_iterator< BidirectionalIterator,T,Reference,
Distance >& iterator) const
Return `true` if my associated iterator is in the same state as `iterator`'s.

!=   *bool operator!=(*
const reverse_bidirectional_iterator< BidirectionalIterator,T,Reference,
Distance >& iterator) const
Return `true` if my associated iterator is not in the same state as
`iterator`'s.

Example <ospace/stl/examples/revbit1.cpp>

```
#include <stl.h>
#include <iostream.h>

int array [] = { 1, 5, 2, 3 };

int main ()
{
  vector<int> v (array, array + 4);
  reverse_bidirectional_iterator<vector<int>::iterator, int,
    vector<int>::reference, vector<int>::difference_type>
    r (v.end ());
  while (r != v.begin ())
    cout << *r++ << endl;
  return 0;
}

3
2
5
1
```

Example <ospace/stl/examples/revbit2.cpp>

```cpp
#include <stl.h>
#include <iostream.h>

int array [] = { 1, 5, 2, 3 };

int main ()
{
  vector<int> v (array, array + 4);
  vector<int>::reverse_iterator r;
  for (r = v.rbegin (); r != v.rend (); r++)
    cout << *r << endl;
  return 0;
}


3
2
5
1
```

reverse_iterator

Description:
 A `reverse_iterator` is an iterator that allows you to reverse the polarity of an existing random access iterator.

Declaration:
```
#include <iterator.h>
template< class RandomAccessIterator,class T, class Reference,
  class Distance >
class stl_reverse_iterator : public
  random_access_iterator< T, Distance >
```

Constructor	*reverse_iterator( )* Construct myself to act as a past-the-end value.
Constructor	*reverse_iterator(RandomAccessIterator iterator)* Construct myself to be associated with `iterator`.
base	*RandomAccessIterator base( )* Return a copy of my associated iterator.
*****	*Reference operator*( )* Return a reference to the item referenced by my associated iterator.
++	*reverse_iterator< RandomAccessIterator, T, Reference, Distance >&* *operator++( )* Retreat my associated iterator by one and a reference to myself.
++	*reverse_iterator< RandomAccessIterator, T, Reference, Distance >* *operator++(int)* Retreat my associated iterator by one and return a copy of my old value.
--	*reverse_iterator< RandomAccessIterator, T, Reference, Distance >&* *operator--( )* Advance my associated iterator and return a reference to myself.
--	*reverse_iterator< RandomAccessIterator, T, Reference, Distance >* *operator--(int)* Advance my associated iterator and return a copy of my old value.
+	*reverse_iterator< RandomAccessIterator, T, Reference, Distance >* *operator+(Distance n) const* Return a copy of my associated iterator retreated by n positions.

+=	*reverse_iterator< RandomAccessIterator, T, Reference, Distance >&* *operator+=(Distance n)* Retreat my associated iterator by n positions and return a reference to myself.
-	*reverse_iterator< RandomAccessIterator, T, Reference, Distance >* *operator-(Distance n) const* Return a copy of my associated iterator advanced by n positions.
-=	*reverse_iterator< RandomAccessIterator, T, Reference, Distance >&* *operator-=(Distance n)* Advance my associated iterator by n positions and return a reference to myself.
[]	*Reference operator[ ](Distance n)* Return a reference to the item that is n positions behind my associated iterator.
==	*bool operator==(const* *reverse_iterator< RandomAccessIterator,T,Reference,Distance >& x)* *const* Return true if my associated iterator is in the same state as x's.
!=	*bool operator!=(const* *reverse_iterator< RandomAccessIterator,T,Reference,Distance >& x)* *const* Return true if my associated iterator is not in the same state as x's.
<	*bool operator<(const* *reverse_iterator< RandomAccessIterator,T,Reference,Distance >& x_* *const* Return true if x_'s associated iterator is less than my own.
-	*Distance operator-(const* *reverse_iterator< RandomAccessIterator,T,Reference,Distance >& x)* *const* Return the distance between x's associated iterator and my own.

Non-Member Functions:

+ *reverse_iterator*
< RandomAccessIterator,T,Reference,Distance > operator+
(
  Distance n,
  const reverse_iterator< RandomAccessIterator, T, Reference,
  Distance >& x
)
  Return a reverse_iterator whose associated iterator is n positions behind
  x.

Example <ospace/stl/examples/reviter1.cpp>

```
#include <stl.h>
#include <iostream.h>

int array [] = { 1, 5, 2, 3 };

int main ()
{
  vector<int> v (array, array + 4);
  reverse_iterator<vector<int>::iterator, int,
    vector<int>::reference, vector<int>::difference_type>
    r (v.end ());
  while (r != v.begin ())
    cout << *r++ << endl;
  return 0;
}

3
2
5
1
```

Example <ospace/stl/examples/reviter2.cpp>

```cpp
#include <stl.h>
#include <iostream.h>

int array [] = { 1, 5, 2, 3 };

int main ()
{
  vector<int> v (array, array + 4);
  vector<int>::reverse_iterator r;
  for (r = v.rbegin (); r != v.rend (); r++)
    cout << *r << endl;
  return 0;
}


3
2
5
1
```

sem_lock

Description:

This template class allows a semaphore to be auto-locked within a scope. It must be instantiated on a semaphore class that understands `lock()` and `unlock()`. When an `os_sem_lock` is constructed with a reference to a semaphore, it calls `lock()` on its associated semaphore. When an `os_sem_lock` is destroyed, it calls `unlock()` on its associated semaphore. An `os_sem_lock` does not own its semaphore, it is merely a helper class.

Declaration:
```
#include <ospace/sync/lock.h>
template< class semaphore >
class os_sem_lock
```

Constructor	*os_sem_lock(Semaphore& semaphore)* Construct myself and immediately block until a lock on `semaphore` is obtained.
Destructor	*~os_sem_lock()* Release my lock on my associated semaphore.

sem_read_lock

Description:
This template class allows a semaphore to be auto-locked within a scope. It must be instantiated on a semaphore class that understands `read_lock()` and `read_unlock()`. When an `os_sem_read_lock` is constructed with a reference to a semaphore, it calls `read_lock()` on its associated semaphore. When an `os_sem_read_lock` is destroyed, it calls `read_unlock()` on its associated semaphore. An `os_sem_read_lock` does not own its semaphore, it is merely a helper class.

Declaration:
```
#include <ospace/sync/lock.h>
class os_sem_read_lock
```

Constructor	*os_sem_read_lock(const os_read_write_semaphore& semaphore)* Construct myself and immediately block until a read lock on `semaphore` is obtained.
Destructor	*~os_sem_read_lock()* Release my read lock on my associated semaphore.

sem_write_lock

Description:

This template class allows a semaphore to be auto-locked within a scope. It must be instantiated on a semaphore class that understands `write_lock()` and `write_unlock()`. When an `os_sem_read_write_lock` is constructed with a reference to a semaphore, it calls `write_lock()` on its associated semaphore. When an `os_sem_write_lock` is destroyed, it calls `write_unlock()` on its associated semaphore. An `os_sem_read_write_lock` does not own its semaphore, it is merely a helper class.

Declaration:
```
#include <ospace/sync/lock.h>
class os_sem_write_lock
```

Constructor

os_sem_write_lock(os_read_write_semaphore& semaphore)
Construct myself and immediately block until a write lock on `semaphore` is obtained.

Destructor

~os_sem_write_lock()
Release my write lock on my associated semaphore.

service

Description:

Most hosts on the Internet provide a set of standard services via some well-known numbered ports. Every service has a description, a set of aliases, a port number and a protocol description (either `tcp` or `udp`). Information about these services is usually stored in `/etc/services`. An `os_service` may be constructed from a description/protocol pair or a port/protocol pair. Most services may be accessed via either `tcp` or `udp` protocols .

Declaration:
```
#include <ospace/socket/service.h>
class os_service;
```

Constructor   *os_service()*
Construct myself to have an empty name.

Constructor   *os_service(const servent& service)*
Construct myself from the `servent` structure `service`.

Constructor   *os_service(const os_service& service)*
Construct myself to be a copy of `service`.

Constructor   *os_service(const string& name, const string& protocol)*
Construct myself to be the service with name `name` and protocol `protocol` (default `tcp`).

    Events: `other`
    On Resumption: I will be in an unusable state.

Constructor   *os_service(int port, const string& protocol)*
Construct myself to be the service with name `name` and protocol `protocol` (default `tcp`).

    Events: `other`
    On Resumption: I will be in an unusable state.

<   *bool operator< (const os_service& service) const*
Return `true` if I'm considered to be less than `service`.

=   *os_service& operator=(const os_service& service)*
Assign myself from `service`.

==   *bool operator==(const os_service& service) const*
Return `true` if my name and protocol is the same as `service`'s.

aliases   *const vector< string >& aliases() const*
Return a vector of my aliases.

defined   *bool defined() const*
Return true if my name is not empty.

name   *string name() const*
Return my name.

port   *int port() const*
Return my port.

print   *void print(ostream& stream) const*
Print my name, port and protocol to stream.

protocol   *string protocol() const*
Return my protocol.

services   */* static */ vector< os_service* > services()*
Return a vector of pointers to objects on the heap representing all of the services in the service database. It is the caller's responsibility to properly delete the objects in the vector.

Non-Member Functions:

<<   *ostream& operator<<(ostream& stream, const os_service& service)*
Print service to stream.

<<   *os_bstream& operator<<(os_bstream& stream, const os_service& service)*
Write service to stream.

>>   *os_bstream& operator>>(os_bstream& stream, os_service& control)*
Read service from stream.

set

Description:

A set is a container that is optimized for fast associative lookup. Items are matched using their == operator. When an item is inserted into a set, it is stored in a data structure that allows the item to be found very quickly. Within the data structure, the items are ordered according to a user-defined comparitor function object. A typical user-supplied function object is less, which causes the items to be ordered in ascending order. Unlike multisets, a set cannot contain multiple copies of the same item.

Declaration:
```
#include <set.h>
template< class Key, class Compare >
class set
```

Constructor   *set()*
Construct myself to be an empty set that orders elements using the compare function specified when my template was instantiated.

Constructor   *set(alloc_type& alloc)*
Construct myself to be an empty set that orders elements using the compare function specified when my template was instantiated. Use alloc to allocate storage.

Constructor   *set(const Compare& compare)*
Construct myself to be an empty set that orders elements using the compare function compare.

Constructor   *set(alloc_type& alloc, const Compare& compare)*
Construct myself to be an empty set that orders elements using the compare function compare. Use alloc to allocate storage.

Constructor   *set(const Key* first, const Key* last)*
Construct myself to contain copies of the elements in the range [first, last), using the compare function specified when my template was instantiated.

Constructor   *set(alloc_type& alloc, const Key* first, const Key* last)*
Construct myself to contain copies of the elements in the range [first, last), using the compare function specified when my template was instantiated. Use alloc to allocate storage.

Constructor	*set(const Key* first, const Key* last, const Compare& compare)* Construct myself to contain copies of the elements in the range `[first, last)`, using `compare` to order the elements.
Constructor	*set(alloc_type& alloc, const Key* first, const Key* last,* *const Compare& compare)* Construct myself to contain copies of the elements in the range `[first, last)`, using `compare` to order the elements. Use `alloc` to allocate storage.
Constructor	*set(const set< Key,Compare >& x)* Construct myself to be a copy of `x`.
Constructor	*set(alloc_type& alloc, const set< Key,Compare >& x)* Construct myself to be a copy of `x`. Use `alloc` to allocate storage.
Destructor	*~set()* Destroy myself, erasing all of my items.
=	*set< Key,Compare >& operator=(const set< Key,Compare >& x)* Replace my contents by a copy of `x`'s.
==	*bool operator==(const set< Key,Compare >& x) const* Return `true` if I contain the same items in the same order as `x`.
<	*bool operator<(const set< Key,Compare >& x) const* Return `true` if I'm lexigraphically less than `x`.
begin	*iterator begin() const* Return an iterator positioned at my first item.
count	*size_type count(const Key& key) const* Return the number of elements that I contain that match `key`.
empty	*bool empty() const* Return `true` if I contain no entries.
end	*iterator end() const* Return an iterator positioned immediately after my last item.
erase[9]	*void erase()* Erase all of my elements.
erase	*void erase(iterator pos)* Erase the element at `pos`.
erase	*void erase(iterator first, iterator last)* Erase the elements in range `[first, last)`.

---

[9] Non-standard, unique to Systems<ToolKit>

set

erase

size_type erase(const Key& key)
Erase all elements that match `key` and return the number of elements that were erased.

find

iterator find(const Key& key) const
If I contain an element that matches `key`, return an iterator positioned at the matching element, otherwise return an iterator positioned at end().

insert

pair< const_iterator, bool > insert(const Key& key)
If I don't contain an element that matches `key`, insert a copy of `key` and return a pair whose first element is an iterator positioned at the new element and whose second element is `true`. If I already contain an element that matches `key`, return a pair whose first element is an iterator positioned at the existing element and whose second element is `false`.

insert

void insert(const Key first, const Key* last)*
Insert copies of the elements in the range `[first, last)`.

insert

iterator insert(iterator pos, const Key& key)
Insert a copy of `key` if I don't already contain an element that matches it, using `pos` as a hint on where to start searching for the correct place to insert.

key_comp

Compare key_comp() const
Return my comparison object.

lower_bound

iterator lower_bound(const Key& key) const
Return an iterator positioned at the first location that `key` could be inserted without violating the ordering criteria. If no such location is found, return an iterator positioned at end().

max_size

size_type max_size() const
Return the maximum number of entries that I can contain.

rbegin

reverse_iterator rbegin() const
Return a reverse iterator positioned at my last item.

rend

reverse_iterator rend() const
Return a reverse_iterator positioned immediately before my first item.

size

size_type size() const
Return the number of entries that I contain.

swap

void swap(set< Key,Compare >& x)
Swap my contents with x's.

upper_bound

iterator upper_bound(const Key& value) const
Return an iterator positioned at the last location that `key` could be inserted without violating the ordering criteria. If no such location is found return an iterator positioned at end().

value_comp   *Compare value_comp( ) const*
Return my comparison object.

shared_memory

Description:

An `os_shared_memory` object represents an area of memory that any process can attach to its own virtual address space and access as if it were local. Shared memory is often used as a very fast way to share information amongst processes, although care must be taken to ensure that access is properly synchronized.

When a shared memory segment is created, it is not attached to the process' address space; this must be done by performing one of the `attach...()` family of functions. A process may detach from its shared memory region by either sending `detach()` to the segment, or by terminating.

Once created, a shared memory segment persists in the system even if no processes are attached to it. To remove a shared memory segment, send it `remove()`; this schedules it for removal when the last process detaches from it.

A superuser can lock a shared memory segment into main memory to prevent it from being paged out using `lock()`. Similarly, `unlock()` may be used to unlock a segment.

Conversions allow `os_shared_memory` and `os_vid_t` (the System V IPC id) to be used interchangeably.

Declaration:
```
#include <ospace/sharemem/sharemem.h>
class os_shared_memory
```

Options:

Legal open control:	O_OPEN, O_CREAT, O_EXCL
Legal I/O control:	O_RDONLY, O_RDWR
Default I/O control:	O_RDWR

Constructor   *os_shared_memory()*
Construct myself with no associated shared memory segment.

Constructor   *os_shared_memory(os_vid_t id)*
Construct myself to reference the shared memory segment with id `id`.

Constructor   *os_shared_memory(const os_key& key)*
Construct myself to reference the existing shared memory segment with key `key`. Don't attach to the new segment; this should be done using one of the `attach...()` family of functions.

> Events: `syscall`
> On Resumption: My id is set to `OS_UNDEFINED`.

Constructor	*os_shared_memory(int size, os_mode_t mode)* Construct myself to reference a new memory segment of `size` bytes that has a private key and mode `mode`. Don't attach to the new segment; this should be done using one of the `attach...()` family of functions.

> Events: `syscall`
> On Resumption: My id is set to `OS_UNDEFINED`.

Constructor	*os_shared_memory(const os_key& key, os_open_t open, int size, os_mode_t mode)* Construct myself to reference a new memory segment of `size` bytes with key `key` and mode `mode`. If a memory segment with key `key` already exists, then reference the existing memory segment instead and ignore the `mode` and `size` parameters. Don't attach to the new segment; this should be done using one of the `attach...()` family of functions.

> Events: `syscall`
> On Resumption: My id is set to `OS_UNDEFINED`.

<	*bool operator<(const os_shared_memory& shared_memory) const* Return `true` if my id is less than `shared_memory`s.
==	*bool operator==(const os_shared_memory& shared_memory) const* Return `true` if my id is the same as `shared_memory`s.
address	*char* address() const* Return the memory address that I am currently attached to within my process's address space. If I'm not currently attached, return `OS_UNDEFINED_SEGMENT`.
attach_aligned_at	*char* attach_aligned_at(char* address, os_ioctl_t control)* Attach myself to the current process' address space at location `address` with control `control` (default `O_RDWR`). Before attaching, round `address` down to the next legal address boundary. Return the address of attachment if successful, otherwise return `OS_UNDEFINED_SEGMENT`. Address boundaries are machine dependent but usually are every 32 bits. On machines where data alignment is a concern, this method of attachment is more desirable than `attach_at()`.

> Events: `syscall, other`
> On Resumption: I will be detached.

attach_at *char* attach_at(char* address, os_ioctl_t control)*
Attach myself to the current process' address space at `address` with control `control` (default `O_RDWR`). Return the address of attachment if successful, otherwise return `OS_UNDEFINED_SEGMENT`. Due to the variance in different platform's memory management policies, this method of attachment should be avoided when creating portable code.

> Events: `syscall`, `other`
> On Resumption: I will be detached.

attach_at first_available

char* attach_at_first_available(os_ioctl_t control)

Attach myself to the current process' address space at the first available address as assigned by the operating system with control `control` (default `O_RDWR`). For portability, this is the best way to attach a segment. Return the address of attachment if successful, otherwise return `OS_UNDEFINED_SEGMENT`.

> Events: `syscall`, `other`
> On Resumption: I will be detached.

creator_group *os_gid_t creator_group() const*
Return my creator's group.

> Events: `syscall`
> On Resumption: Returns 0.

creator_process *os_pid_t creator_process() const*
Return the process that created my shared memory segment.

> Events: `syscall`
> On Resumption: Returns 0.

creator_user *os_uid_t creator_user() const*
Return my creator's user.

> Events: `syscall`
> On Resumption: Returns 0.

defined *bool defined() const*
Return `true` if my id is not `OS_UNDEFINED`.

detach *void detach()*
Detach myself from the operating system IPC structure. After detachment, the current process can no longer access the previous shared memory space. My address will be set to `OS_UNDEFINED_SEGMENT`.

> Events: `syscall`

id *void id(os_vid_t id)*
Set my id to `id`.

id   *os_vid_t id() const*
Return my id.

key   *os_key key() const*
Return my key.

> Events: `syscall`
> On Resumption: Returns a default `os_key` object.

last_attach_time   *os_time_and_date last_attach_time() const*
Return the last time that a process attached to my shared memory segment.

> Events: `syscall`
> On Resumption: Returns `os_time_and_date( 0 )`.

last_change_time   *os_time_and_date last_change_time() const*
Return the last time that my shared memory segment was changed.

> Events: `syscall`
> On Resumption: Returns `os_time_and_date( 0 )`.

last_detach_time   *os_time_and_date last_detach_time() const*
Return the last time that a process detached from my shared memory segment.

> Events: `syscall`
> On Resumption: Returns `os_time_and_date( 0 )`.

last_op_process   *os_pid_t last_op_process() const*
Return the last process that operated on my shared memory segment.

> Events: `syscall`
> On Resumption: Returns 0.

lock   *void lock()*
Lock myself into memory. This function may only be executed by a superuser.

> Events: `syscall`

mode   *os_mode_t mode() const*
Return my mode.

> Events: `syscall`
> On Resumption: Returns 0.

mode   *void mode(os_mode_t mode)*
Set my mode to `mode`.

> Events: `syscall`

number_attached　　*int number_attached() const*
Return the number of processes that are attached to my shared memory segment.

> Events: `syscall`
> On Resumption: Returns 0.

os_vid_t　　*operator os_vid_t() const*
Return my id.

owner_group　　*void owner_group(os_gid_t group)*
Set my owner's group to `group`.

> Events: `syscall`.

owner_group　　*os_gid_t owner_group() const*
Return my owner's group.

> Events: `syscall`
> On Resumption: Returns 0.

owner_user　　*void owner_user(os_uid_t user)*
Set my owner's user to `user`.

> Events: `syscall`

owner_user　　*os_uid_t owner_user() const*
Return my owner's user.

> Events: `syscall`
> On Resumption: Returns 0.

print　　*void print(ostream& stream) const*
Print my id to `stream`.

> Events: `syscall`

remove　　*void remove()*
Schedule my memory segment to be removed from the system and prevent any processes from using its key. The memory segment is automatically removed when no processes are attached to it. Any processes already attached to the segment are unaffected by this operation.

> Events: `syscall`

size　　*int size() const*
Return the size of my shared memory segment in bytes.

> Events: `syscall`
> On Resumption: Returns 0.

slot_sequence number

    int slot_sequence_number() const

    Return my slot usage sequence number.

        Events: `syscall`
        On Resumption: Returns 0.

unlock

    void unlock()
    Unlock myself from memory. This function may only be executed by a superuser.

        Events: `syscall`

Non-Member Functions:

<<

    ostream& operator<<(ostream& stream, const os_shared_memory& memory)
    Print `memory` to `stream`.

signal

Description:

A signal is a software interrupt; UNIX supports about 30 signals, each of which has a unique integer code. The signals are numbered sequentially, starting from 1. A programmer may choose for the current process to react to a particular signal in one of three ways:

— react in the default way, which is often to terminate and possibly dump core

— ignore the signal

— execute a user-supplied signal handler function

In addition, `os_this_process` may be told to block certain signals; blocked signals are queued and only delivered if they are later unblocked. Some signals are so commonly sent that they have a function named after them in `os_process` and `os_this_process`.

Conversions allow `os_signal` and `os_sig_t` to be used interchangeably.

Declaration:

```
#include <ospace/process/signal.h>
class os_signal
```

Constructor	*os_signal(const os_signal& signal)* Construct myself to be a copy of `signal`.
Constructor	*os_signal(os_sig_t code)* Construct myself with signal code `code` (default `OS_UNDEFINED`).
<	*bool operator<(const os_signal& signal) const* Return `true` if my code is less than `signal`'s.
=	*os_signal& operator=(os_sig_t signal)* Assign myself from `signal`.
=	*os_signal& operator=(const os_signal& signal)* Assign myself from `signal`.
==	*bool operator==(const os_signal& signal) const* Return `true` if my code is the same as `signal`'s.
code	*void code(os_sig_t code)* Set my code to `code`.
code	*os_sig_t code() const* Return my code.
defined	*bool defined() const* Return `true` if my code is a valid system signal.

os_sig_t	*operator os_sig_t() const* Return my code.
print	*void print(ostream& stream) const* Print my code and description to `stream`.

Non-Member Functions:

<<	*ostream& operator<<(ostream& stream, const os_signal& signal)* Print `signal` to `stream`.
<<	*os_bstream& operator<<(os_bstream& stream, const os_signal& signal)* Write `signal` to `stream`.
>>	*os_bstream& operator>>(os_bstream& stream, os_signal& signal)* Read `signal` from `stream`.

signal_action

Description:

To take total control over how the current process reacts to a particular signal or set of signals, use `os_this_process::action()`. This function takes a signal or a signal set as its first argument and an `os_signal_action` object as its second.

An `os_signal_action` specifies how a process reacts to signals. The default constructor creates a signal action that reacts to the signal in the default way. Another constructor creates a signal action that calls a used-supplied handler, and takes the following parameters:

- A pointer to a user-supplied handler with prototype `void (*handler)( int )`. When the handler is called, the signal number is passed as its argument. If `handler` is equal to `SIG_DFL`, the default action is performed. If `handler` is equal to `SIG_IGN`, the signal is ignored. We recommend that you use `restore_default()` and `ignore()` instead of using these options.

- An optional set of signals that should be added to the set of blocked signals during the execution of the handler and removed after the handler has finished.

- An optional set of bitwise-ored `SA_INTERRUPT` (on some platforms), `SA_RESETHAND` and `SA_NOCLDSTOP` flags.

The meaning of the flags are as follows:

- `SA_RESETHAND`: Resets the handler to be the default action after the signal is received once.

- `SA_NOCLDSTOP`: If the specified signal is `SIGCHLD` and this flag is set, then `SIGCHLD` signals will not be sent to the current process when one of its children terminates.

- `SA_INTERRUPT`: If a reentrant system call is being executed when the signal is received, do not automatically restart it.

Conversions allow `os_signal_action` and `os_sigaction_t` to be used interchangeably.

Declaration:
```
#include <ospace/process/sigactn.h>
class os_signal_action
```

Typedefs:
```
typedef struct sigaction os_sigaction_t;
```

Constructor	*os_signal_action(const os_sigaction_t& action)* Construct myself from `action`.
Constructor	*os_signal_action(const os_signal_action& action)* Construct myself to be a copy of `action`.

Constructor	*os_signal_action()* Construct myself to represent the default action.
Constructor	*os_signal_action(void (*new_handler)(int),* *const vector< os_sig_t >& signals, int flags)* Construct myself with handler `new_handler`, blocked signal set `signals` (default empty set) and flags `flags` (default 0). If this action is installed for a signal using these default values, it will not block any additional signals during the execution of `new_handler`, will restart any interrupted system call (where possible), will stay installed for repeated signals, and will not block the delivery of `SIGCHLD`.
=	*os_signal_action& operator=(const os_sigaction_t& action)* Assign myself from `action`.
=	*os_signal_action& operator=(const os_signal_action& action)* Assign myself from `action`.
==	*bool operator==(const os_signal_action& action) const* Return `true` if I'm the same as `action`.
added_blocking	*vector< os_sig_t > added_blocking() const* Return the signal set that is added to the current process's blocked signals during handler execution.
added_blocking	*void added_blocking(const vector< os_sig_t >& signals)* Set the signal set that will be added to the current process's blocked signals during execution of the signal handler to `signals`. Events: `syscall`
block_child_stop	*void block_child_stop(bool flag)* If `flag` is `true` and this action is installed for `SIGCHILD`, a `SIGCHILD` signal will not be generated when a child process terminates. If `flag` is `false` and this action is installed for `SIGCHILD`, a `SIGCHILD` signal will be generated when a child process terminates.
block_child_stop	*bool block_child_stop() const* Return `true` if I am set to block the delivery of `SIGCHLD` when a child process stops.
get_default	*bool get_default() const* Return `true` if my action is "perform default."
handle_once	*void handle_once(bool flag)* If `flag` is `true`, reset the signal handler when the signal is delivered. This means that the handler will only execute once unless its specifically re-enabled. If `flag` is `false` the handler will remain installed and will execute every time the signal is delivered.

handle_once   *bool handle_once() const*
Return `true` if I am set to handle only the first signal reception.

handler   *void handler(void (*handler)(int))*
Set my action to "execute `handler`."

ignore   *bool ignore() const*
Return `true` if I my action is "ignore."

os_sigaction_t   *operator os_sigaction_t() const*
Return myself as a `sigaction` structure.

print   *void print(ostream& stream) const*
Print myself to `stream`.

restart_system_calls   *bool restart_system_calls() const*
Return `true` if I am set to restart interrupted system calls.

restart_system_calls   *void restart_system_calls(bool flag)*
If `flag` is `true`, restart an interrupted system call after the signal handler returns. If `flag` is `false`, the system call will return with an error `EINTR`.

set_default   *void set_default()*
Set my action to "perform default."

set_ignore   *void set_ignore()*
Set my action to "ignore." Note that the kill and stop signals cannot be ignored.

Non-Member Functions:

<<   *ostream& operator<<(ostream& stream, const os_signal_action& action)*
Print `action` to `stream`.

simple_time_zone_rule

Description:
Represents a simple rule used to determine DST adjustments.

Declaration:
```
#include <ospace/time/simple.h>
class os_simple_time_zone_rule : public os_time_zone_rule
```

Constructor	*os_simple_time_zone_rule(const os_calendar_date& start_point, const os_calendar_date& end_point, os_year_t start_year, os_year_t end_year)* Construct a DST rule that is valid between `start_point` in the year `start_year` through `end_point` in the year `end_year`. Assume a 60-minute DST adjustment value.
Constructor	*os_simple_time_zone_rule(const os_calendar_date& start_point, const os_calendar_date& end_point, os_year_t start_year, os_year_t end_year, const os_time_period& adjustment)* Construct a DST rule that is valid between `start_point` in the year `start_year` through `end_point` in the year `end_year`. When DST is in effect, the time will be corrected by an `adjustment` time period.
is_in_effect	*/* virtual */ bool is_in_effect(const os_time& time, const os_date& date) const* Return `true` if this rule is in effect on `date` at `time`.

socket

Description:

This is the abstract base of the Systems<ToolKit> socket hierarchy. It defines all the behaviors common to all types of socket elements, including:

- descriptor management
- parameter access
- shutdown

The two derived classes of os_socket are os_tcp_connection_server and os_connectable_socket.

Conversions allow os_socket and os_desc_t (UNIX descriptor) to be used interchangeably.

Declaration:

```
#include <ospace/socket/socket.h>
class os_socket
```

Destructor	/* virtual */ ~os_socket() Destroy myself, closing my descriptor if necessary.
<	*bool operator<(const os_socket& socket) const* Return true if my descriptor is less than socket's.
==	*bool operator==(const os_socket& socket) const* Return true if my descriptor is the same as socket's.
auto_close	*void auto_close(bool flag)* If flag is true, close my descriptor on destruction.
auto_close	*bool auto_close() const* Return true if I close my descriptor on destruction.
bind_to	*void bind_to(const os_socket_address& address)* Bind myself to the IP socket address address (AF_INET only).
close	*void close()* Close myself. Events: syscall On Resumption: My descriptor may be unchanged.
descriptor	*void descriptor(os_desc_t descriptor)* Set my descriptor to descriptor.

descriptor	*os_desc_t descriptor() const* Return my descriptor.
get_and_clear_error	*int get_and_clear_error()* Clear my error status and return its previous value. The kernel maintains this value using the same encoding scheme as `errno`.

> Events: `syscall`
> On Resumption: Error status will be unknown and return value may be invalid.

io_control	*os_ioctl_t io_control() const* Return my I/O control setting.

> Events: `syscall`
> On Resumption: Return value may be invalid.

io_control	*void io_control(os_desc_t control)* Set my I/O control setting to `control`.

> Events: `syscall`
> On Resumption: My I/O control settings may be unchanged.

is_open	*bool is_open() const* Return `true` if I'm open.
linger_information	*void linger_information(bool flag, int seconds)* This option affects the way that I process unsent messages when I'm closed. If `flag` is `false`, I return immediately on `close()` and the system tries to deliver the unsent messages. If `flag` is `true`, the system tries to deliver unsent messages for up to `seconds` seconds and then discards any remaining unsent messages. If `flag` is `true` and `seconds` is 0, I process a `close()` by discarding unsent messages and returning immediately.

> Events: `syscall`
> On Resumption: Linger settings may be unchanged.

linger_information	*bool linger_information(int& seconds) const* Return my linger information in `seconds` and in the return value.

> Events: `syscall`
> On Resumption: Return values may be invalid.

os_desc_t	*operator os_desc_t() const* Return my descriptor.
print	*/* virtual */ void print(ostream& stream) const* Print myself to `stream`.

receive_buffer_size   *int receive_buffer_size() const*
Return the size, in bytes, of my receive buffer.

> Events: `syscall`
> On Resumption: Return value may be invalid.

receive_buffer_size   *void receive_buffer_size(int size)*
Set the size of my receive buffer to be `size` bytes. Increasing the size of this buffer past its default size can sometimes increase performance.

> Events: `syscall`
> On Resumption: Buffer size will be unknown.

reuse_local_addresses *void reuse_local_addresses(bool flag)*
Set local address reuse to `flag`.

> Events: `syscall`
> On Resumption: Reuse state will be unknown.

reuse_local_addresses *bool reuse_local_addresses() const*
Return `true` if I can reuse local address.

> Events: `syscall`
> On Resumption: Return value may be invalid.

route   *void route(bool flag)*
Set regular routing to `flag`.

> Events: `syscall`
> On Resumption: Routing state will be unknown.

route   *bool route() const*
Return `true` if regular routing is enabled. If regular routing is disabled, messages are sent directly to the network interface specified by the network portion of the destination address.

> Events: `syscall`
> On Resumption: Return value may be invalid.

send_buffer_size   *int send_buffer_size() const*
Return the size, in bytes, of my send buffer.

> Events: `syscall`
> On Resumption: Return value may be invalid.

send_buffer_size   *void send_buffer_size(int size)*
Set the size of my send buffer to be `size` bytes. Increasing the size of this buffer past its default size can sometimes increase performance.

> Events: `syscall`
> On Resumption: Buffer size will be unknown.

shutdown	*void shutdown()* Shutdown my send and receive channels. Further sends and receives will be disallowed. Events: `syscall` On Resumption: My send and receive channels will be in an unknown state.
shutdown	*void shutdown(int code)* Shutdown according to `code`. Events: `syscall` On Resumption: My descriptor may not be shutdown.
shutdown_receives	*void shutdown_receives()* Shutdown my receive channel. Further receives will be disallowed. Events: `syscall` On Resumption: My receive channel will be in an unknown state.
shutdown_sends	*void shutdown_sends()* Shutdown my send channel. Further sends will be disallowed. Events: `syscall` On Resumption: My send channel will be in an unknown state.
socket_address	*os_socket_address socket_address() const* Return my IP socket address (`AF_INET` only). Events: `syscall` On Resumption: Return value may be invalid.
type	*int type() const* Return the standard value encoding of my type. (`SOCK_STREAM` = 1, `SOCK_DGRAM` = 2, `SOCK_RAW` = 3, `SOCK_RDM` = 4, ...) Events: `syscall` On Resumption: Return value may be invalid.

socket_address

Description:

An os_socket_address represents an address of a socket endpoint on a machine. Socket addresses are used for three primary purposes:

— as addresses for construction of an os_tcp_socket or os_tcp_connection_server.

— as an argument for connect_to().

— as an argument for send_to() or receive_from(), used with UDP sockets.

Conversions allow os_socket_address and sockaddr_in to be used interchangeably.

Declaration:

```
#include <ospace/socket/sockaddr.h>
class os_socket_address
```

Constructor	*os_socket_address(const string& filepath)*
	Construct myself to reference the UNIX style socket with file system name filepath.
	
	    Events: other
	    On Resumption: I may not be in a usable state.

Constructor	*os_socket_address(const sockaddr_un& address)* Construct myself from the encoded UNIX style socket address address.
Constructor	*os_socket_address(int n)* Construct myself to represent the port n on the local host.
Constructor	*os_socket_address(const sockaddr_in& address)* Construct myself from the encoded IP socket address address.
Constructor	*os_socket_address(const os_ip_address& address, int n)* Construct myself to reference the port n (default 0) at IP address address.
Constructor	*os_socket_address(const os_socket_address& address)* Construct myself to be a copy of address.
<	*bool operator<(const os_socket_address& address) const* Return true if I'm considered to be less than address.
=	*os_socket_address& operator=(const sockaddr_un& address)* Assign myself from address.
=	*os_socket_address& operator=(const os_socket_address& address)* Assign myself from address.

=	*os_socket_address& operator=(const sockaddr_in& address)* Assign myself from `address`.
==	*bool operator==(const os_socket_address& address) const* Return `true` if my address and port are the same as `address`'s.
defined	*bool defined() const* Return `true` if my port is non-zero.
domain	*short domain() const* Return my domain.
ip_address	*os_ip_address ip_address() const* Return my IP address.
ip_address	*void ip_address(const os_ip_address& address)* Set my IP address to `address`.
path	*string path() const* Return the path to my socket as a string.
path	*void path(const string& filepath)* Set my socket identifier to be `filepath`. Events: `other` On Resumption: I may be in an unusable state.
port	*void port(int port)* Set my port to `port`.
port	*int port() const* Return my port number.
print	*void print(ostream& stream) const* Print my IP address and port to `stream`.
sockaddr_in	*operator sockaddr_in() const* Return myself as a `sockaddr_in` structure.
sockaddr_un	*operator sockaddr_un() const* Return myself as a `sockaddr_un` structure.

Non-Member Functions:

<<	*ostream& operator<<(ostream& stream, const os_socket_address& sockaddr)* Print `sockaddr` to `stream`.
<<	*os_bstream& operator<<(os_bstream& stream, const os_socket_address& address)* Write `address` to `stream`.

socket_address

>>   *os_bstream& operator>>(os_bstream& stream, os_socket_address& address)*
Read `address` from `stream`.

stack

Description:

A stack is an adapter that allows you to use any container that supports push_back() and pop_back() as a first-in, last-out data structure.

Declaration:

```
#include <stack.h>
template< class Container >
class stack
```

Constructor	*stack()* Construct myself to be an empty stack.
Constructor	*stack(Container::alloc_type& alloc)* Construct myself to be an empty stack. Use alloc to allocate storage.
Destructor	*~stack()* Destroy myself, erasing all of my items.
=	*stack< Containe r>& operator=(const stack< Container >& x)* Replace my contents by a copy of x's.
==	*bool operator==(const stack< Container >& x) const* Return true if I contain the same items in the same order as x.
<	*bool operator<(const stack< Container >& x) const* Return true if I'm lexigraphically less than x.
empty	*bool empty() const* Return true if I contain no entries.
max_size	*size_type max_size() const* Return the maximum number of entries that I can contain.
pop	*void pop()* Erase my top element. Events: other (os_empty_error)
push	*void push(const_reference& value)* Push a copy of value.
size	*size_type size() const* Return the number of entries that I contain.
swap	*void swap(stack< Container >& x)* Swap my contents with x's.

stack

top   *reference& top()*
                   Return a reference to my top element.

top   *const_reference& top() const*
                   Return a reference to my top element.

stopwatch

Description:
An `os_stopwatch` supports traditional stopwatch facilities and is handy for timing operations and general benchmarking. Although a stopwatch stores its start and stop times down to microsecond levels, the inherent delays due to operating system paging and context switching tends to make stopwatches accurate to only +/- 1 second.

Declaration:
```
#include <ospace/time/stopwtch.h>
class os_stopwatch
```

Constructor	*os_stopwatch(const os_stopwatch& stopwatch)* Construct myself to be a copy of `stopwatch`.
Constructor	*os_stopwatch()* Construct me as a reset stopwatch that is not yet running.
=	*os_stopwatch& operator=(const os_stopwatch& stopwatch)* Assign myself from `stopwatch`.
==	*bool operator==(const os_stopwatch& stopwatch) const* Return `true` if I have the same state as `stopwatch`.
lap	*os_time_period lap() const* Return the current accumulated time period without affecting whether or not I am running.
os_time_period	*operator os_time_period() const* Return myself as a time period.
print	*void print(ostream& stream) const* Print myself to `stream`.
reset	*void reset()* Reset the stopwatch to a time period of 0 seconds and stop it if it is running.
running	*bool running() const* Return `true` if I'm running.
start	*void start()* Start me.
stop	*void stop()* Stop me.

Non-Member Functions:

<<   *ostream& operator<<(ostream& stream, const os_stopwatch& watch)*
       Print `watch` to `stream`.

<<   *os_bstream& operator<<(os_bstream& stream, const os_stopwatch& watch)*
       Write `watch` to `stream`.

>>   *os_bstream& operator>>(os_bstream& stream, os_stopwatch& watch)*
       Read `watch` from `stream`.

string

Description:

string is a typedef of an instantation of the ANSI basic_string template with its element type equal to char. basic_string uses two template parameters to define the following:

- **Type of element**—the first template parameter specifies the type of element comprising the string. For example, you can instantiate a basic_string of char to obtain a traditional C-like string, or a basic_string of wchar_t (wide characters) to obtain an international string.
- **String traits**—the second template parameter specifies the string's traits. A trait class is an auxiliary helper class controlling how the basic_string class assigns and compares elements, calculates the length of strings and defines the value denoting end-of-string. This approach allows you to vary specific low-level characteristics of each string type without having to alter the code for basic_string.

Although use of a template allows you to create a wide variety of different strings, most C++ programs only require a couple of common string types. Systems<ToolKit> includes the following typedefs that handle most situations:

```
// Regular string of characters.
typedef basic_string< char, string_char_traits_char > string

// Regular string of wide characters.
typedef basic_string< wchar_t, string_char_traits< wchar_t > >
  wstring
```

string_char_traits is a standard template class containing the default behaviors for a string's traits. string_char_traits_char is a class derived from the string_char_traits class that contains specialized behaviors for a string of regular chars. The header file <ospace/string/traits.h> contains the definition of these trait classes.

Errors:

This template class uses the Systems<ToolKit> error handling mechanism instead of throwing exceptions as specified by the ANSI Draft Working Paper.

The member functions can directly generate two kinds of events in addition to out-of-memory events. The os_string_range_error is generated to indicate a subscript out of range. The os_string_length_error is much rarer and serves to indicate that a string with an illegal length (e.g. -1 elements) was implied by the operation of the function; that is, the length overflowed a size_t. Note that strings can be so long as to run out of memory without generating an os_string_length_error.

In general, input parameters are checked. Typically, a range is specified as a starting position `pos` and a length `n`. The `pos` parameter is *strictly* checked to refer to a legal position within the string. An `os_string_range_error` is generated if it does not. The `n` parameter is more flexible—it is clamped to the available length. So, a too-large value of `n` is not an error, but will take all remaining characters. The descriptions below uses the language "clamped length" to refer to the shorter of the specified value and available length.

The value `os_npos` is defined as the largest number a `size_t` can represent is used as both an input value and a return value. When functions return this value, it typically means something was not found, such as a specific character, an index of a character, etc.

Errors from elements:

The `basic_string` template does not make special considerations for errors occurring during manipulation of the underlying elements. The container is not designed to handle an element which has constructors, a destructor, or an assignment operator which can fail.

Declaration:

```
#include <ospace/string.h>
template< class CHAR_T, class TRAITS >
class os_basic_string
```

Typedefs:

```
// Note that when you define OS_ALTERNATIVE_NAMES these become
// os_string and os_wstring.
typedef os_basic_string< char, string_char_traits_char >
  string

typedef os_basic_string< wchar_t, string_char_traits< wchar_t > >
  wstring
```

Constructor	*string()* Construct myself to be an empty string.
Constructor	*string(const string& str)* Construct myself to be a copy of `str`. Events: `memory` On Resumption: Constructs an empty string
Constructor	*string(const string& str, size_t pos, size_t n)* Constructs myself to be a copy of a portion of `str`. The portion starts at `pos` and is the clamped value of `n` in length. Events: `memory`, `string_range_error` On Resumption: Constructs an empty string.

Constructor	*string(const char* str, size_t n)*
	Construct myself to be a copy of the array `str`. Exactly n elements are copied from `str`; any `nul`s contained within that length have no significance.
	
	    Events: `memory`
	    On Resumption: Constructs an empty string.

Constructor	*string(const char* str)*
	Construct myself to be a copy of the `nul`-terminated array of elements `str`. The terminating element is not taken as part of the input.
	
	    Events: `memory`
	    On Resumption: Constructs an empty string.

Constructor	*string(char c, size_t n)*
	Construct myself to contain n repetitions of the element c.
	
	    Events: `memory`
	    On Resumption: Constructs an empty string.

Constructor[10]	*string(const substring& sub)* Construct myself to be a copy of the substring `sub`.
Destructor	*~string()* Destructor.

+=	*string& operator+=(const char* str)*
	Append a copy of the `nul`-terminated array of elements `str`. The terminating element is not taken as part of the input. Return a reference to myself. This function is a synonym for `append()`.
	
	    Events: `memory`
	    On Resumption: Leaves `*this` unmodified.

+=	*string& operator+=(const string& str)*
	Append a copy of `str` to myself. This function is a synonym for `append()`. Return a reference to myself.
	
	    Events: `memory`
	    On Resumption: Leaves `*this` unmodified.

+=	*string& operator+=(char c)*
	Append a copy of element c to myself. Return a reference to myself. This function is a synonym for `append()`.
	
	    Events: `memory`
	    On Resumption: Leaves `*this` unmodified.

---

[10] Non-standard extension.

=   *string& operator=(const char* str)*
Assign myself to be a copy of the `nul`-terminated array of elements `str`. The terminating element is not taken as part of the input. Return a reference to myself. This function is a synonym for `assign()`.

> Events: `memory`
> On Resumption: Leaves `*this` unmodified.

=   *string& operator=(char c)*
Assign myself to contains a single element with value `c`. Return a reference to myself.

> Events: `memory`
> On Resumption: Leaves `*this` unmodified.

=   *string& operator=(const string& str)*
Assign myself from `str`. Return a reference to myself. This is a synonym for `assign()`.

> Events: `memory`
> On Resumption: Leaves `*this` unmodified.

[]   *char& operator[ ](size_t pos)*
Return a reference to the element at index `pos`.

> Events: `memory`, `string_range_error`
> On Resumption: Returns a reference to an internal static scratch element.

[]   *char operator[ ](size_t pos) const*
Return the element at index `pos`. It is legal to access one past the end (`pos == size()`) in which case the `nul` character is returned.
This function has more overhead than `get_at()` because of the one-past-the-end testing.

> Events: `string_range_error`
> On Resumption: Returns a meaningless value.

()[11]   *substring operator()(size_t pos, size_t len)*
Return a substring of myself whose length is `len` bytes and whose start index is `pos`.

append   *string& append(const string& str, size_t pos, size_t n)*
Append to myself a portion of `str`. The portion begins at offset `pos` (default 0) and is the clamped length of `n` (default `os_npos`). Returns a reference to myself.

> Events: `memory`
> On Resumption: Leaves `*this` unmodified.

---

[11] Non-standard extension.

append	*string& append(const char* str, size_t n)* Append to myself a copy of the array `str`. Exactly n elements are copied from `str`; any `nuls` contained within that length have no significance. Return a reference to myself. Events: `memory` On Resumption: Leaves `*this` unmodified.
append	*string& append(char c, size_t)* Append a n (default 1) copies of element `c` to myself. Return a reference to myself. This function is more general than `operator+=()` as it has an optional second argument. Events: `memory` On Resumption: Leaves `*this` unmodified.
append	*string& append(const char* str)* Append a copy of the `nul`-terminated array of elements `str`. The terminating element is not taken as part of the input. Return a reference to myself. Events: `memory` On Resumption: Leaves `*this` unmodified.
assign	*string& assign(const string& str, size_t pos, size_t n)* Assign myself to be a copy of a portion of `str`. The portion starts at `pos` and is the clamped value of n (default `os_npos`) in length. Returns a reference to myself Events: `memory, string_range_error` On Resumption: Leaves `*this` unmodified.
assign	*string& assign(const string& str)* Assign myself from `str`. Return a reference to myself. This is a synonym for `operator=()`. Events: `memory` On Resumption: Leaves `*this` unmodified.
assign	*string& assign(const char* str, size_t n)* Assign myself to be a copy of the array `str`. Exactly n elements are copied from `str`; any `nuls` contained within that length have no significance. Returns a reference to myself. Events: `memory` On Resumption: Leaves `*this` unmodified.

assign

string& assign(const char str)*
Assign myself to be a copy of the `nul`-terminated array of elements `str`. The terminating element is not taken as part of the input. Return a reference to myself. This function is a synonym for `operator=()`.

> Events: `memory`
> On Resumption: Leaves `*this` unmodified.

assign

string& assign(char c, size_t n)
Assign myself to contain `n` (default 1) repetitions of the element `c`.

> Events: `memory`
> On Resumption: Constructs an empty string.

at

char& at(size_t pos)
Return a reference to the element at index `pos`. This function is a synonym for `operator[]()`.

> Events: `memory, string_range_error`
> On Resumption: Returns a reference to an internal static scratch element.

at

char at(size_t pos) const
Return the element at index `pos`. This function is a synonym for `get_at()`.

> Events: `string_range_error`
> On Resumption: Returns a meaningless value.

c_str

const char c_str() const*
Return a pointer to the beginning of a sequence of `size()+1` elements containing elements I control followed by an `nul` terminating value. The pointer returned refers to internal storage and may become invalid when a non-const function or `c_str()` (again) or `data()` is executed on myself.

> Events: `memory`
> On Resumption: Returns a 0 pointer.

compare

int compare(const char str, size_t pos, size_t n) const*
Equivalent to `compare(string(str,n),pos)` (though implemented in a more efficient form; it does not offer the possibility of a memory error implied by this equivalence). Note carefully that `n` applies to the size of the array `str` and *not* to the range in me to compare.

You might think that this function would be equivalent to `compare(string(str,n),pos,n)`, but it is not. Instead, the entire remainder of this string after `pos` is compared with the specified length of `str`.

compare	*int compare(char c, size_t pos, size_t rep) const* Equivalent to `compare(string(c,rep),pos)`. Note that this form is not mentioned in the April ANSI Draft Working Paper. It was in the September '94 draft and was left in place. The default value of `pos` is 0, and the default value of `rep` is 1.
compare	*int compare(const char* s, size_t pos) const* Equivalent to `compare(string(str),pos)`. The default value of `pos` is 0.
compare	*int compare(const string& str, size_t pos, size_t n) const* Compare a portion of myself (from position `pos` (default 0) running through the clamped length of n (default os_npos)) against the entire value of `str`. The return value is zero when the compared portion of the strings are equal, negative when my compared portion is less than the other string, and positive when greater than the other string.
copy	*size_t copy(char* str, size_t n, size_t pos) const* Copy the elements starting at `pos` (default 0) running the clamped length of n to the area specified with `str`. This is a safe way to read multiple elements from a string—make your own local copy of them. Pay careful attention to the order of the parameters. They are in a different order than most of the other functions, due to the nature of the function (n becomes the capacity of `str`) and the desire to make `pos` take a default argument.
data	*const char* data() const* This returns the internal data of the string as an array of elements. No special terminating value is added For a zero-length string, the return value is unspecified (it may or may not be NULL). The pointer returned refers to internal storage and may become invalid when a non-const function or `c_str()` (again) or `data()` is executed on myself. This is a very efficient function. See also `c_str()` and `copy()`.
empty	*bool empty() const* Return `true` if I don't contain any elements.
exchange	*void exchange(string& str)* Swap my contents with that of `str`. This is a particularly fast operation.
find	*size_t find(char c, size_t pos) const* Equivalent to `find(string(c), pos)`
find	*size_t find(const char* str, size_t pos) const* Equivalent to `find(string(str), pos)`

find
      size_t find(const char* str, size_t pos, size_t n) const
Equivalent to `find(string(str,n), pos)`.

find
      size_t find(const string& str, size_t pos) const
Starting the search from index `pos` of myself, return the index of the first occurrence of `str`, or `os_npos` if no such index exists. Note that unlike most other members, a value of `pos` which is out of range is not an error. Instead, the string will never be found.

      Events: `memory`

find_first_not_of
      size_t find_first_not_of(const char& c, size_t pos) const
Equivalent to `find_first_not_of(string(c),pos)`.

find_first_not_of
      size_t find_first_not_of(const string& str, size_t pos) const
Return the lowest index greater than or equal to `pos` which contains an element that does not also occur in `str`. If no such index exists, return `os_npos`.

      Events: `memory`

find_first_not_of
      size_t find_first_not_of(const char* str, size_t pos) const
Equivalent to `find_first_not_of(string(str),pos)`.

find_first_not_of
      size_t find_first_not_of(const char* str, size_t pos, size_t n) const
Equivalent to `find_first_not_of(string(str,n),pos)`.

find_first_of
      size_t find_first_of(const string& str, size_t pos) const
Return the lowest index greater than or equal to `pos` which contains an element that also occurs in `str`. If no such index exists, return `os_npos`.

      Events: `memory`

find_first_of
      size_t find_first_of(const char& c, size_t pos) const
Equivalent to `find_first_of(string(c),pos)`.

find_first_of
      size_t find_first_of(const char* str, size_t pos, size_t n) const
Equivalent to `find_first_of(string(str,n),pos)`.

find_first_of
      size_t find_first_of(const char* str, size_t pos) const
Equivalent to `find_first_of(string(str),pos)`.

find_last_not_of
      size_t find_last_not_of(const string& str, size_t pos) const
Return the highest index less than or equal to `pos` which contains an element that is not also present in `str`. If no such index exists, return `os_npos`.

      Events: `memory`

find_last_not_of
      size_t find_last_not_of(const char* str, size_t pos) const
Equivalent to `find_last_not_of(string(str),pos)`.

find_last_not_of	*size_t find_last_not_of(const char& c, size_t pos) const* Equivalent to `find_last_not_of(string(c),pos)`.
find_last_not_of	*size_t find_last_not_of(const char* str, size_t pos, size_t n) const* Equivalent to `find_last_not_of(string(str,n),pos)`.
find_last_of	*size_t find_last_of(const char& c, size_t pos) const* Equivalent to `find_last_of(string(c),pos)`.
find_last_of	*size_t find_last_of(const string& str, size_t pos) const* Return the highest index less than or equal to `pos` which contains an element that also occurs in `str`. If no such index exists, return `os_npos`. Events: `memory`
find_last_of	*size_t find_last_of(const char* str, size_t pos) const* Equivalent to `find_last_of(string(str),pos)`.
find_last_of	*size_t find_last_of(const char* str, size_t pos, size_t n) const* Equivalent to `find_last_of(string(str,n),pos)`.
get_at	*char get_at(size_t pos) const* Return the element at index `pos`. Events: `string_range_error` On Resumption: Returns a meaningless value.
insert	*string& insert(size_t pos, char c, size_t)* Insert n (default 1) copies of `c` at position `pos`. Return a reference to myself. Events: `memory` On Resumption: Leaves `*this` unmodified.
insert	*string& insert(size_t pos, const char* str, size_t n)* Insert at position `pos` a copy of the array `str`. Exactly n elements are copied from `str`; any `nuls` contained within that length have no significance. Returns a reference to myself. Events: `memory` On Resumption: Leaves `*this` unchanged.
insert	*string& insert(size_t pos, const char* str)* Insert at position `pos` a copy of the `nul`-terminated array of elements `str`. The terminating element is not taken as part of the input. Events: `memory` On Resumption: Leaves `*this` unmodified.

insert

string& insert(size_t pos1, const string& str, size_t pos2, size_t n_npos)
Insert at index `pos1` a portion of `str` starting from `pos2` (default 0) running for the clamped length of `n` (default `os_npos`). Returns a reference to myself.

> Events: `memory`
> On Resumption: Constructs an empty string.

length

size_t length() const
Return the number of elements that I contain.

NOTE: `length()` is deprecated, due to renaming of the function in later editions of the ANSI Draft Working Paper. Use `size()` instead.

put_at

void put_at(size_t pos, char c)
Change the element at position `pos` into `c`. You may put one element past the end of the string, which will append to the string.

> Events: `memory, string_range_error`
> On Resumption: The string is unmodified.

remove

string& remove()
Become an empty string. Return a reference to myself. This is a particularly efficient operation. Calling `remove()` with no arguments is equivalent in meaning to `remove(0,os_npos)` but is implemented as a special form (rather than defaulting the first argument to 0 in the other form) so that it can be implemented specially. This specialization is much more efficient and is immune from error conditions.

remove

string& remove(size_t pos, size_t n)
Remove the elements which start at index `pos` and run for the clamped length of `n` (default `os_npos`). Returns a reference to myself.

> Events: `memory`
> On Resumption: Leaves `*this` unmodified.

replace

string& replace(size_t pos, size_t n1, const char str)*
Target the sequence of elements starting at `pos` whose length is the clamped value of `n1`. Replace the targeted sequence with a copy of the `nul`-terminated array of elements `str`. The terminating element is not taken as part of the input. Return a reference to myself.

> Events: `memory`
> On Resumption: Leaves `*this` unmodified.

replace	*string& replace(size_t pos1, size_t n1, const string& str, size_t pos2, size_t n2)*

Target the sequence of elements starting at `pos1` whose length is the clamped value of `n1`. Replace the targeted sequence with a portion of `str` starting at `pos2` (default 0) running for the clamped length of `n2` (default `os_npos`). Return a reference to myself.

> Events: `memory`
> On Resumption: Leaves `*this` unmodified.

replace	*string& replace(size_t pos, size_t n1, const char* str, size_t n2)*

Target the sequence of elements starting at `pos1` whose length is the clamped value of `n1`. Replace the targeted sequence with a copy of the array `str`. Exactly n elements are copied from `str`; any `nul` contained within that length have no significance. Return a reference to myself.

> Events: `memory`
> On Resumption: Leaves `*this` unmodified.

replace	*string& replace(size_t pos, size_t n1, char c, size_t n2)*

Target the sequence of elements starting at `pos1` whose length is the clamped value of `n1`. Replace the targeted sequence with a n2 (default 1) copies of `c`. Return a reference to myself.

> Events: `memory`
> On Resumption: Leaves `*this` unmodified.

reserve	*void reserve(size_t size)*

If necessary, expand my internal storage so that it can hold at least `size` characters. This will optimize subsequent `append()` and `operator+=()` calls. The string can grow, through appending, up to a total length of `size` before having to reallocate storage. Calling other functions to manipulate me, or assigning me to another string will disable the reserve effect.

> Events: `memory`
> On Resumption: Leaves `*this` unmodified.

reserve	*size_t reserve() const*

Return the number of characters that I can hold without reallocating my internal storage.

resize	*void resize(size_t n)*

Equivalent to `resize(n,nul)`.

resize	*void resize(size_t n, char c)*

If my size is less than n, append n - `size()` copies of c to myself; otherwise, truncate myself to become n characters long.

> Events: `memory`
> On Resumption: Leaves `*this` unmodified.

rfind   *size_t rfind(const char* str, size_t pos) const*
Equivalent to `rfind(string(str), pos)`

rfind   *size_t rfind(char c, size_t pos) const*
Equivalent to `rfind(string(c), pos)`

rfind   *size_t rfind(const char* str, size_t pos, size_t n) const*
Equivalent to `rfind(string(str,n), pos)`.

rfind   *size_t rfind(const string& str, size_t pos) const*
Return the index of the last occurrence of `str` that starts before or at `pos`, or returns `os_npos` if no such index exists. Note that unlike most other functions, a value of `pos` out of range is not an error. Instead, a very large value of `pos` will specify that the entire string be searched.

> Events: `memory`

size   *size_t size() const*
Return the number of elements that I contain.

substr   *string substr(size_t pos, size_t n) const*
Return a string whose length is the smaller of `n` (default `os_npos`) and `size() - pos` and whose contents are copied from index `pos` (default 0) of myself.

Non-Member Functions:

+   *string operator+(const char* left, const string& right)*
Concatenates the two operands together.

> Events: `memory`
> On Resumption: Returns an empty string.

+   *string operator+(const char left, const string& right)*
Concatenates the two operands together.

> Events: `memory`
> On Resumption: Returns an empty string.

+   *string operator+(const string& left, const char right)*
Concatenates the two operands together.

> Events: `memory`
> On Resumption: Returns an empty string.

+   *string operator+(const string& left, const char* right)*
Concatenates the two operands together.

> Events: `memory`
> On Resumption: Returns an empty string.

+
string operator+ (const string& left_hand_side,
const string& right_hand_side)
Concatenates the two operands together.

> Events: `memory`
> On Resumption: Returns an empty string.

>,<,>=,<=,==,!=
various relational operators
A full complement of relational operators are provided, which make the use of `compare()` much simpler.

<<
ostream& operator<<(ostream& stream, const string& str)
Print `str` to `stream`.

<<
os_bstream& operator<<(os_bstream& stream, const string& str)
Write `str` to `stream`.

>>
os_bstream& operator>>(os_bstream& stream, string& str)
Read `str` from `stream`.

substring

Description:

Substrings are a non-ANSI extension to the string class. Given the declaration:

```
string a_string; // Declare a string.
```

the syntax:

```
a_string( pos, length )
```

specifies a substring of `a_string` starting at offset `pos` whose length is no greater than `length`. When used as `lvalue`, the specified portion of the target string is replaced by the right hand argument. The specified portion of the target string does not have to be the same size as its replacement value.

Declaration:
```
#include <ospace/string.h>
class string::substring // Nested class.
```

Constructor

substring(string& str, size_t pos, size_t len)
This constructs a substring object to refer to a portion of `str`, starting at `pos` and up to `len` characters in length. The argument values are just remembered and are not applied to anything so no error conditions are detected.

=

void operator=(const string& str) const
This will replace the controlled region of the substring with the right-hand side - `str` and will also update the substring object to reflect the new region if the length of the replacement is different from the original length.

system

Description:

The os_system class is comprised wholly of static functions that allow you to access general information about your operating system. It is useful for obtaining system-wide information such as the name and release number of the operating system, as well as pre-defined system limits. Note that there are specific interfaces for limit access in the os_this_process class. You cannot instantiate os_system.

Declaration:
```
#include <ospace/system/system.h>
class os_system
```

clock_ticks_per_second

/* static */ long clock_ticks_per_second()
Return the number of "clock ticks" per second. This is a constant and is used to maintain some internal statistics as well as provide an underlying heartbeat of the operating system.

hardware_version

/* static */ string hardware_version()
Return my version identification.

Events: other
On Resumption: Returns empty string.

host_name

/* static */ string host_name()
Return my host name.

Events: other
On Resumption: Returns empty string.

limit

/* static */ long limit(int n)
Return the limit associated with the resource encoded by n.

Events: other
On Resumption: Returns -1.

machine

/* static */ string machine()
Return the name of my hardware architecture.

Events: other
On Resumption: Returns empty string.

page_size

/* static */ long page_size()
Return the number of bytes in one of my pages. This is the granularity of many memory management calls. This page size does not necessarily reflect the size of pages on my underlying hardware.

platform_version /* *static* */ *string platform_version( )*
Return my release identification.

> Events: `other`
> On Resumption: Returns empty string.

posix_version /* *static* */ *long posix_version( )*
Return my `POSIX.1` version number

print /* *static* */ *void print(ostream& stream)*
Print my name to `stream`.

system_name /* *static* */ *string system_name( )*
Return the name of my operating system.

> Events: `other`
> On Resumption: Returns empty string.

xpg_version /* *static* */ *long xpg_version( )*
Return my `XPG` version number.

sysv_semaphore

Description:

An `os_sysv_semaphore` is an object that is used to manage one or more shared resources. Unlike most synchronization classes, System V semaphores can be used between processes. They are primarily used for synchronization of resources shared by multiple processes. The number of available resources is specified when a semaphore is constructed and is stored inside the semaphore as a counter.

When a process uses `obtain()` to obtain n resources from a semaphore and the semaphore's counter is greater than or equal to n, the counter is decremented by n and the function returns immediately. However, if the counter is less than n, the process is suspended until the resources become available.

When a process uses `release()` to release n resources to a semaphore, the semaphore's counter is incremented by n and the function returns immediately.

It can be a problem if a process obtains a resource and then terminates abnormally before releasing it. To avoid this, you may specify the `O_UNDO` flag when using `obtain()` or `release()`, which classifies the operation as "undoable." When a process terminates, all "undoable" operations are automatically reversed. For example, if a resource was obtained, it is released. Similarly, if a resource was released, it is obtained. You may specify that an operation is non-blocking by using the `O_NONBLOCK` option. If an operation is performed that would block, it generates an `EAGAIN` error and immediately returns.

An `os_sysv_semaphore` contains a pointer to an `os_sysv_semaphore_array`. You can access its underlying array and obtain additional status information directly from the semaphores. You may copy and assign an `os_sysv_semaphore` object and it will reference count the underlying `os_sysv_semaphore_array`, allowing efficient pass by value.

Declaration:
```
#include <ospace/sync/sysvsem.h>
class os_sysv_semaphore
```

Options:

Legal open control:	`O_OPEN, O_CREAT, O_EXCL`
Legal I/O control:	`O_NONBLOCK, O_UNDO`
Default I/O control:	0 (blocking, no undo)

Constructor	*os_sysv_semaphore(os_vid_t id)* Construct myself to reference the existing semaphore with `id`. Events: `memory`
Constructor	*os_sysv_semaphore(const os_key& key)* Construct myself to reference the existing semaphore with `key`. Events: `syscall`, `memory` On Resumption: My id is set to `OS_UNDEFINED`.
Constructor	*os_sysv_semaphore(int initial_value, os_mode_t mode)* Construct myself to reference a new semaphore with a private key, `initial_value` and access permissions `mode`. Events: `syscall`, `memory` On Resumption: My id is set to `OS_UNDEFINED`.
Constructor	*os_sysv_semaphore(const os_key& key, os_open_t open, int initial_value, os_mode_t mode)* Construct myself to reference a new semaphore with `key`, `initial_value` open control flags `open` and access permissions `mode`. If a semaphore with `key` already exists, then reference the existing semaphore and ignore the `mode` and `initial_value` parameters. Events: `syscall`, `memory` Os Resumption: id is set to `OS_UNDEFINED`.
Constructor	*os_sysv_semaphore(const os_sysv_semaphore& semaphore)* Construct myself to reference the same semaphore as `semaphore`.
Destructor	*~os_sysv_semaphore()* Destroy myself. I disconnect from my semaphore array, which will self-destruct if it was allocated on the heap and I was the last semaphore to reference it.
<	*bool operator<(const os_sysv_semaphore& semaphore) const* Return `true` if I am considered less than `semaphore`.
=	*const os_sysv_semaphore& operator=(* *const os_sysv_semaphore& semaphore)* Reference the same semaphore as `semaphore`.
==	*bool operator==(const os_sysv_semaphore& semaphore) const* Return `true` if I am the same semaphore as `semaphore`.
array	*const os_sysv_semaphore_array& array() const* Return a reference to my semaphore array.
clear	*void clear()* Flush any pending operations without executing them.

count_waiting for_increase

>*int count_waiting_for_increase() const*
>
>Return the number of processes that are waiting for my value to increase.
>
>>Events: `syscall`
>>On Resumption: Returns `OS_UNDEFINED`.

count_waiting for_zero

>*int count_waiting_for_zero() const*
>
>Return the number of processes that are waiting for my value to become zero.
>
>>Events: `syscall`
>>On Resumption: Returns `OS_UNDEFINED`.

defined

>*bool defined() const*
>Return `true` if I reference a valid semaphore array.
>
>>Events: `syscall`
>>On Resumption: Returns `false`.

down

>*void down(os_ioctl_t control)*
>Same as `obtain( 1, control )`. The default value of `control` is 0.

execute

>*void execute()*
>Execute all of the operations that are pending for my associated semaphore array.
>
>>Events: `syscall`
>>On Resumption: All pending operations are still in the queue.

index

>*int index() const*
>Return my index in my semaphore array.

last_operator

>*os_pid_t last_operator() const*
>Return the last process that operated on me.
>
>>Events: `syscall`
>>On Resumption: Returns `OS_UNDEFINED`.

lock

>*void lock(os_ioctl_t control)*
>Same as `obtain( 1, control )`.

obtain

>*void obtain(int amount, os_ioctl_t control)*
>Decrement my value by `amount`, using the I/O control `control` (default 0). This function may be recorded.
>
>>Events: `syscall`, `other`

obtain

void obtain()
Decrement my value by 1. This function may be recorded.

Events: `syscall`, `other`

os_vid_t

operator os_vid_t() const
Return my IPC id.

print

void print(ostream& stream) const
Print my id and index to `stream`.

P

void P(os_ioctl_t control)
Same as `obtain( 1, control )`.

record

void record(bool flag)
Set the record mode of my associated semaphore array to `flag` (default `true`).

record

bool record() const
Return `true` if my associated semaphore array is in record mode.

release

void release(int amount, os_ioctl_t control)
Increment my value by `amount`, using the I/O control `control` (default 0). This function may be recorded.

Events: `syscall`, `other`

release

void release()
Increment my value by 1. This function may be recorded.

Events: `syscall`, `other`

remove

void remove()
Remove my associated semaphore array from the operation system. Any process that attempts to access any of its semaphores after this operation will error.

Events: `syscall`

signal

void signal(os_ioctl_t control)
Same as `release( 1, control )`.

unlock

void unlock(os_ioctl_t control)
Same as `release( 1, control )`.

up

void up(os_ioctl_t control)
Same as `release( 1, control )`.

value	*int value() const* Return my current value. Events: `syscall` On Resumption: Returns `OS_UNDEFINED`.
value	*void value(int new_value)* Set my value to `new_value`. Events: `syscall`
V	*void V(os_ioctl_t control)* Same as `release( 1, control )`.
wait	*void wait(os_ioctl_t control)* Same as `obtain( 1, control )`.
wait_until_zero	*void wait_until_zero(os_ioctl_t control)* Block the current process until my value becomes zero. If `control` (default 0) is set to `O_NONBLOCK`, do not block but return an `EAGAIN`. This function may be recorded. Events: `syscall`

Non-Member Functions:

<<	*ostream& operator<<(ostream& stream, const os_sysv_semaphore& semaphore)* Print `semaphore` to `stream`.

sysv_semaphore_array

Description:

An os_sysv_semaphore_array is an array of System V semaphores. Unlike most synchronization classes, System V semaphores can be used between processes. They are primarily used for synchronization of resources shared by multiple processes

You may create an array of semaphores by constructing an os_sysv_semaphore_array with the number of semaphores as the count. To access the n'th semaphore in the array, use semaphore(n). By default, any operation that you perform on a semaphore is executed immediately. However, it is sometimes useful to be able to execute a series of operations as a single transaction. To do this, place the semaphore or semaphore array into record mode using record(true), which causes all operations that obtain, release, or wait on resources to be queued. To execute all of the queued operations in an atomic manner, use execute(). No resources are obtained/released by an execute() until all of the queued operations succeed. To turn off record mode, use record(false).

Conversions allow os_sysv_semaphore_array and os_vid_t (the System V IPC id) to be used interchangeably.

Declaration:

```
#include <ospace/sync/semarray.h>
class os_sysv_semaphore_array
```

Options:

Legal open control:	O_OPEN, O_CREAT, O_EXCL
Legal I/O control:	O_NONBLOCK, O_UNDO
Default I/O control:	0

Constructor	*os_sysv_semaphore_array(os_vid_t id)* Construct myself to reference the existing semaphore array with id id.
Constructor	*os_sysv_semaphore_array(const os_key& key)* Construct myself to reference the existing semaphore array with key. Events: syscall On Resumption: My id is set to OS_UNDEFINED.
Constructor	*os_sysv_semaphore_array(int count, os_mode_t mode)* Construct myself to reference a new array of count semaphores, with a private key and access mode mode. Events: syscall On Resumption: My id is set to OS_UNDEFINED.

Constructor	*os_sysv_semaphore_array(const os_key& key, os_open_t open, int count, os_mode_t mode)* Construct myself to reference a new array of `count` semaphores with `key`, `open` control flags and `mode`. If a semaphore array with `key` already exists, then reference the existing semaphore array and ignore the `mode` parameter. Events: `syscall` On Resumption: My id is set to `OS_UNDEFINED`.
<	*bool operator< (const os_sysv_semaphore_array& array) const* Return `true` if my id is less than `array`'s.
==	*bool operator== (const os_sysv_semaphore_array& array) const* Return `true` if my id is the same as `array`'s.
clear	*void clear()* Flush any pending operations without executing them.
creator_group	*os_gid_t creator_group() const* Return my creator's group id. Events: `syscall` On Resumption: Returns 0.
creator_user	*os_uid_t creator_user() const* Return my creator's user id. Events: `syscall` On Resumption: Returns 0.
defined	*bool defined() const* Return `true` if my id is not `OS_UNDEFINED`.
execute	*void execute()* Atomically execute all of the operations in my pending operation queue and then clear the queue. Events: `syscall` On Resumption: All pending operations are still in the queue.
id	*os_vid_t id() const* Return my IPC id.
id	*void id(os_vid_t id)* Set my id to `id`.
is_legal_index	*bool is_legal_index(int index) const* Return `true` is index is a legal semaphore index. Events: `syscall` On Resumption: Returns `false`.

key
os_key key() const
Return my key.

> Events: `syscall`
> On Resumption: Returns a default `os_key` object.

last_change_time
os_time_and_date last_change_time() const
Return the last time that any of my semaphores were changed.

> Events: `syscall`
> On Resumption: Returns `os_time_and_date( 0 )`.

last_op_time
os_time_and_date last_op_time() const
Return the last time that an operation was performed on any of my semaphores.

> Events: `syscall`
> On Resumption: Returns `os_time_and_date( 0 )`.

mode
os_mode_t mode() const
Return my mode.

> Events: `syscall`
> On Resumption: Returns 0.

mode
void mode(os_mode_t mode)
Set my mode to `mode`.

> Events: `syscall`

op
void op(int index, int operation, os_ioctl_t control)
Perform operation on semaphore `index` with the specified `control` flags (default is `blocking` and `undo`). If I'm in record mode, append the operation to my pending operations queue, else perform the operation immediately.

> Events: `syscall`, `other`

os_vid_t
operator os_vid_t() const
Convert myself to my IPC id.

owner_group
os_gid_t owner_group() const
Return my owner's group id.

> Events: `syscall`
> On Resumption: Returns 0.

owner_group
void owner_group(os_gid_t group)
Set my owner's group to `group`.

> Events: `syscall`

owner_user	*os_uid_t owner_user() const*
	Return my owner's user id.
	
	    Events: `syscall`
	    On Resumption: Returns 0.

owner_user	*void owner_user(os_uid_t user)* Set my owner's user to `user`. Events: `syscall`
print	*void print(ostream& stream) const* Print my id and index to `stream`.
record	*bool record() const* Return `true` if I'm in record mode.
record	*void record(bool flag)* Set my record mode to `flag`.
remove	*void remove()* Immediately remove the semaphore array from the operating system. Any process still trying to access the semaphores will get errors. Events: `syscall`
semaphore	*os_sysv_semaphore semaphore(int index)* Return a semaphore that references my `index`'th semaphore. Events: `other`
semaphore	*const os_sysv_semaphore semaphore(int index) const* Return a semaphore that references my `index`'th semaphore. Events: `other`

size	*int size() const*
	Return the number of semaphores in my array.
	
	    Events: `syscall`
	    On Resumption: Returns 0.

slot_sequence number	*int slot_sequence_number() const*
	Return my slot usage sequence number.
	
	    Events: `syscall`
	    On Resumption: Returns 0.

Non-Member Functions:

<<   *ostream& operator<<(ostream& stream, const*
                          os_sysv_semaphore_array & semarray)
                          Print `semarray` to `stream`.

tcp_connection_server

Description:

An `os_tcp_connection_server` accepts incoming TCP connections on a particular address. It should be used in conjunction with `os_tcp_socket`s. Refer to the chapter on sockets in the *Systems<ToolKit> User's Manual* for detailed information on establishing connections using `os_tcp_connection_server`.

Conversions allow `os_tcp_connection_server` and `os_desc_t` (UNIX descriptor) to be used interchangeably.

Declaration:
```
#include <ospace/socket/tcpsrvr.h>
class os_tcp_connection_server : public os_socket
```

Constructor	*os_tcp_connection_server(os_desc_t descriptor)* Construct myself to reference the socket with descriptor `descriptor`.
Constructor	*os_tcp_connection_server(const os_socket_address& address, os_desc_t control, int backlog)* Construct myself to bind to `address` and serve connections with a backlog of up to `backlog` (default 5) incoming connections (`AF_INET` only). Set my I/O control to be `control` (default 0). Events: `syscall` On Resumption: I will be in an unknown state.
accept	*bool accept(os_tcp_socket& socket)* Extract the first pending connection request and associate it with the socket `socket`. If `socket` is already open, close it first. If an error occurs, or I'm in non-blocking mode and no connections were pending, return `false`; otherwise, return `true`. Events: `syscall` On Resumption: Returns `false`.
listen	*void listen(int backlog)* Set the maximum backlog of incoming connections to `backlog`. Events: `syscall` On Resumption: My backlog maximum will be unknown.

tcp_socket

Description:

An `os_tcp_socket` allows reliable connection-oriented communication between a server socket and a client socket. The server process constructs an `os_tcp_connection_server` and binds it to an address that is known to its client. It then waits for an incoming connection request using `accept()`. A client process creates a stream socket and connects it to the server socket using `connect_to()`. When the connection is made, the server's `accept()` function connects its socket argument to the client socket. Any data written to the server socket will appear as input to the client socket and visa-versa.

TCP sockets may be bound to a UNIX file system path, although this is only useful for TCP connections between processes that have access to the same file system.

Conversions allow `os_tcp_socket` and `os_desc_t` (UNIX descriptor) to be used interchangeably.

Declaration:
```
#include <ospace/socket/tcpsock.h>
class os_tcp_socket : public os_connectable_socket
```

Constructor
os_tcp_socket(os_desc_t descriptor)
Construct myself to reference the socket with descriptor `descriptor`.

Constructor
os_tcp_socket()
Construct myself to have a unique local IP address.

> Events: `syscall`
> On Resumption: I will be in an unknown state.

Constructor
os_tcp_socket(const os_socket_address& address, os_ioctl_t control)
Construct myself to have IP socket address `address` with an I/O control of `control` (default 0).

> Events: `syscall`
> On Resumption: I will be in an unknown state.

keep_alive
void keep_alive(bool flag)
Set "keep alive" to `flag`.

> Events: `syscall`
> On Resumption: My "keep alive" state will be unknown.

keep_alive
bool keep_alive() const
Return `true` if I should transmit periodically to keep my connection alive.

> Events: `syscall`
> On Resumption: Return value may be invalid.

os_adapter   *operator os_adapter() const*
Return an `os_adapter` to myself.

Events: `syscall`
On Resumption: The attachment count of the adapter may be incorrect.

this_process

Description:

The `os_this_process` class represents the current running process. It is comprised solely of static member functions that provide a wide set of functions for controlling the current process. You cannot instantiate `os_this_process`.

The functions of `os_this_process` may be grouped into several categories:

- Process id's
- Signals
- Process group membership
- Child process status
- Executing a program in the current process
- Process environment - `os_environment` is a `typedef` to an STL `map< string, string >` containing the key/value pairs that define the environment.
- Signal actions
- Signal blocking
- Current working directory
- Execution permissions
- Execution priority
- Timers
- Resource limits

These functions make use of `os_resource`, `os_interval_timer`, `os_signal`, `os_signal_action`, `os_process_status` and `os_process` objects. See these classes for more information.

Declaration:
```
#include <ospace/process/thisproc.h>
class os_this_process
```

Typedefs:
```
typedef os_environment
os_map< string, string, less< string > >
```

_exit   */* static */ void _exit(int code)*
                    Terminate me immediately with exit code `code` without flushing or
                    closing my I/O buffers.

action /* static */ os_signal_action action(os_sig_t signal)
Return the action that I would perform if I received `signal`.

> Events: `syscall`
> On Resumption: Returns a default `os_signal_action` object.

action /* static */ void action(const vector< os_sig_t >& signals,
const os_signal_action& action)
Set the action associated with all signals in `signals` to `action`.

> Events: `syscall`

action /* static */ void action(os_sig_t signal, const os_signal_action& action)
Set the action associated with `signal` to `action`.

> Events: `syscall`

add_exit_function /* static */ void add_exit_function(void (*f)())
Add `f` to my list of functions to be automatically executed when I exit.
These functions are executed immediately prior to the standard I/O exit
processing.

> Events: `other`

add_exit_function /* static */ void add_exit_function(void (*f)(int, ...), caddr_t arg)
Add `f` to my list of functions to be automatically executed with argument
`arg` when I exit. These functions are executed immediately prior to the
standard I/O exit processing. On exit, the registered functions will be
called as `f (status, arg)` where `status` is the argument passed to exit()
that caused me to terminate.

> Events: `other`

argument_limit /* static */ long argument_limit()
Return the system limit for the total length of the argument list passed to
exec (in bytes).

> Events: `other`
> On Resumption: Returns -1.

become_process group_leader

/* static */ void become_process_group_leader()

Make me a process group leader.

> Events: `syscall`

become_session leader

> /* static */ void become_session_leader()

> Make me a session leader. If I am already a session leader, this will fail. Otherwise, I will become a new session leader and the leader of a new process group.

>> Events: `syscall`

block

> /* static */ void block(const vector< os_sig_t >& signals)
> Add the signals in `signals` to the set of signals that are blocked.

>> Events: `syscall`

block

> /* static */ void block(os_sig_t signal)
> Add `signal` to the set of signals that are blocked.

>> Events: `syscall`

blocked_signals

> /* static */ vector< os_sig_t > blocked_signals()
> Return the current vector of signals being blocked. Note that this does not imply the signal is actually pending, but that it will pend if sent to the process. To determine which signals in the blocked vector are pending delivery, use `pending_signals()`.

>> Events: `syscall`
>> On Resumption: Returns an empty vector.

blocked_signals

> /* static */ void blocked_signals(const vector< os_sig_t >& signals)
> Set my vector of signals to be blocked to `signals`.

cd

> /* static */ void cd(const string& dirpath)
> Same as the UNIX or shell command `cd [dirpath]`.

>> Events: `syscall`
>> On Resumption: The current working directory is not altered.

children_limit

> /* static */ long children_limit()
> Return the system limit for the maximum number of processes per real user id.

>> Events: `other`
>> On Resumption: Returns -1.

core_resource

> /* static */ os_resource core_resource()
> Return the maximum number of bytes that I could core dump.

core_resource

> /* static */ void core_resource(const os_resource& resource)
> Set the maximum number of bytes in my core file to `resource`.

>> Events: `syscall`

cpu_resource	/* static */ os_resource cpu_resource() Return the maximum number of cpu seconds that I can use. When this soft limit is exceeded, I am sent a SIGXCPU signal.
cpu_resource	/* static */ void cpu_resource(const os_resource& resource) Set my maximum number of cpu seconds to resource. Events: syscall
data_resource	/* static */ os_resource data_resource() Return the maximum size of my data segment, in bytes. When this soft limit is exceeded, the new operator returns nil (0).
data_resource	/* static */ void data_resource(const os_resource& resource) Set my maximum data segment size, in bytes, to resource. Events: syscall
effective_group	/* static */ void effective_group(os_gid_t group) Set my effective group to group. I must have superuser privileges or have a real, effective, or saved group equal to group. Events: syscall
effective_group	/* static */ os_gid_t effective_group() Return my effective group.
effective_user	/* static */ os_uid_t effective_user() Return my effective user.
effective_user	/* static */ void effective_user(os_uid_t user) Set my effective user to user. I must be have superuser privileges or have a real, effective, or saved user equal to user. Events: syscall
environment	/* static */ void environment(const os_environment& env) Set my environment to a copy of env. Events: memory
environment	/* static */ os_environment environment() Return a copy of my environment. Events: memory
execute	/* static */ void execute(const os_environment* env, os_desc_t send, os_desc_t receive, os_desc_t error, const char* name, const char* argv[]) Execute the program called name using the null-terminated argument list argv, environment env, send channel send, receive channel receive and error channel error. Events: syscall.

execute
/* static */ void execute(const os_environment* env, os_desc_t send, os_desc_t receive, os_desc_t error, const char* name)
Execute the program called `name` using environment `env`, send channel `send`, receive channel `receive` and error channel `error`.

Events: `syscall`

execute
/* static */ void execute(int (*f)())
Execute the function `f`.

execute
/* static */ void execute(const char* shell, const char* command)
Execute the command `command` using the shell `shell`.

Events: `syscall`

execute
/* static */ void execute(const os_environment* env, os_desc_t send, os_desc_t receive, os_desc_t error, int (*f)(int argc, const char* argv[]), const char* argv [])
Execute the function `f` using the null-terminated argument list `argv`, environment `env`, send channel `send`, receive channel `receive` and error channel `error`.

Events: `syscall`.

execute
/* static */ void execute(const os_environment* env, os_desc_t send, os_desc_t receive, os_desc_t error, const char* shell, const char* command)
Execute the command `command` using the shell `shell`, environment `env`, send channel `send`, receive channel `receive` and error channel `error`.

Events: `syscall`.

execute
/* static */ void execute(const os_environment* env, os_desc_t send, os_desc_t receive, os_desc_t error, int (*f)())
Execute the function `f` using the environment `env`, send channel `send`, receive channel `receive` and error channel `error`.

Events: `syscall`.

execute
/* static */ void execute(int (*f)(int argc, const char* argv []), const char* arg0, const char* arg1, ...)
Execute the function `f` using the null-terminated variable argument list.

Events: `other`

execute /* static */ void execute(const os_environment* env, os_desc_t send, os_desc_t receive, os_desc_t error, int (*f)(int argc, const char* argv[]), const char* arg0, const char* arg1, ...)
Execute the function f using the null-terminated variable argument list, environment env, send channel send, receive channel receive and error channel error.

> Events: syscall, memory, other
> On Resumption: The current process remains unaltered.

execute /* static */ void execute(const char* name, const char* arg1, const char* arg2, ...)
Execute the program called name using the null-terminated variable argument list.

> Events: other, syscall
> On Resumption: The current process remains unaltered.

execute /* static */ void execute(const char* name, const char* argv[])
Execute the program called name using the null-terminated argument list argv.

> Events: syscall
> On Resumption: Generates a panic event.

execute /* static */ void execute(const char* name)
Execute the program called name.

> Events: syscall
> On Resumption: Generates a panic event.

execute /* static */ void execute(const os_environment* env, os_desc_t send, os_desc_t receive, os_desc_t error, const char* name, const char* arg1, const char* arg2, ...)
Execute the program called name using the null-terminated variable argument list, environment env, send channel send, receive channel receive and error channel error.

> Events: syscall, memory, other
> On Resumption: The current process remains unaltered.

execute /* static */ void execute(int (*f)(int argc, const char* argv[]), const char* argv[])
Execute the function f using the null-terminated argument list argv. Remember to end your argv list with a zero.

exit /* static */ void exit(int code)
Terminate me with exit code code after flushing and closing my I/O buffers. Be aware though that exit can cause your static object destructors to be called, which in turn could potentially generate events.

file_size_resource   /* *static* */ *void file_size_resource(const os_resource& resource)*
Set the maximum size of file that I can create, in bytes, to `resource`.

> Events: `syscall`

file_size_resource   /* *static* */ *os_resource file_size_resource()*
Return the maximum size of file that I may create, in bytes. When this soft limit is exceeded, I am sent a `SIGXFSZ` signal and subsequent writes to the file will fail.

fork   /* *static* */ *os_pid_t fork()*
Create a child process. Return thc child process to the parent and the parent process to the child. The child process will contain every thread that I do.

> Events: `syscall`
> On Resumption: Returns -1.

fork_alone   /* *static* */ *os_pid_t fork_alone()*
Create a child process. Return the child process to the parent and the parent process to the child. The child process will only contain the thread that caused the fork.

> Events: `syscall`
> On Resumption: Returns -1.

fork_and_is_child   /* *static* */ *bool fork_and_is_child()*
Spawn a child. Both the parent and child will return from this function. The parent returns `false` and the child returns `true`.

> Events: `syscall`
> On Resumption: Returns `false`.

group   /* *static* */ *os_gid_t group()*
Return my real group.

hangup   /* *static* */ *void hangup()*
Send me a hangup signal.

> Events: `syscall`.

has_job_control   /* *static* */ *bool has_job_control()*
Return `true` if the system supports job control.

> Events: `other`
> On Resumption: Returns `false`.

has_saveable_ids   /* *static* */ *bool has_saveable_ids()*
Returns `true` if the system supports saved set-group-ids and saved set-user-ids.

> Events: `other`
> On Resumption: Returns `false`.

ignore	/* *static* */ *void ignore(const vector< os_sig_t >& signals)* Ignore the signals in `signals`. Events: `syscall`
ignore	/* *static* */ *void ignore(os_sig_t signal)* Ignore the signal `signal`. Events: `syscall`
interrupt	/* *static* */ *void interrupt()* Send me an interrupt signal. Events: `syscall`.
keyboard_suspend	/* *static* */ *void keyboard_suspend()* Send me a keyboard stop signal. This is normally generated by a `Ctrl-Z` and will suspend my execution. Events: `syscall`.
kill	/* *static* */ *void kill()* Send me a kill signal. Events: `syscall`.
lock_data	/* *static* */ *void lock_data()* Lock my data segment into physical memory. Events: `syscall`
lock_text	/* *static* */ *void lock_text()* Lock my text segment into physical memory. Events: `syscall`
lock_text_and_data	/* *static* */ *void lock_text_and_data()* Lock my text and data segments into physical memory. Events: `syscall`
memory_resource	/* *static* */ *os_resource memory_resource()* Return the maximum size of my address space, in bytes.
memory_resource	/* *static* */ *void memory_resource(const os_resource& resource)* Set the maximum size of my address space, in bytes, to `resource`. Events: `syscall`

open_file_limit	/* *static* */ *long open_file_limit()*
	 Return the system limit for the maximum number of open files per process.
	
	      Events: `other`
	      On Resumption: Returns -1.

open_file_resource
/* static */ void open_file_resource(const os_resource& resource)
Set the maximum number of files that I may have simultaneously open to
`resource`.

> Events: `syscall`

open_file_resource
/* static */ os_resource open_file_resource()
Return the maximum number of files that I may have simultaneously open.
When this soft limit is exceeded, subsequent file opens and duplications
will fail.

open_stream_limit
/* static */ long open_stream_limit()
Return the system limit for the maximum number of standard I/O streams
per process at any given time.

> Events: `other`
> On Resumption: Returns -1.

parent
/* static */ os_pid_t parent()
Return my parent process.

pause
/* static */ void pause(const vector< os_sig_t >& signals)
Wait for any signal that is not currently being ignored and is not in
`signals`. Any actions associated with the incoming signal are executed
before I return from this call.

> Events: `syscall`

pause
/* static */ void pause()
Wait for any signal that is not currently being ignored. Any actions
associated with the incoming signal are executed before I return from this
call.

> Events: `syscall`

pending_signals
/* static */ vector< os_sig_t > pending_signals()
Return the vector of currently pending signals. Any signal that is being
blocked will be pending in the operating system and not be delivered until
unblocked. This message can be used to determine which signals are
pending without actually unblocking them.

> Events: `syscall`
> On Resumption: Returns an empty vector.

pid
/* static */ os_pid_t pid()
Return my process id.

priority
/* static */ void priority(int value)
Set my execution priority (nice) value to `value`. The range varies between
platforms, but is usually -20 (highest priority) to 20 (lowest priority). Only
superuser can lower a priority.

> Events: `syscall`

priority   /* static */ int priority()
                       Return my execution priority (nice) value. The range varies some between platforms, but is usually -20 (highest priority) to 20 (lowest priority).

> Events: `syscall`
> On Resumption: Returns -1. Be careful though, this is a valid priority and therefore cannot be used exclusively as an error indicator.

process_group   /* static */ void process_group(os_pid_t group)
                       Set my process group to `group`.

> Events: `syscall`

process_group   /* static */ os_pid_t process_group()
                       Return my process group.

> Events: `syscall`
> On Resumption: Returns `OS_UNDEFINED`.

process_group_limit /* static */ long process_group_limit()
                         Return the system limit for the maximum number of supplementary process group ids per process.

> Events: `other`
> On Resumption: Returns -1.

profile_timer   /* static */ os_interval_timer profile_timer()
                       Return my profile interval timer.

quit   /* static */ void quit()
                       Send me a quit signal.

> Events: `syscall`.

real_and effective_group

  /* static */ void real_and_effective_group(os_gid_t group)

  Set my real and effective group to `group`. I must have superuser privileges or have a real, effective, or saved group equal to `group`.

> Events: `syscall`

real_and effective_user

  /* static */ void real_and_effective_user(os_uid_t user)

  Set my real and effective user to `user`. I must have superuser privileges or have a real, effective, or saved user equal to `user`.

> Events: `syscall`

real_group   /* static */ os_gid_t real_group()
                       Return my real group.

real_timer   */* static */ os_interval_timer real_timer()*
Return my real interval timer.

real_user   */* static */ os_uid_t real_user()*
Return my real user.

resident_set_resource */* static */ void resident_set_resource(const os_resource& resource)*
Set the maximum size of my resident set size, in bytes, to `resource`.

> Events: `syscall`

resident_set_resource */* static */ os_resource resident_set_resource()*
Return the maximum size of my resident set size, in bytes. When this limit is exceeded, my resident pages are likely to be paged out.

restore_default */* static */ void restore_default(const vector< os_sig_t >& signals)*
Set the actions associated with the signals in `signals` to their defaults.

> Events: `syscall`

restore_default */* static */ void restore_default(os_sig_t signal)*
Set the action associated with `signal` to its default.

> Events: `syscall`

resume   */* static */ void resume()*
Send me a continue signal. This signal will resume my execution if I was suspended.

> Events: `syscall`.

root_directory */* static */ void root_directory(const string& dirpath)*
Set my root directory to `dirpath`.

> Events: `syscall`

set_alarm   */* static */ os_interval_timer set_alarm(const os_time_period& interval)*
Set my real time interval timer to expire in `interval` and return the timer.

> Events: `syscall`

set_repeat_alarm */* static */ os_interval_timer set_repeat_alarm(
const os_time_period& interval)*
Set my real time interval timer to expire every `interval` time period and return the timer.

> Events: `syscall`

signal /* *static* */ *void signal(os_sig_t signal)*
Send me the signal with code `signal`. The caller must have superuser privileges or an effective or saved user id that matches my real or effective user id. An exception is the `SIGCONT` signal, which can be sent to any process in the same session as the sender.

    Events: `syscall`, `other`

signal_all /* *static* */ *void signal_all(os_sig_t signal)*
Send the signal with code `signal` to all processes that have my real or effective user id.

    Events: `syscall`

sleep /* *static* */ *os_time_period sleep(const os_time_period& interval)*
Suspend my execution until the `interval` of time expires. This message called sleep(). If a signal is received during the sleep, the amount of remaining time is returned. In a multi-threaded environment, os_this_thread::sleep() should be used instead.

stack_resource /* *static* */ *void stack_resource(const os_resource& resource)*
Set the maximum size of my stack, in bytes, to `resource`.

    Events: `syscall`

stack_resource /* *static* */ *os_resource stack_resource()*
Return the maximum size of my stack, in bytes.

supplemental_groups /* *static* */ *void supplemental_groups(
const vector< os_gid_t >& groups)*
Set my supplementary groups to be the `groups`. You must have superuser permissions to execute this function.

    Events: `memory`, `syscall`

supplemental_groups *vector< os_gid_t > supplemental_groups()*
Return a vector of my group ids. This vector is the same as obtained by `os_this_process::user().groups()` unless modified by `supplemental_groups( groups )`.

    Events: `memory`

suspend /* *static* */ *void suspend()*
Send me a stop signal. This will suspend my execution and is only valid for systems that support job control.

    Events: `syscall`.

system /* *static* */ *os_process_status system(const string& command)*
Execute `command` using the library function system() and return its status.

terminate
/* *static* */ *void terminate()*
Send me a terminate signal. This is the signal sent by default when the
kill(1) UNIX command is executed.

    Events: `syscall`.

umask
/* *static* */ *void umask(os_mode_t mask)*
Set my file creation mask to `mask`.

umask
/* *static* */ *os_mode_t umask()*
Return my file creation mask.

unblock
/* *static* */ *void unblock(const vector< os_sig_t>& signals)*
Remove the signals in `signals` from the vector of signals that are
blocked.

    Events: `syscall`

unblock
/* *static* */ *void unblock(os_sig_t signal)*
Remove `signal` from the vector of signals that are blocked.

    Events: `syscall`

unlock
/* *static* */ *void unlock()*
Unlock my text and data segments.

    Events: `syscall`

usage
/* *static* */ *os_resource_usage usage()*
Return my current resource usage.

usage_for terminated_children

/* *static* */ *os_resource_usage usage_for_terminated_children()*

Return the sum of resource usage for all of the terminated children that I
have waited for.

user
/* *static* */ *os_uid_t user()*
Return my real user.

virtual_timer
/* *static* */ *os_interval_timer virtual_timer()*
Return my virtual interval timer.

wait_for_any_child
/* *static* */ *os_process_status wait_for_any_child(int flags)*
Wait for any of my children using `flags` and return its status.

    Events: `syscall`
    On Resumption: Returns a default `os_process_status` object.

wait_for_any child_in

> */* static */ os_process_status wait_for_any_child_in(os_pid_t pgid,*
>
> *int flags)*
> Wait for any child in the process group `pgid` using `flags` and return its status.
>
> > Events: `syscall`
> > On Resumption: Returns a default `os_process_status` object.

wait_for_any child_in_my_group

> */* static */ os_process_status wait_for_any_child_in_my_group(*
>
> *int flags)*
> Wait for any child in my process group using `flags` and return its status.
>
> > Events: `syscall`
> > On Resumption: Returns a default `os_process_status` object.

wait_for_child   */* static */ os_process_status wait_for_child(os_pid_t pid, int flags)*
Wait for any of my child with pid `pid` using `flags` and return its status.

> Events: `syscall`
> On Resumption: Returns a default `os_process_status` object.

working_directory   */* static */ os_path working_directory()*
Return my current working directory.

> Events: `syscall`
> On Resumption: Returns an empty path.

working_directory   */* static */ void working_directory(const string& dirpath)*
Change my current working directory to `dirpath`, which may be absolute or relative.

       Events: `syscall`

this_thread

Description:

`os_this_thread` is comprised entirely of static member functions that represent the current thread of control. It allows the manipulation of several aspects of the current thread, including:

- thread specific data
- current thread priority
- suspending execution pending another threads completion or intervention
- terminating this thread
- yielding control to another thread

The priority interfaces use enumerations defined in `os_thread_priority`. See `os_thread` for details.

Declaration:
```
#include <ospace/thread/thisthrd.h>
class os_this_thread
```

allocate	*/* static */ os_thread_key_t allocate()* Allocate a new key for thread specific data. See `release()`, `get()` and `set()`.
get	*/* static */ void* get(const os_thread_key_t& handle)* This returns the thread specific data associated with `handle`.
milli_sleep	*/* static */ void milli_sleep(long milliseconds)* Suspend the current thread for a duration of at least `milliseconds`.
priority	*/* static */ void priority(os_thread_priority::group_t group,* *os_thread_priority::level_t level)* Change the current thread's priority to group `group` and level `level`.
priority_group	*/* static */ os_thread_priority::group_t priority_group()* Return the priority group of the current thread.
priority_level	*/* static */ os_thread_priority::level_t priority_level()* Return the priority level of the current thread.
release	*/* static */ void release(os_thread_key_t& handle)* Release a key for thread specific data that was created with `allocate()`.

set /* static */ void set(const os_thread_key_t& handle, void* data)
This stores thread specific data. The value of the `data` pointer is
associated with the `handle` (created with `allocate()`) and the current
thread and subsequent calls to `get()` with the same `handle` called in the
context of this same thread will return `data`.

sleep /* static */ void sleep(int seconds)
Suspend the current thread for a duration of at least `seconds`.

suspend /* static */ void suspend()
Suspend the current thread.

terminate /* static */ void terminate(void* status)
Terminate the current thread, setting its exit status to `status`. On Solaris:
If the current thread is not detached, its id and exit status are retained until
another thread waits for it. If the current thread is the last non-daemon
thread in the process, the process terminates with an exit code of 0. If the
current thread is the initial thread, the process terminates with an exit code
of `status`.

tid /* static */ os_thread_t tid()
Return a handle to the current thread.

wait_for_any_thread /* static */ void* wait_for_any_thread(os_thread_t* thread)
Suspend the current thread until any other thread terminates and then
return the terminating thread's exit status. The handle of the terminating
thread is stored in `*thread` (if non-null). This function is only available
for Solaris.

wait_for_thread /* static */ void* wait_for_thread(os_thread_t thread)
Suspend the current thread until the specified `thread` terminates and then
return its exit status.

yield /* static */ void yield()
If a thread with the same priority is waiting to execute, suspend myself
and allow the waiting thread to execute.

thread

Description:

A thread is a program that is executing. A thread can access almost all of its own attributes, but only a small subset of attributes for other threads. Thread objects are therefore modeled using two classes: `os_this_thread`, which represents the current thread, and `os_thread`, which represents other threads.

To create a new thread, construct an `os_thread` with the address of a function and a pointer to an optional argument. This creates a thread that executes the specified function with the supplied pointer as its argument. The function must take be able to take a `void*` argument and return a `void*`.

Once constructed, an `os_thread` object contains functions that allow you to suspend, resume, terminate and change the priority of the thread object. The new thread executes concurrently with other threads in the process and terminates when it reaches the end of the specified function.

It is associated with a priority defined by two enumerations defined below. These enumerators are scoped in the class `os_thread_priority`. A thread priority is defined by a `group` and a `level`. Adopting these conventions will allow portable prioritization across most major platforms.

Conversions allow `os_thread` and `os_thread_t` to be used interchangeably.

Declaration:

```
#include <ospace/threads/thread.h>
class os_thread
```

Enums:
```
class os_thread_priority
  {
  public:
    enum group_t
      {
      critical = 0,
      server,
      standard,
      idle
      };

    enum level_t
      {
      highest = 0,
      above_normal,
      normal,
      below_normal,
      lowest
      };
  };
```

Typedefs:
```
void* (*os_thread_func_t)( void* arg )
// Pointer to a function that takes a void* argument and returns
// a void*.
```

Constructor	*os_thread(os_thread_func_t f, void* arg, size_t stack_size)* Construct myself to be a new thread. By default, when I'm constructed, immediately execute the function pointed to by `f` with the single argument `arg`. The default value for `flags` (0) causes the thread to run non-detached. The default value for `stack_size` (0) causes a default stack size to be allocated for the thread.
Constructor	*os_thread(const os_thread& thread)* Construct myself to represent the same thread as `thread`.
Constructor	*os_thread(os_thread_t tid)* Construct myself to represent the thread whose identifier is `tid`.
<	*bool operator<(const os_thread& thread) const* Return `true` if my id is less than `thread`'s.
=	*os_thread& operator=(os_thread_t tid)* Associate myself with the thread whose id is `tid`.
==	*bool operator==(const os_thread& thread) const* Return `true` if my id is equal to `thread`'s.

concurrency	*/* static */ void concurrency(int level)* Set my concurrency level to `level`.
concurrency	*/* static */ int concurrency()* Return my concurrency level.
create_thread	*/* static */ os_thread_t create_thread(os_thread_func_t f, void* arg,* *size_t stack_size)* Construct a new thread and return its handle. The arguments are the same as those described in the `os_thread` constructor.
exists	*bool exists() const* Return `true` if I represent a thread that has not terminated.
os_thread_t	*operator os_thread_t() const* Return my id.
print	*void print(ostream& stream) const* Print myself to `stream`.
priority	*void priority(os_thread_priority::group_t group,* *os_thread_priority::level_t level)* Change my priority to group `group` and level `level`.
priority_group	*os_thread_priority::group_t priority_group() const* Return my priority group.
priority_level	*os_thread_priority::level_t priority_level() const* Return my priority level.
resume	*void resume() const* Resume my execution.
suspend	*void suspend() const* Suspend my execution.
terminate	*void terminate(void* status)* Terminate myself with exit code `status`. Not available on Solaris.
tid	*os_thread_t tid() const* Return my id.

Non-Member Functions:

<<	*ostream& operator<<(ostream& stream, const os_thread& thread)* Print `thread` to `stream`.

times

Description:

times is a binary function object that returns the product of its two operands.

Declaration:
```
#include <function.h>
template< class T >
struct times : binary_function< T, T, T >
```

()
bool operator()(const T& x, const T& y) const
Return x * y.

Example <ospace/stl/examples/times.cpp>

```
#include <stl.h>
#include <iostream.h>

int input [4] = { 1, 5, 7, 2 };

int main ()
{
   int total = accumulate (input, input + 4, 1, times<int> ());
   cout << "total = " << total << endl;
   return 0;
}

total = 70
```

time

Description:

Represents a time between 00:00:00 and 23:59:59, inclusive, to microsecond accuracy. Time arithmetic will wrap around within this range.

Declaration:
```
#include <ospace/time/time.h>
class os_time
```

Typedefs:
```
typedef unsigned short os_hour_t;
typedef unsigned short os_minute_t;
typedef unsigned short os_second_t;
typedef unsigned long  os_usecond_t;
```

Constructor	*os_time()* Construct myself to represent midnight (00:00:00).
Constructor	*os_time(long seconds)* Construct myself to represent the time that is `seconds` past midnight.
Constructor	*os_time(os_hour_t hour, os_minute_t minute, os_second_t second,* *os_usecond_t microsecond)* Construct myself to be the time that is `hour`, `minute`, `second` and `microsecond` since midnight.
Constructor	*os_time(const os_time_period& period)* Construct myself to be a time that is `period` after midnight.
Constructor	*os_time(const tm& value)* Construct myself to be the time encoded by the `tm` structure `value`.
Constructor	*os_time(const os_time& time)* Construct myself to be a copy of `time`.
!=	*bool operator!=(const os_time& time) const* Return `true` if I am not equal to `time`.
+	*os_time operator+(const os_time_period& period) const* Return myself added to `period`.
+=	*os_time& operator+=(const os_time_period& period)* Add `period` to myself and return a reference to myself.
−	*os_time operator−(const os_time_period& period) const* Return `period` subtracted from myself.

–
> *os_time_period operator–(const os_time& time) const*
> Return the period between myself and `time`.

–=
> *os_time& operator–=(const os_time_period& period)*
> Subtract `period` from myself and return a reference to myself.

<
> *bool operator<(const os_time& time) const*
> Return `true` if I am earlier than `time`.

<=
> *bool operator<=(const os_time& time) const*
> Return `true` if I am earlier than or equal to `time`.

=
> *os_time& operator=(const os_time& time)*
> Assign myself from `time`.

==
> *bool operator==(const os_time& time) const*
> Return `true` if I am equal to `time`.

>
> *bool operator>(const os_time& time) const*
> Return `true` if I am later than `time`.

>=
> *bool operator>=(const os_time& time) const*
> Return `true` if I am later than or equal to `time`.

am_name
> */* static */ const string& am_name()*
> Return the string that is used to denote times before noon.

am_name
> */* static */ void am_name(const string& am)*
> Set the string that is used to denote times before noon to `am`. [MT UNSAFE]

default_format
> */* static */ void default_format(const string& format)*
> Set the default format to `format`. [MT UNSAFE]

default_format
> */* static */ string default_format()*
> Return the default format.

hours
> *os_hour_t hours() const*
> Return my hours field (0-23).

is_am
> *bool is_am() const*
> Return `true` if I'm before noon.

is_hour
> */* static */ bool is_hour(os_hour_t hour)*
> Return `true` if `hour` is a valid hour (0-23).

is_microsecond
> */* static */ bool is_microsecond(os_usecond_t microsecond)*
> Return `true` if `microsecond` is a valid microsecond. A microsecond for an `os_time` must be non-negative, unlike one for an `os_time_period`.

is_minute
> */* static */ bool is_minute(os_minute_t minute)*
> Return `true` if `minute` is a valid minute (0-59).

is_pm	*bool is_pm() const* Return `true` if I'm after noon.
is_second	*/* static */ bool is_second(os_second_t second)* Return `true` if `second` is a valid second (0-59).
max_time	*/* static */ const os_time& max_time()* Return the maximum time value.
microseconds	*os_usecond_t microseconds() const* Return my microseconds field (0-999999).
min_time	*/* static */ const os_time& min_time()* Return the minimum time value.
minutes	*os_minute_t minutes() const* Return my minutes field (0-59).
now	*/* static */ os_time now()* Return the current local time.
os_time_period	*operator os_time_period() const* Return me as a time period representing the number of seconds since midnight.
pm_name	*/* static */ void pm_name(const string& pm)* Set the string that is used to denote times after noon to `pm`. [MT UNSAFE]
pm_name	*/* static */ const string& pm_name()* Return the string that is used to denote times after noon.
print	*void print(ostream& stream) const* Print myself to `stream`.
seconds	*os_second_t seconds() const* Return my seconds field (0-59).
time	*void time(const tm& value)* Set the time from the `tm` structure `value`. All fields except the `tm_sec`, `tm_min` and `tm_hour` are cleared and ignored.
time	*void time(os_hour_t hour, os_minute_t minute, os_second_t second, os_usecond_t microsecond)* Set my time to `hour` (0-23), `minute` (0-59), `second` (0-59) and `microsecond` (0-999999).
to_string	*string to_string() const* Return myself as a formatted string using the default format.
to_string	*string to_string(const string& format) const* Return myself as a formatted string using `format`.

Non-Member Functions:

<<   *ostream& operator<<(ostream& stream, const os_time& time)*
                   Print `time` to `stream` using the current format.

<<   *os_bstream& operator<<(os_bstream& stream, const os_time& time)*
                   Write `time` to `stream`.

>>   *os_bstream& operator>>(os_bstream& stream, os_time& time)*
                   Read `time` from `stream`.

time_and_date

Description:

The `os_time_and_date` class represents a point in time in a particular time zone between 00:00 Jan 1, 4713 BC and 23:59 Dec 31, 32766 AD.

Declaration:
```
#include <ospace/time/timedate.h>
class os_time_and_date
```

Typedefs and Enums:

See catalog entries for `os_time` and `os_date`.

Constructor	*os_time_and_date()* Construct myself to be Jan 1, 1970, 00:00:00.
Constructor	*os_time_and_date(const os_time_period& period)* Construct me from `period`, which is the number of seconds since 00:00:00 Jan 1, 1970 GMT
Constructor	*os_time_and_date(const os_time_period& period , const os_date& date)* Construct me from `period`, which is the number of seconds since `date`.
Constructor	*os_time_and_date(const tm& tm_struct)* Construct me from the `tm` structure `tm_struct`, interpreted as a local time.
Constructor	*os_time_and_date(const time_t seconds)* Construct me from the `time_t` value `seconds`, interpreted as a local time.
Constructor	*os_time_and_date(const os_time& time, const os_date& date)* Construct me to have the date `date`, time `time` and the default time zone.
Constructor	*os_time_and_date(const os_time& time, const os_date& date,* *const os_time_zone& tzone)* Construct me to have the date `date`, time `time` and time zone `tzone`.
Constructor	*os_time_and_date(const os_time_and_date& time_and_date)* Construct myself to be a copy of `time_and_date`.
!=	*bool operator!=(const os_time_and_date& time_and_date) const* Return `true` if I am not equal to `time_and_date`.
+	*os_time_and_date operator+(const os_time_period& period) const* Return myself added to `period`.

+= *os_time_and_date& operator+=(const os_time_period& period)*
Add `period` to myself and return a reference to myself.

– *os_time_period operator–(const os_time_and_date& time_and_date) const*
Return the period between myself and `time_and_date`.

– *os_time_and_date operator–(const os_time_period& period) const*
Return `period` subtracted from myself.

–= *os_time_and_date& operator–=(const os_time_period& period)*
Subtract `period` from myself and return a reference to myself.

< *bool operator<(const os_time_and_date& time_and_date) const*
Return `true` if I am earlier than `time_and_date`.

<= *bool operator<=(const os_time_and_date& time_and_date) const*
Return `true` if I am earlier then or equal to `time_and_date`.

= *os_time_and_date& operator=(*
const os_time_and_date& time_and_date)
Assign myself from `time_and_date`.

= *os_time_and_date& operator=(const tm& tm_struct)*
Assign myself from `tm_struct`.

== *bool operator==(const os_time_and_date& time_and_date) const*
Return `true` if I am equal to `time_and_date`.

> *bool operator>(const os_time_and_date& time_and_date) const*
Return `true` if I am later than `time_and_date`.

>= *bool operator>=(const os_time_and_date& time_and_date) const*
Return `true` if I am later than or equal to `time_and_date`.

tm *operator tm() const*
Return myself encoded as a `tm` structure.

date *os_date date() const*
Return my date.

date *void date(const os_date& date)*
Set my date to `date`.

default_format */* static */ string default_format()*
Return my default format. [not MTSAFE]

default_format */* static */ void default_format(const string& format)*
Set my default format to `format`. [not MTSAFE]

default_time_zone */* static */ const os_time_zone& default_time_zone()*
Return a pointer to my default time zone.

is_dst	*bool is_dst( ) const* Return `true` if I am on daylight savings time.
max_date	*/* static */ const os_date& max_date( )* Return the maximum date value.
max_time	*/* static */ const os_time& max_time( )* Return the maximum time value.
min_date	*/* static */ const os_date& min_date( )* Return the minimum date value.
min_time	*/* static */ const os_time& min_time( )* Return the minimum time value.
now	*/* static */ os_time_and_date now( )* Return the current local time and date.
print	*void print(ostream& stream) const* Print myself to `stream`.
std_date	*os_date std_date( ) const* Return my standard date.
std_time	*os_time std_time( ) const* Return my standard time.
time	*void time(const os_time& time)* Set my time to `time`.
time	*os_time time( ) const* Return my wall time.
time_and_date	*void time_and_date(const time_t seconds)* Set myself to me the date that is `seconds` seconds after 00:00:00 Jan 1, 1970 GMT
time_and_date	*void time_and_date(const os_time_period& period,* *const os_date& date)* Set my time and date to be a time period `period` after `date`.
time_and_date	*void time_and_date(const os_time& time, const os_date& date)* Set my date to `date` and my time to `time`.
time_and_date	*void time_and_date(const os_time_period& period)* Set my time and date from the a time that is (00:00:00.0, Jan 1, 1970 BC + `period`).
time_and_date	*void time_and_date(const tm& tm_struct)* Set my time and date from the `tm` structure `tm_struct`.

time_and_date	*void time_and_date(const os_time& time, const os_date& date, const os_time_zone& tzone)* Set my date to `date`, my time to `time` and my time zone to `tzone`.
time_zone	*void time_zone(const os_time_zone& tzone)* Set my time zone to `tzone`.
time_zone	*const os_time_zone& time_zone() const* Return a pointer to my time zone.
utc_date	*os_date utc_date() const* Return my utc date.
utc_time	*os_time utc_time() const* Return my utc time.
utc_time_and_date	*void utc_time_and_date(const os_time& time, const os_date& date)* Set my date to `date` and my time to `time`.

Non-Member Functions:

+	*os_time_and_date operator+ (const os_time_period& period, const os_time_and_date& time_and_date)* Return `time_and_date` added to `period`.
+	*os_time_and_date operator+ (const os_time_period& period, const os_time_and_date& time_and_date);* Return `period` added to `time_and_date`.
<<	*ostream& operator<<(ostream& stream, const os_time_and_date& time_and_date)* Print `time_and_date` to `stream` using the current format.
<<	*os_bstream& operator<<(os_bstream& stream, const os_time_and_date& time_and_date)* Write `time_and_date` to `stream`.
>>	*os_bstream& operator>>(os_bstream& stream, os_time_and_date& time_and_date)* Read `time_and_date` from `stream`.

time_period

Description:

An `os_time_period` represents a period of time with microsecond accuracy. Arithmetic operations on time periods are supported, as well as conversions to an integral number of days, hours, minutes, or seconds using one of the `to_...()` family of functions.

For backwards compatibility, you can construct a time period from a `timeval` (where available) or `time_t`. Similarly, you can convert a time period into a `timeval` or `time_t` using one of its conversion operators.

Declaration
```
#include <ospace/time/tperiod.h>
class os_time_period
```

Constructor	*os_time_period()* Construct myself to represent a zero second time period.
Constructor	*os_time_period(const timeval& time)* Construct me from the `timeval` structure `time`.
Constructor	*os_time_period(long days, long hours, long minutes, long seconds, long microseconds)* Construct me to be the interval that is the sum of the days, hours, minutes, seconds and microseconds given. For a negative period, all values must be zero or negative.
Constructor	*os_time_period(const os_time_period& time)* Construct myself to be a copy of `time`.
Constructor	*os_time_period(const timestruc_t& time)* Construct me from the `timestruc_t` structure time, converting from nanoseconds to microseconds.
Constructor	*os_time_period(long seconds, long microseconds)* Construct me to have `seconds` seconds and `microseconds` microseconds. Note that there are 1 million microseconds in a second. All values are assumed reduced such that seconds and microseconds are below these rollover points. For example, 2.3 seconds would be 2 seconds, 300000 microseconds. It would not be accepted as 2300000 microseconds. For negative time periods, both values must be zero or negative.
!=	*bool operator!=(const os_time_period& time) const* Return `true` if I'm not the same as `time`.

%	*os_time_period operator%(long value) const* Return myself modulus `value`.
%=	*os_time_period& operator%=(long value)* Become modulus `value` and return a reference to myself.
*=	*os_time_period& operator*=(long value)* Multiply myself by `time` and return a reference to myself.
+	*os_time_period operator+(const os_time_period& time) const* Return myself added to `time`.
+=	*os_time_period& operator+=(const os_time_period& time)* Add `time` to myself and return a reference to myself.
–	*os_time_period operator–(const os_time_period& time) const* Return `time` subtracted from myself.
–	*os_time_period operator–() const* Return myself negated.
–=	*os_time_period& operator–=(const os_time_period& time)* Subtract `time` from myself and return a reference to myself.
/	*os_time_period operator/(long value) const* Return a time period that is `value` times smaller than myself.
/=	*os_time_period& operator/=(long value)* Become `value` times smaller and return a reference to myself.
<	*bool operator<(const os_time_period& time) const* Return `true` if I'm less than `time`.
<=	*bool operator<=(const os_time_period& time) const* Return `true` if I'm less than or equal to `time`.
=	*os_time_period& operator=(long time)* Construct myself to have `time` seconds.
=	*os_time_period& operator=(const timestruc_t& time)* Assign myself to be the time period encoded by `time`.
=	*os_time_period& operator=(const os_time_period& time)* Assign myself from `time`.
=	*os_time_period& operator=(const timeval& time)* Assign myself to be the time period encoded by `time`.
==	*bool operator==(const os_time_period& time) const* Return `true` if I'm the same as `time`.

>	*bool operator>(const os_time_period& time) const* Return `true` if I'm greater than `time`.
>=	*bool operator>=(const os_time_period& time) const* Return `true` if I'm greater than or equal to `time`.
timestruc_t	*operator timestruc_t() const* Return myself encoded as a `time_struc_t` structure.
is_microsecond	*/* static */ bool is_microsecond(long microsecond)* Return `true` if `microsecond` is a valid microsecond. Note that unlike a microsecond for an `os_time`, `microsecond` may be negative.
microseconds	*long microseconds() const* Return my microseconds.
print	*void print(ostream& stream) const* Print myself to `stream`.
time_period	*void time_period(const timestruc_t& time)* Assign myself to be the time period encoded by `time`.
time_period	*void time_period(const timeval& time)* Set myself to the specified time period `time`.
time_period	*void time_period(long seconds, long microseconds)* Set myself to the specified time period. For a negative period, all values must be zero or negative.
time_period	*void time_period(long days, long hours, long minutes, long seconds, long microseconds)* Set myself to the interval that is the sum of the `days`, `hours`, `minutes`, `seconds` and `microseconds` given. For a negative period, all values must be zero or negative.
timeval	*operator timeval() const* Return myself encoded as a `timeval` structure.
to_days	*long to_days() const* Return the number of complete days in my period.
to_hours	*long to_hours() const* Return the number of complete hours in my period.
to_minutes	*long to_minutes() const* Return the number of complete minutes in my period.
to_seconds	*long to_seconds() const* Return my seconds.

time_period

to_string   *string to_string() const*
                          Return a string representation of myself.

Non-Member Functions:

*   *os_time_period operator*(long value, const os_time_period& time)*
                          Return a time period that is `value` times greater than `time`.

<<   *ostream& operator<<(ostream& stream, const os_time_period& period)*
                          Print `period` to `stream`.

<<   *os_bstream& operator<<(os_bstream& stream, const os_time_period& period)*
                          Write `period` to `stream`.

>>   *os_bstream& operator>>(os_bstream& stream, os_time_period& period)*
                          Read `period` from `stream`.

time_zone

Description:
This represents a logical time zone with an optional daylight savings time adjustment.

Declaration
```
#include <ospace/time/timezone.h>
class os_time_zone
```

Constructor	*os_time_zone(const os_time_period& offset)* Construct myself to be a time zone with offset `offset`.
Constructor	*os_time_zone(const os_time_period& offset, const string& name,* *const string& dst_name)* Construct myself to be a time zone with offset `offset`, Standard Time `name` and Daylight Savings Time `dst_name`.
Destructor	*~os_time_zone()* Destroy myself.
aleutian	*/* static */ const os_time_zone& aleutian()* Return the Aleutian (AST/ADT) time zone.
atlantic	*/* static */ const os_time_zone& atlantic()* Return the Atlantic (AST/ADT) time zone.
central	*/* static */ const os_time_zone& central()* Return the Central (CST,CDT) time zone.
central_european	*/* static */ const os_time_zone& central_european()* Return the Central European (CET/CETDST) time zone.
dst_adjustment	*os_time_period dst_adjustment(const os_time& time,* *const os_date& date) const* Return my DST adjustment value for `time` and `date`.
dst_name	*string dst_name() const* Return my Daylight Savings name.
dst_observed	*bool dst_observed() const* Return `true` if I observe daylight savings time.
eastern	*/* static */ const os_time_zone& eastern()* Return the Eastern (EST/EDT) time zone.
greenwich	*/* static */ const os_time_zone& greenwich()* Return the Greenwich (GMT/BST) time zone.

insert   *bool insert(os_time_zone_rule& rule)*
                           Insert a Daylight Savings Time `rule` for this time zone.

is_dst   *bool is_dst(const os_time& time, const os_date& date) const*
                           Return `true` if `time` and `date` has daylight savings time.

mountain   */* static */ const os_time_zone& mountain()*
                           Return the Mountain (MST,MDT) time zone.

name   *string name() const*
                           Return my standard name.

name   *string name(const os_time& time, const os_date& date) const*
                           Return the name of the time zone associated with `time` and `date`.

newfoundland   */* static */ const os_time_zone& newfoundland()*
                           Return the Newfoundland (NST/NDT) time zone.

offset   *os_time_period offset(const os_time& time, const os_date& date) const*
                           Return the offset for `time` and `date`.

offset   *os_time_period offset() const*
                           Return my offset.

pacific   */* static */ const os_time_zone& pacific()*
                           Return the Pacific (PST/PDT) time zone.

portuguese   */* static */ const os_time_zone& portuguese()*
                           Return the Portuguese (PWT/PST) time zone.

print   *void print(ostream& stream) const*
                           Print.

south_africa   */* static */ const os_time_zone& south_africa()*
                           Return the South African (SAS/SADT) time zone.

western_european   */* static */ const os_time_zone& western_european()*
                           Return the Western European (WET/WETDST) time zone.

yukon   */* static */ const os_time_zone& yukon()*
                           Return the Yukon (YST/YDT) time zone.

Non-Member Functions:

<<   *ostream& operator<<(ostream& stream, const os_time_zone&*
                           time_zone)
                           Print `time_zone` to `stream`.

time_zone_rule

Description:

    `os_time_zone_rule` is the abstract base class of all time zone rules.

Declaration
```
#include <ospace/time/rule.h>
class os_time_zone_rule
```

Destructor	*~os_time_zone_rule()* Destructor.
<	*bool operator<(const os_time_zone_rule& rule) const* Returns `true` if this rule is appropriate for a time range before `rule`s time range.
adjustment	*const os_time_period& adjustment() const* Return the DST adjustment value for this rule.
end_point	*void end_point(const os_calendar_date& point)* Set the ending time and date for this rule to `point`.
end_point	*const os_calendar_date& end_point() const* Return the ending time and date for this rule.
end_year	*os_year_t end_year() const* Return the last year this rule is in effect. If 0, the rule is does not expire.
end_year	*void end_year(os_year_t year)* Set the last year this rule is effective to `year`. If `year` is 0, the rule does not expire.
is_open_ended	*bool is_open_ended() const* Return `true` if the rule has no expiration year.
print	*void print(ostream& stream) const* Print myself to `stream`.
start_point	*const os_calendar_date& start_point() const* Return the starting time and date for this rule.
start_point	*void start_point(const os_calendar_date& point)* Set the starting time and date for this rule to `point`.
start_year	*void start_year(os_year_t year)* Set the first year this rule is effective to `year`.

start_year   *os_year_t start_year() const*
                               Return the first year this rule is in effect.

Non-Member Functions:

<<   *ostream& operator<<(ostream& stream,*
                               const os_time_zone_rule& rule)
                               Print `rule` to `stream`.

tokenizer

Description:

This class provides functions to break a string into tokens. A token is a portion of a string identified by its relationship to separators. Once constructed, a tokenizer is a factory for tokens, taking an input string and returning a vector of tokens.

`os_tokenizer` is conceptually similar to the C `strtok()` function.

Declaration:
```
#include <ospace/string/tokenize.h>
class os_tokenizer
```

Constructor	*os_tokenizer()* Construct with defaults. See the full blown constructor for default values.
Constructor	*os_tokenizer(const string& separators, bool allow_empty_tokens,* *const string& ignore, const string& terminators, const string& terminals,* *bool include_separators)* Construct myself to tokenize strings using the separators `separators` (default " "), ignoring all characters in `ignore` (default ""), terminating at a nul or any character in `terminators` (default "\n") and treating all characters in `terminals` (default "") as individual tokens. If `allow_empty_tokens` (default `false`) is `true`, then two consecutive separators are treated as an empty token sandwich. If `include_separators` (default `false`) is `true`, include separators in the tokens.
Constructor	*os_tokenizer(const os_tokenizer& tokenizer)* Construct myself to be a copy of `tokenizer`.
=	*os_tokenizer& operator=(const os_tokenizer& tokenizer)* Assign myself from `tokenizer`.
allow_empty_tokens	*void allow_empty_tokens(bool flag)* If `flag` is `true` (default), then consider empty tokens valid.
allow_empty_tokens	*bool allow_empty_tokens() const* Return `true` if I allow empty tokens.
ignore	*const string& ignore() const* Return my ignore characters.
ignore	*void ignore(const string& str)* Set my ignore characters to `str`.

include_separators	*bool include_separators() const* Return `true` if I include my separators.
include_separators	*void include_separators(bool flag)* If `flag` (default `true`) is `true`, include separators in the tokens.
print	*void print(ostream& stream) const* Print myself to `stream`.
separators	*const string& separators() const* Return my separators.
separators	*void separators(const string& str)* Set my separator characters to `str`.
terminals	*const string& terminals() const* Return my terminal characters.
terminals	*void terminals(const string& str)* Set my terminal characters to `str`.
terminators	*const string& terminators() const* Return my terminator characters.
terminators	*void terminators(const string& str)* Set my terminator characters to `str`.
tokenize	*vector< string > tokenize(const string& str)* Return the vector of the tokens found by parsing `str` with my current settings.

Non-Member Functions:

<<	*ostream& operator<<(ostream& stream,* *const os_tokenizer& tokenizer)* Print `tokenizer` to `stream`.
<<	*os_bstream& operator<<(os_bstream& stream, const os_tokenizer& tokenizer)* Write `tokenizer` to `stream`.
>>	*os_bstream& operator>>(os_bstream& stream,* *os_tokenizer& tokenizer)* Read `tokenizer` from `stream`.

tstream

Description:
A text stream is an instance of `os_tstream`. `os_tstream` is derived from the standard `iostream` class and thus inherits all of its behaviors. When an `os_tstream` is constructed, it is associated with a particular I/O device via an intermediate adapter object called an `os_adapter`. When an item is streamed to an `os_tstream`, it is converted into a text format and then sent to the I/O device via the adapter. This technique allows the text streaming mechanism to be fully decoupled from details of any particular I/O device.

Declaration:
```
#include <ospace/stream/tstream.h>
class os_tstream : public iostream
```

Constructor	*os_tstream( )* Construct myself to use my internal `streambuf`.
Constructor	*os_tstream(const os_adapter& adapter)* Stream items to the device associated with `adapter`.
clear_event	*void clear_event( )* Clear my last event.
close	*void close()* Close the device I am attached to.
last_event	*const os_event* last_event() const* Return a pointer to my last event.

udp_socket

Description:

An `os_udp_socket` allows unreliable connectionless communication. A datagram is a single packet of information that is sent from one socket to another. The sender must know the address of the destination socket. Since datagram communication is unreliable, there is no guarantee that the receiver will actually get the datagram.

Although datagram communication is connectionless, a UDP socket may be "connected" to a destination address. If you call `connect_to()` in a UDP socket, all datagrams that are subsequently sent using `send()` are automatically routed to the "connected" address. Every use of `connect_to()` overrides the previous connection address.

Conversions allow `os_udp_socket` and `os_desc_t` (UNIX descriptor) to be used interchangeably.

Declaration:

```
#include <ospace/socket/udpsock.h>
class os_udp_socket : public os_connectable_socket
```

Constructor	*os_udp_socket(os_desc_t descriptor)* Construct myself to reference the socket with descriptor `descriptor`.
Constructor	*os_udp_socket()* Construct myself to have a unique IP socket address. Events: `syscall` On Resumption: I will be in an unknown state.
Constructor	*os_udp_socket(const os_socket_address& address, os_desc_t control)* Construct myself to be a new datagram socket bound to the IP socket address `address` with I/O control of `control` (default 0). Events: `syscall` On Resumption: I will be in an unknown state.
broadcast	*void broadcast(bool flag)* Set broadcast enabling to `flag`. Events: `syscall` On Resumption: Broadcast state will be unknown.
broadcast	*bool broadcast() const* Return `true` if broadcasting is enabled. Events: `syscall` On Resumption: Return value may be invalid.

send_to
                  int send_to(const os_socket_address& address, const char* buffer,
long bytes)
Send `bytes` bytes from `buffer` to the socket with IP socket address
`address`. Return the number of bytes that were successfully written, or
`-1` on error. [MT UNSAFE on Solaris.]

    Events: `syscall`
    On Resumption: Returns `-1`.

unary_compose, compos1

Description:

unary_compose is a unary function object that returns the result of executing its two operations in a specific sequence. Its associated adapter function compose1() allows you to conveniently construct a unary_compose object directly from two functions.

Declaration:

```
#include <function.h>
template< class Operation1, class Operation2 >
class unary_compose : public unary_function
  < Operation2::argument_type, Operation1::result_type >
```

Adapter:

```
template< class Operation1, class Operation2 >
binary_compose< Operation1, Operation2 >
compose1( const Operation1& op1, const Operation2& op2 )
```

Constructor	*unary_compose(const Operation1& op1, const Operation2& op2)* Construct myself with associated operators op1 and op2.
()	*Operation1::result_type operator()* *(const Operation2::argument_type& x) const* Return op1(op2(x)).

Example <ospace/stl/examples/ucompos1.cpp>

```cpp
#include <iostream.h>
#include <math.h>
#include <stl.h>

struct square_root : public unary_function<double, double>
{
  square_root () {}
  double operator () (double x_) const { return sqrt (x_); }
};

int input [3] = { -1, -4, -16 };

int main ()
{
  int output [3];
  transform (input, input + 3, output,
    unary_compose<square_root, negate<int> > (square_root (),
    negate<int> ()));
  for (int i = 0; i < 3; i++)
    cout << output[i] << endl;
  return 0;
}

1
2
4
```

Example <ospace/stl/examples/ucompos2.cpp>

```
#include <iostream.h>
#include <math.h>
#include <stl.h>

struct square_root : public unary_function<double, double>
{
  square_root () {}
  double operator () (double x_) const { return sqrt (x_); }
};

int input [3] = { -1, -4, -16 };

int main ()
{
  int output [3];
  transform (input, input + 3, output,
    compose1 (square_root (), negate<int> ()));
  for (int i = 0; i < 3; i++)
   cout << output[i] << endl;
  return 0;
}


1
2
4
```

unary_function

Description:

unary_function is the abstract base structure of all unary function objects. It defines two useful typedefs that are used by most of its derived classes.

Declaration:
```
#include <function.h>
template< class Arg, class Result >
struct unary_function
   {
   typedef Arg argument_type;
   typedef Result result_type;
   };
```

unary_negate, not1

Description:

unary_negate is a unary function object that returns the logical negation of executing its unary predicate. Its associated adapter function not1() allows you to conveniently construct a unary_negate object directly from a predicate.

Declaration:
```
#include <function.h>
template< class Predicate >
class unary_negate : public unary_function
  < Predicate::argument_type, bool >
```

Adapter:
```
template< class Predicate >
unary_negate< Predicate > not1( const Predicate& pred );
```

Constructor   *unary_negate(const Predicate& pred)*
                         Construct myself with predicate pred.

()   *bool operator()(const argument_type& x) const*
                         Return the result of pred(x)

Example <ospace/stl/examples/unegate1.cpp>

```
#include <iostream.h>
#include <stl.h>

struct odd : public unary_function<int, bool>
{
  odd () {}
  bool operator () (int n_) const { return (n_ % 2) == 1; }
};

int array [3] = { 1, 2, 3 };

int main ()
{
  int* p = find_if (array, array + 3, unary_negate<odd> (odd ()));
  if (p != array + 3)
    cout << *p << endl;
  return 0;
}
```

2 is not odd

Example <ospace/stl/examples/unegate2.cpp>

```
#include <iostream.h>
#include <stl.h>

struct odd : public unary_function<int, bool>
{
  odd (_) {}
  bool operator () (int n_) const { return (n_ % 2) == 1; }
};

int array [3] = { 1, 2, 3 };

int main ()
{
  int* p = find_if (array, array + 3, not1 (odd ()));
  if (p != array + 3)
    cout << *p << endl;
  return 0;
}
```

2 is not odd

unnamed_pipe

Description:

An unnamed pipe allows two related processes to communicate; typically a parent and its child. One process sends output to the write end of the pipe, whereas the other process receives input from the read end of the pipe. A pipe automatically buffers its input up to a maximum of 4K (BSD) or 40K (System V).

An `os_unnamed_pipe` is often used in conjunction with the `os_process` constructors to fork a child using pipes for communication.

Declaration:
```
#include <ospace/pipe/upipe.h>
class os_unnamed_pipe
```

Options:

Legal I/O control:	`O_NONBLOCK, O_CLOSE_ON_EXEC, O_ASYNC`
Default I/O control:	0 (blocking)

Constructor   *os_unnamed_pipe(os_ioctl_t control)*
Construct myself to reference a new unnamed pipe with I/O control setting `control` (default 0, which means "blocking").

> Events: `syscall`
> On Resumption: I will be in an unknown state.

Destructor   *~os_unnamed_pipe()*
Destroy myself, closing my descriptor if necessary.

<   *bool operator<(const os_unnamed_pipe& pipe) const*
Return `true` if I'm considered to be less than `pipe`.

==   *bool operator==(const os_unnamed_pipe& pipe) const*
Return `true` if my read and write ends are the same as `pipe`'s.

auto_close   *bool auto_close() const*
Return `true` if I close my pipe ends on destruction.

auto_close   *void auto_close(bool flag)*
If `flag` is `true`, close my pipe ends on destruction.

clear   *void clear()*
Set my state to good.

close	*void close()*
	Close both of my ends.
	
	    Events: `syscall`
	    On Resumption: Any remaining pipe end will attempt to be closed.

eof	*bool eof() const* Return `true` if I'm at the end of my input.
event_on_eof	*void event_on_eof(bool flag)* If flag is `true`, I will generate an event on eof.
event_on_eof	*bool event_on_eof() const* Return `true` if I will generate an event on eof.
good	*bool good() const* Return `true` if I'm in a good state and not at eof.
is_open	*bool is_open() const* Return `true` if either of my ends is open.
ok	*bool ok() const* Return `true` if I'm not failed.

read	*int read(void* buffer, int bytes)*
	Read up to `bytes` bytes into `buffer`. Return the number of bytes actually read, or `-1` on error.
	
	    Events: `syscall`
	    On Resumption: Returns `-1`.

read_end	*os_desc_t read_end()* Return a reference to my read end.

write	*int write(const void* buffer, int bytes)*
	Write `bytes` bytes from `buffer`. Return the number of bytes actually written, or `-1` on error.
	
	    Events: `syscall`
	    On Resumption: Returns `-1`.

write_end	*os_desc_t write_end()* Return a reference to my write end.

Non-Member Functions:

<<	*ostream& operator<<(ostream& stream, const os_unnamed_pipe& pipe)* Print `pipe` to `stream`.

user

Description:
An os_user represents a user. Most entities such as processes, files and IPC mechanisms are owned by a user. An os_user object may be constructed from either a numeric user id or from a symbolic user name. Once constructed, an os_user allows easy access to information about a user, such as their name, home directory and associated groups. In addition, a super-user can access and modify the priority of all the processes owned by a particular user.

Conversions allow os_user and os_uid_t to be used interchangeably.

Declaration:
```
#include <ospace/security/user.h>
class os_user
```

Constructor	*os_user(os_uid_t user)* Construct myself with user id user (default OS_UNDEFINED). Events: other On Resumption: Set my user id to OS_UNDEFINED.
Constructor	*os_user(const struct passwd& pwd)* Construct myself from pwd.
Constructor	*os_user(const os_user& user)* Construct myself to be a copy of user.
Constructor	*os_user(const string& name)* Construct myself to represent the user with name name. Events: other On Resumption: Set my user id to OS_UNDEFINED.
<	*bool operator<(const os_user& user) const* Return true if my user id is less than user's.
=	*os_user& operator=(const os_user& user)* Assign myself from user.
=	*os_user& operator=(os_uid_t user)* Assign myself from user.
==	*bool operator==(const os_user& user) const* Return true if my user id is the same as user's.
comment	*string comment() const* Return my associated comment. If this information cannot be obtained from the user database, return an empty string.

defined	*bool defined() const* Return `true` if my user id is not `OS_UNDEFINED`.
gid	*os_gid_t gid() const* Return the id of my primary group. If this information cannot be obtained from the user database, return `OS_UNDEFINED`.
groups	*vector< os_gid_t > groups() const* Return a vector of all my group's ids.
home_directory	*string home_directory() const* Return my home directory path. If this information cannot be obtained from the user database, return an empty string.
name	*string name() const* Return my name. If this information cannot be obtained from the user database, return an empty string.
os_uid_t	*operator os_uid_t() const* Return my user id.
password	*string password() const* Return my password. If this information cannot be obtained from the user database, return an empty string.
print	*void print(ostream& stream) const* Print my name and user id to `stream`.
shell	*string shell() const* Return the name of my shell. If this information cannot be obtained from the user database, return an empty string.
super_user	*bool super_user() const* Return `true` if I'm a superuser.
uid	*void uid(os_uid_t user)* Set my user id to `user`.
uid	*os_uid_t uid() const* Return my user id.
users	*/* static */ vector< os_uid_t > users()* Return a vector of all user ids.

Non-Member Functions:

<<   *ostream& operator<<(ostream& stream, const os_user& user)*
                      Print user to stream.

<<   *os_bstream& operator<<(os_bstream& stream, const os_user& user)*
                      Write user to stream.

>>   *os_bstream& operator>>(os_bstream& stream, os_user& user)*
                      Read user from stream.

vector

Description:
A `vector` is a sequential container that is very similar to a regular C array except that it can expand to accommodate new elements.

Declaration:
```
#include <vector.h>
template< class T >
class vector
```

Constructor	*vector()* Construct myself to be empty.
Constructor	*vector(alloc_type& alloc)* Construct myself to be empty. Use `alloc` to allocate storage.
Constructor	*vector(size_type n)* Construct me to contain n elements set to their default value.
Constructor	*vector(alloc_type& alloc, size_type n)* Construct me to contain n elements set to their default value. Use `alloc` to allocate storage.
Constructor	*vector(size_type n, const T& value)* Construct me to contain n copies of `value`.
Constructor	*vector(alloc_type& alloc, size_type n, const T& value)* Construct me to contain n copies of `value`. Use `alloc` to allocate storage.
Constructor	*vector(const T* first, const T* last)* Construct me to contain copies of all of the elements in the range `[first, last)`.
Constructor	*vector(alloc_type& alloc, const T* first, const T* last)* Construct me to contain copies of all of the elements in the range `[first, last)`. Use `alloc` to allocate storage.
Constructor	*vector(const vector< T >& x)* Construct myself to be a copy of x.
Constructor	*vector(alloc_type& alloc, const vector< T >& x)* Construct myself to be a copy of x. Use `alloc` to allocate storage.
Destructor	*~vector()* Destroy myself, erasing all of my items.

=	*vector<T>& operator=(const vector< T >& x)* Replace my contents by a copy of x's.
==	*bool operator==(const vector< T >& x) const* Return `true` if I contain the same items in the same order as x.
<	*bool operator<(const vector< T >& x) const* Return `true` if I'm lexigraphically less than x.
[]	*T& operator [ ](int index)* Return a reference to my `index`th element. 　　　Events: `other (os_illegal_index)`
[]	*const T& operator [ ](int index) const* Return a reference to my `index`th element. 　　　Events: `other (os_illegal_index)`
back	*T& back( )* Return a reference to my last element. 　　　Events: `other (os_empty_error)`
back	*const T& back( ) const* Return a reference to my last element. 　　　Events: `other (os_empty_error)`
begin	*iterator begin( )* Return an iterator positioned at my first item.
begin	*const_iterator begin( ) const* Return an iterator positioned at my first item.
capacity	*size_type capacity( ) const* Return the number of elements that I can contain without allocating more memory.
empty	*bool empty( ) const* Return `true` if I contain no entries.
end	*iterator end( )* Return an iterator positioned immediately after my last item.
end	*const_iterator end( ) const* Return an iterator positioned immediately after my last item.
erase[12]	*void erase( )* Erase all of my elements.

---

[12] Non-standard, unique to Systems<ToolKit>

erase	*void erase(iterator pos)* Erase the element at `pos`.
erase	*void erase(iterator first, iterator last)* Erase the elements in range `[first, last)`.
front	*T& front()* Return a reference to my first element. Events: `other (os_empty_error)`
front	*const T& front() const* Return a reference to my first element. Events: `other (os_empty_error)`
insert	*iterator insert(iterator pos, const T& value)* Insert `value` at `pos` and return an iterator pointing to the new element's position.
insert	*void insert(iterator pos, size_type n, const T& value)* Insert `n` copies of `value` at `pos`.
insert	*void insert(iterator pos, const T* first, const T* last)* Insert copies of the elements in the range `[first, last)` at `pos`.
max_size	*size_type max_size() const* Return the maximum number of entries that I can contain.
push_back	*void push_back(const T& value)* Add `value` at my end.
pop_back	*void pop_back()* Erase my last element. Events: `other (os_empty_error)`
rbegin	*reverse_iterator rbegin()* Return a reverse iterator positioned at my last item.
rbegin	*const_reverse_iterator rbegin() const* Return a reverse iterator positioned at my last item.
rend	*reverse_iterator rend()* Return a reverse_iterator positioned immediately before my first item.
rend	*const_reverse_iterator rend() const* Return a reverse_iterator positioned immediately before my first item.
reserve	*void reserve(size_type n)* Pre-allocate enough space to hold up to `n` elements. This operation does not change the value returned by size().

vector

size　　　　　　*size_type size() const*
　　　　　　　　　Return the number of entries that I contain.

swap　　　　　　*void swap(vector< T >& x)*
　　　　　　　　　Swap my contents with x's.

Algorithm Catalog

This section contains a concise description of every STL algorithm, including the ObjectSpace helper algorithms that are denoted using an `os_` prefix.

Every entry contains the following information:

- *A Synopsis.* A short description of the algorithm.

- *A Signature.* This shows the various forms of the function signature.

- *A Description.* A longer specification of what the algorithm does.

- *Complexity.* Information about the time and space complexity of the algorithm.

- *Examples.* Examples of using the algorithm with other classes.

Optionally, there may be another section labeled *Helper* which lists the helper algorithms supplied by ObjectSpace that make the STL algorithm easier to use.

accumulate

Synopsis:

Sum the values in a range.

Declaration:
```
template< class InputIterator, class T >
T accumulate( InputIterator first, InputIterator last, T init )

template< InputIterator, T, BinaryOperation >
T accumulate
  (
  InputIterator first,
  InputIterator last,
  T init,
  BinaryOperation binary_op
  )
```

Description:

Add the value of each element in the range [first, last) to init and return the new value of init. Note that init is not automatically initialized prior to this operation. The first version uses operator+ to perform the addition, whereas the second version uses the binary function binary_op.

Complexity:

Time Complexity: is linear. Space Complexity: is constant.

Example <ospace/stl/examples/accum1.cpp>

```
#include <stl.h>
#include <iostream.h>

int main ()
{
  vector <int> v (5);
  for (int i = 0; i < v.size (); i++)
    v[i] = i + 1;

  int sum = accumulate (v.begin (), v.end (), 0);

  cout << "Sum = " << sum << endl;
  return 0;
}
```

```
Sum = 15
```

Example <ospace/stl/examples/accum2.cpp>

```
#include <stl.h>
#include <iostream.h>

int mult (int initial, int element)
{
  return initial * element;
}

int main ()
{
  vector <int> v (5);
  for (int i = 0; i < v.size (); i++)
    v[i] = i + 1;

  int prod = accumulate (v.begin (), v.end (), 1, mult);

  cout << "Prod = " << prod << endl;
  return 0;
}
```

```
Prod = 120
```

adjacent_difference

Synopsis:

Calculate and sum the difference between adjacent pairs of values.

Declaration:

```
template< class InputIterator, class OutputIterator >
OutputIterator adjacent_difference
    (
    InputIterator first,
    InputIterator last,
    OutputIterator result
    )

template
    <
    class InputIterator,
    class OutputIterator,
    class BinaryOperation
    >
OutputIterator adjacent_difference
    (
    InputIterator first,
    InputIterator last,
    OutputIterator result,
    BinaryOperator binary_op
    )
```

Description:

Iterate through every element in the range `[first+1..last)` and write the difference between the element and its preceding element to `result`. Return an iterator equal to `result` + n where n = `last - first`. Assignment back into the original range is allowed. The first version of this algorithm uses `operator-` to calculate the difference, whereas the second version of this algorithm uses the binary function `binary_op`.

Complexity:

Time Complexity: is linear as operator- or binary_op are applied (`last - first - 1`) times. Space Complexity: is constant.

Example <ospace/stl/examples/adjdiff0.cpp>

```
#include <stl.h>
#include <iostream.h>

int numbers[5] = { 1, 2, 4, 8, 16 };

int main ()
{
  int difference[5];
  adjacent_difference (numbers, numbers + 5, difference);

  for (int i = 0; i < 5; i++)
    cout << numbers[i] << ' ';
  cout << endl;
  for (i = 0; i < 5; i++)
    cout << difference[i] << ' ';
  cout << endl;

  return 0;
}
```

```
1 2 3 8 16
1 1 2 4 8
```

Example <ospace/stl/examples/adjdiff1.cpp>

```
#include <stl.h>
#include <iostream.h>

int main ()
{
  vector <int> v (10);
  for (int i = 0; i < v.size (); i++)
    v[i] = i * i;
  vector <int> result (v.size ());

  adjacent_difference (v.begin (), v.end (), result.begin ());

  ostream_iterator<int> iter (cout, " ");
  copy (v.begin (), v.end (), iter);
  cout << endl;
  copy (result.begin (), result.end (), iter);
  cout << endl;
  return 0;
}
```

```
0 1 4 9 16 25 36 49 64 81
0 1 3 5 7 9 11 13 15 17
```

Example <ospace/stl/examples/adjdiff2.cpp>

```cpp
#include <stl.h>
#include <iostream.h>

int mult (int a, int b)
{
  return a * b;
}

int main ()
{
  vector <int> v (10);
  for (int i = 0; i < v.size (); i++)
    v[i] = i + 1;
  vector <int> result (v.size ());

  adjacent_difference (v.begin (), v.end (), result.begin (), mult);

  ostream_iterator<int> iter (cout, " ");
  copy (v.begin (), v.end (), iter);
  cout << endl;
  copy (result.begin (), result.end (), iter);
  cout << endl;

  return 0;
}

1 2 3 4 5 6 7 8 9 10
1 2 6 12 20 30 42 56 72 90
```

adjacent_find

Synopsis:

Locate a consecutive sequence in a range.

Declaration:
```
template< class InputIterator >
InputIterator adjacent_find
  (
  InputIterator first,
  InputIterator last
  )

template< class InputIterator, class BinaryPredicate >
InputIterator adjacent_find
  (
  InputIterator first,
  InputIterator last,
  BinaryPredicate binary_pred
  )
```

Description:

Return an input iterator positioned at the first pair of matching consecutive elements. If no match is found, return `last`. The first version performs matching using `operator==`, whereas the second version uses the binary function `binary_pred`.

Complexity:

Time Complexity: is linear, as a maximum of (`last` - `first`) comparisons are performed.
Space Complexity: is constant.

Example <ospace/stl/examples/adjfind0.cpp>

```
#include <stl.h>
#include <iostream.h>

int numbers1 [5] = { 1, 2, 4, 8, 16 };
int numbers2 [5] = { 5, 3, 2, 1, 1 };

int main ()
{
  int* location = adjacent_find (numbers1, numbers1 + 5);

  if (location != numbers1 + 5)
    cout
      << "Found adjacent pair of: "
      << *location
      << " at offset "
      << location - numbers1
      << endl;
  else
    cout << "No adjacent pairs" << endl;

  location = adjacent_find (numbers2, numbers2 + 5);

  if (location != numbers2 + 5)
    cout
      << "Found adjacent pair of: "
      << *location
      << " at offset "
      << location - numbers2
      << endl;
  else
    cout << "No adjacent pairs" << endl;

  return 0;
}
```

No adjacent pairs
Found adjacent pair of: 1 at offset 3

Example <ospace/stl/examples/adjfind1.cpp>

```cpp
#include <stl.h>
#include <iostream.h>

int main ()
{
  typedef vector<int> IntVector;

  IntVector v (10);
  for (int i = 0; i < v.size (); i++)
    v[i] = i;
  IntVector::iterator location;

  location = adjacent_find (v.begin (), v.end ());

  if (location != v.end ())
    cout << "Found adjacent pair of: " << *location << endl;
  else
    cout << "No adjacent pairs" << endl;
  v[6] = 7;

  location = adjacent_find (v.begin (), v.end ());

  if (location != v.end ())
    cout << "Found adjacent pair of: " << *location << endl;
  else
    cout << "No adjacent pairs" << endl;

  return 0;
}
```

No adjacent pairs
Found adjacent pair of: 7

adjacent_find

Example <ospace/stl/examples/adjfind2.cpp>

```
#include <stl.h>
#include <iostream.h>
#include <string.h>

typedef vector <char*> CStrVector;

int equal_length (const char* v1, const char* v2)
{
  return ::strlen (v1) == ::strlen(v2);
}

char* names[] = { "Brett", "Graham", "Jack", "Mike", "Todd" };

int main ()
{
  const int nameCount = sizeof (names)/sizeof(names[0]);
  CStrVector v (nameCount);
  for (int i = 0; i < nameCount; i++)
    v[i] = names[i];
  CStrVector::iterator location;

  location = adjacent_find (v.begin (), v.end (), equal_length);

  if (location != v.end ())
    cout
      << "Found two adjacent strings of equal length: "
      << *location
      << " -and- "
      << *(location + 1)
      << endl;
  else
    cout << "Didn't find two adjacent strings of equal length.";

  return 0;
}
```

Found two adjacent strings of equal length: Jack -and- Mike

advance

Synopsis:
Change the current position of an iterator.

Declaration:
```
template< class InputIterator, class Distance >
void advance
  (
  InputIterator& i,
  Distance n
  )
```

Description:
Increment the iterator reference i by n. n may be negative (meaning decrement instead of increment) for random access and bidirectional iterators only.

Complexity:
Time Complexity: is constant for random access iterators and linear for all other iterators.
Space Complexity: is constant.

Example <ospace/stl/examples/advance.cpp>

```
#include <stl.h>
#include <iostream.h>

int
main()
  {
  typedef list< int > IntList;

  IntList v;
  for (int i = 0; i < 10; i++)
    v.push_back( 100 + i );

  IntList::iterator location = v.begin();
  cout << "first: " << *location << endl;

  advance( location, 8 );
  cout << "first + 8: " << *location << endl;

  advance( location, -3 );
  cout << "first + 5: " << *location << endl;

  return 0;
  }
```

```
first: 100
first + 8: 108
first + 5: 105
```

binary_search

Synopsis:
Locate an item in a sorted sequence.

Declaration:
```
template< class ForwardIterator, class T >
bool binary_search
  (
  ForwardIterator first,
  ForwardIterator last,
  const T& value
  )

template< class ForwardIterator, class T, class Compare >
bool binary_search
  (
  ForwardIterator first,
  ForwardIterator last,
  const T& value,
  Compare compare
  )
```

Description:
Return `true` if `value` is in the range `[first..last)`. The first version assumes that the elements in `[first..last)` are already sorted using operator<, whereas the second version assumes that the elements are already sorted using the comparison function `compare`.

Complexity:
Time Complexity: is O(log(N)) for random access iterators and O(N) for all other iterators.
Space Complexity: is constant.

Helper:
```
bool os_binary_search( const Container& c, const T& value )
```

Example <ospace/stl/examples/binsrch1.cpp>

```
#include <stl.h>
#include <iostream.h>

int main ()
{
  int vector[100];
  for (int i = 0; i < 100; i++)
    vector[i] = i;

  if (binary_search (vector, vector + 100, 42))
    cout << "found 42" << endl;
  else
    cout << "did not find 42" << endl;
  return 0;
}
```

found 42

Example <ospace/stl/examples/binsrch2.cpp>

```
#include <stl.h>
#include <iostream.h>
#include <string.h>

bool str_compare (const char* a, const char* b)
{
  return ::strcmp (a, b) < 0 ? 1 : 0;
}

char* labels[] = { "aa", "dd", "ff", "jj", "ss", "zz" };

int main ()
{
  const unsigned count = sizeof (labels) / sizeof (labels[0]);

  if (binary_search (labels, labels + count, "ff", str_compare))
    cout << "ff is in labels." << endl;
  else
    cout << "ff is not in labels." << endl;

  return 0;
}
```

ff is in labels

copy

Synopsis:

Copy a range of items to another area.

Declaration:

```
template< class InputIterator, class OutputIterator >
OutputIterator copy
   (
   InputIterator first,
   InputIterator last,
   OutputIterator result
   )
```

Description:

Copy the elements from the range [first, last) into a range of the same size starting at result, using operator= to replace the existing elements. Return an iterator of the same type as result positioned immediately after the last new element.

Complexity:

Time Complexity: is linear, as (last - first) assignments are performed. Space Complexity: is constant.

Example <ospace/stl/examples/copy1.cpp>

```
#include <stl.h>
#include <iostream.h>
#include <string.h>

char string[23] = "A string to be copied.";

int main ()
{
   char result[23];

   copy (string, string + 23, result);

   cout << " Src: " << string << "\nDest: " << result << endl;
   return 0;
}

  Src: A string to be copied.
 Dest: A string to be copied.
```

Example <ospace/stl/examples/copy2.cpp>

```
#include <stl.h>
#include <iostream.h>

int main ()
{
  vector <int> v (10);
  for (int i = 0; i < v.size (); i++)
    v[i] = i;
  ostream_iterator<int> iter (cout, " ");

  copy (v.begin (), v.end (), iter);

  return 0;
}
```

0 1 2 3 4 5 6 7 8 9

Example <ospace/stl/examples/copy3.cpp>

```
#include <stl.h>
#include <iostream.h>

int main ()
{
  vector <int> v1 (10);
  for (int i = 0; i < v1.size (); i++)
    v1[i] = i;
  vector <int> v2 (10);

  copy (v1.begin (), v1.end (), v2.begin ());

  ostream_iterator<int> iter (cout, " ");
  copy (v2.begin (), v2.end (), iter);

  return 0;
}
```

0 1 2 3 4 5 6 7 8 9

Example <ospace/stl/examples/copy4.cpp>

```
#include <stl.h>
#include <iostream.h>

int main ()
{
  typedef vector <int> IVec;

  vector <int> v1 (10);
  for (int loc = 0; loc < v1.size (); loc++)
    v1[loc] = loc;
  vector <int> v2;

  // When templates are better supported, below will read:
  //   insert_iterator <IVec> iter (v2, v2.begin ());
  insert_iterator<IVec, int, IVec::iterator> i(v2, v2.begin ());

  copy (v1.begin (), v1.end (), i);

  ostream_iterator<int> outIter (cout, " ");
  copy (v2.begin (), v2.end (), outIter);

  return 0;
}

0 1 2 3 4 5 6 7 8 9
```

copy_backward

Synopsis:

Copy a range of items backwards to another area.

Declaration:

```
template< class BidirectionalIterator1, class BidirectionalIterator2 >
BidirectionalIterator2 copy_backward
  (
  BidirectionalIterator1 first,
  BidirectionalIterator1 last,
  BidirectionalIterator2 result
  )
```

Description:

Copy the elements from the range [first..last) into a range of the same size ending immediately before result, using operator= to replace the existing elements. Return an iterator of the same type as result, positioned at the start of the newly created sequence. The elements in result will be in the same order as the elements in [first, last).

Complexity:

Time Complexity: is linear, as (last - first) assignments are performed. Space Complexity: is constant.

Example <ospace/stl/examples/copyb0.cpp>

```
#include <stl.h>
#include <iostream.h>

int numbers[5] = { 1, 2, 3, 4, 5 };

int main ()
{
  int result[5];

  copy_backward (numbers, numbers + 5, result + 5);

  for (int i = 0; i < 5; i++)
    cout << numbers[i] << ' ';
  cout << endl;
  for (i = 0; i < 5; i++)
    cout << result[i] << ' ';
  cout << endl;

  return 0;
}
```

```
1 2 3 4 5
1 2 3 4 5
```

Example <ospace/stl/examples/copyb1.cpp>

```
#include <stl.h>
#include <iostream.h>

int main ()
{
  vector <int> v1 (10);
  for (int i = 0; i < v1.size (); i++)
    v1[i] = i;
  vector <int> v2(v1.size ());

  copy_backward (v1.begin (), v1.end (), v2.end ());

  ostream_iterator<int> iter (cout, " ");
  copy (v2.begin (), v2.end (), iter);

  return 0;
}
```

```
0 1 2 3 4 5 6 7 8 9
```

count

Synopsis:

Count items in a range that match a value.

Declaration:

```
template< class InputIterator, class T, class Size >
void count
   (
   InputIterator first,
   InputIterator last,
   const T& value,
   Size& n
   )
```

Description:

Count the number of elements in the range `[first, last)` that match `value` using `operator==` and add this count to `n`. Note that n is not automatically initialized to zero prior to the counting procedure.

Complexity:

Time Complexity: is linear, as `(last - first)` comparisons are performed. Space Complexity: is constant.

Helper:

```
int os_count( const Container& c, const T& value )
```

Example <ospace/stl/examples/count0.cpp>

```
#include <stl.h>
#include <iostream.h>

int main ()
{
  int numbers[10] = { 1, 2, 4, 1, 2, 4, 1, 2, 4, 1 };
  int result = 0;

  count (numbers, numbers + 10, 1, result);

  cout << "Found " << result << " 1's." << endl;

  return 0;
}
```

Found 4 1's.

Example <ospace/stl/examples/count1.cpp>

```
#include <stl.h>
#include <iostream.h>

int main ()
{
  vector <int> numbers(100);
  for (int i = 0; i < 100; i++)
    numbers[i] = i % 3;
  int elements = 0;

  count (numbers.begin (), numbers.end (), 2, elements);

  cout
    << "Found " << elements << " 2's." << endl;

  return 0;
}
```

Found 33 2's.

count_if

Synopsis:

Count items in a range that satisfy a predicate.

Declaration:
```
template< class InputIterator, class Predicate, class Size >
void count_if
   (
   InputIterator first,
   InputIterator last,
   Predicate pred,
   Size& n
   )
```

Description:

Count the number of elements in the range [first, last) that cause pred to return true and add this count to n. Note that n is not automatically initialized to zero prior to the counting procedure.

Complexity:

Time Complexity: is linear, as (last - first) comparisons are performed. Space Complexity: is constant.

Helper:
```
int os_count_if( const Container& c, Predicate pred )
```

Example <ospace/stl/examples/countif1.cpp>

```
#include <stl.h>
#include <iostream.h>

int odd (int a)
{
  return a % 2;
}

int main ()
{
  vector <int> numbers(100);
  for (int i = 0; i < 100; i++)
    numbers[i] = i % 3;
  int elements = 0;

  count_if (numbers.begin (), numbers.end (), odd, elements);

  cout
    << "Found " << elements << " odd elements." << endl;

  return 0;
}
```

Found 33 odd elements.

distance

Synopsis:

Calculate the span between two iterators.

Declaration:
```
template< class InputIterator, class Distance >
void distance
    (
    InputIterator first,
    InputIterator last,
    Distance& n
    )
```

Description:

Increment `n` by the number of steps it takes to traverse from `first` to `last`.

Complexity:

Time Complexity: is constant for random access iterators and linear for all other iterators.
Space Complexity: is constant.

Example <ospace/stl/examples/distance.cpp>

```cpp
#include <stl.h>
#include <iostream.h>

int
main()
  {
  typedef vector< int > IntVector;

  IntVector v( 10 );
  for( int i = 0; i < v.size(); i++ )
    v[ i ] = 100 + i;

  // Find something in the middle.
  IntVector::iterator location = v.begin();
  advance( location, 8 );

  IntVector::difference_type n = 0;
  distance( v.begin(), location, n );
  cout << n << endl;

  // Notice that n is incremented, not reset.
  distance( location, v.end(), n );
  cout << n << endl;

  distance( v.begin(), v.end(), n );
  cout << n << endl;

  return 0;
  }
```

8
10
20

equal

Synopsis:

Check that two sequences match.

Declaration:

```
template< class InputIterator1, class InputIterator2 >
bool equal
  (
  InputIterator1 first1,
  InputIterator1 last1,
  InputIterator2 first2
  )

template
  <
  class InputIterator1,
  class InputIterator2,
  class BinaryPredicate
  >
bool equal
  (
  InputIterator1 first1,
  InputIterator1 last1,
  InputIterator2 first2,
  BinaryPredicate binary_pred
  )
```

Description:

Compare the sequence [first1..last1) with a sequence of the same size starting at first2. Return true if every corresponding pair of elements match. The first version uses operator== to perform the matching, whereas the second version uses the binary function binary_pred.

Complexity:

Time Complexity: is linear as N comparisons are performed. Space Complexity: is constant.

Example <ospace/stl/examples/equal0.cpp>

```cpp
#include <stl.h>
#include <iostream.h>

int numbers1[5] = { 1, 2, 3, 4, 5 };
int numbers2[5] = { 1, 2, 4, 8, 16 };
int numbers3[2] = { 1, 2 };

int main ()
{
  if (equal (numbers1, numbers1 + 5, numbers2))
    cout << "numbers1 is equal to numbers2" << endl;
  else
    cout << "numbers1 is not equal to numbers2" << endl;

  if (equal (numbers3, numbers3 + 2, numbers1))
    cout << "numbers3 is equal to numbers1" << endl;
  else
    cout << "numbers3 is not equal to numbers1" << endl;

  return 0;
}
```

```
numbers1 is not equal to numbers2
numbers3 is equal to numbers1
```

Example <ospace/stl/examples/equal1.cpp>

```
#include <stl.h>
#include <iostream.h>

int main ()
{
  vector <int> v1 (10);
  for (int i = 0; i < v1.size (); i++)
    v1[i] = i;
  vector <int> v2 (10);

  if (equal (v1.begin (), v1.end (), v2.begin ()))
    cout << "v1 is equal to v2" << endl;
  else
    cout << "v1 is not equal to v2" << endl;

  copy (v1.begin (), v1.end (), v2.begin ());
  if (equal (v1.begin (), v1.end (), v2.begin ()))
    cout << "v1 is equal to v2" << endl;
  else
    cout << "v1 is not equal to v2" << endl;

  return 0;
}
```

v1 is not equal to v2
v1 is equal to v2

Example <ospace/stl/examples/equal2.cpp>

```
#include <stl.h>
#include <iostream.h>

bool values_squared (int a, int b)
{
  return a_*a == b ? 1 : 0;
}

int main ()
{
  vector <int> v1 (10);
  vector <int> v2 (10);
  for (int i = 0; i < v1.size (); i++)
  {
    v1[i] = i;
    v2[i] = i * i;
  }

  if (equal (v1.begin (), v1.end (), v2.begin (), values_squared))
    cout << "v2[i] == v1[i]*v1[i]" << endl;
  else
    cout << "v2[i] != v1[i]*v1[i]" << endl;

  return 0;
}
```

v2[i] == v1[i]*v1[i]

equal_range

Synopsis:

Return the lower and upper bounds within a range.

Declaration:
```
template< class ForwardIterator, class T >
pair< ForwardIterator, ForwardIterator > equal_range
  (
  ForwardIterator first,
  ForwardIterator last,
  const T& value
  )

template< class ForwardIterator, class T, class Compare >
pair< ForwardIterator, ForwardIterator > equal_range
  (
  ForwardIterator first,
  ForwardIterator last,
  const T& value,
  Compare compare
  )
```

Description:

Search a pair of iterators equal to the lower bound and upper bound for `value`. The first version assumes that the elements in the range are already sorted using `operator<`. The second version assumes that the elements in the range are already sorted using `compare`. For information about lower and upper bounds, consult the algorithm catalog entries for `lower_bound()` and `upper_bound()`.

Complexity:

Time Complexity: is O(log(N)) for random access iterators, O(N) for all other iterators. Space Complexity: is constant.

Example <ospace/stl/examples/eqlrnge0.cpp>

```
#include <stl.h>
#include <iostream.h>

int numbers[10] = { 0, 0, 1, 1, 2, 2, 2, 2, 3, 3 };

int main ()
{
  pair <int*, int*> range;
  range = equal_range (numbers, numbers + 10, 2);

  cout
    << "2 can be inserted from before index "
    << range.first - numbers
    << " to before index "
    << range.second - numbers
    << endl;

  return 0;
}
```

2 can be inserted from before index 4 to before index 8

Example <ospace/stl/examples/eqlrng1.cpp>

```cpp
#include <stl.h>
#include <iostream.h>

int main ()
{
  typedef vector <int> IntVec;
  IntVec v (10);
  for (int i = 0; i < v.size (); i++)
    v[i] = i / 3;
  ostream_iterator<int> iter (cout, " ");
  cout << "Within the collection:\n\t";
  copy (v.begin (), v.end (), iter);
  pair <IntVec::iterator, IntVec::iterator> range;

  range = equal_range (v.begin (), v.end (), 2);

  cout
    << "\n2 can be inserted from before index "
    << range.first - v.begin ()
    << " to before index "
    << range.second - v.begin ()
    << endl;

  return 0;
}
```

```
Within the collection:
        0  0  0  1  1  1  2  2  2  3
2 can be inserted from before index 6 to before index 9
```

Example <ospace/stl/examples/eqlrng2.cpp>

```
#include <stl.h>
#include <iostream.h>
#include <string.h>

char chars[] = "aabbccddggghhklllmqqqqssyyzz";

int main ()
{
  const unsigned count = sizeof (chars) - 1;

  ostream_iterator<char> iter (cout);
  cout << "Within the collection:\n\t";
  copy (chars, chars + count, iter);

  pair <char*, char*> range;
  range = equal_range (chars, chars + count, 'q', less<char>());

  cout
    << "\nq can be inserted from before index "
    << range.first - chars
    << " to before index "
    << range.second - chars
    << endl;

  return 0;
}
```

```
Within the collection
        aabbccddggghhklllmqqqqssyyzz
q can be inserted from before index 18 to before index 22
```

fill

Synopsis:

Set every item in a range to a particular value.

Declaration:

```
template< class ForwardIterator, class T >
void fill
  (
  ForwardIterator first,
  ForwardIterator last,
  const T& value
  )
```

Description:

Assign `value` to each element in the range `[first..last)`. Return an iterator equal to `result + n` where n = `last - first`.

Complexity:

Time Complexity: is linear as `(last - first)` assignments are performed. Space Complexity: is constant.

Example <ospace/stl/examples/fill1.cpp>

```cpp
#include <stl.h>
#include <iostream.h>

int main ()
{
  vector <int> v (10);

  fill (v.begin (), v.end (), 42);

  for (int i = 0; i < 10; i++)
    cout << v[i] << ' ';
  cout << endl;

  return 0;
}

42 42 42 42 42 42 42 42 42 42
```

fill_n

Synopsis:
Set n items to a particular value.

Declaration:
```
template< class OutputIterator, class Size, class T >
void fill_n( OutputIterator first, Size n, const T& value )
```

Description:
Assign `value` to the n elements starting at position `first`. Return an iterator equal to
`result + n`.

Complexity:
Time Complexity: is linear as exactly n assignments are performed. Space Complexity: is
constant.

Example <ospace/stl/examples/filln1.cpp>
```
#include <stl.h>
#include <iostream.h>

int main ()
{
  vector <int> v (10);

  fill_n (v.begin (), v.size (), 42);

  for (int i = 0; i < 10; i++)
    cout << v[i] << ' ';
  cout << endl;

  return 0;
}

42 42 42 42 42 42 42 42 42 42
```

find

Synopsis:

Locate an item in a sequence.

Declaration:
```
template< class InputIterator, class T >
InputIterator find
  (
  InputIterator first,
  InputIterator last,
  const T& value
  )
```

Description:

Search for an element within `[first..last)` that matches `value` using `operator==`. Return an iterator to the first matching value, or `last` if no such element exists.

Complexity:

Time Complexity: is linear, as a maximum of `(last - first)` comparisons are performed. Space Complexity: is constant.

Helper:
```
void os_find( Container& c, const T& value, T*& result )
```

Example <ospace/stl/examples/find0.cpp>

```
#include <stl.h>
#include <iostream.h>

int numbers[10] = { 0, 1, 4, 9, 16, 25, 36, 49, 64 };

int main ()
{
  int* location;
  location = find (numbers, numbers + 10, 25);

  cout
    << "Found 25 at offset "
    << location - numbers
    << endl;

  return 0;
}
```

Found 25 at offset 5

Example <ospace/stl/examples/find1.cpp>

```
#include <stl.h>
#include <iostream.h>

int years[] = { 1942, 1952, 1962, 1972, 1982, 1992 };

int main ()
{
  const unsigned yearCount = sizeof (years) / sizeof (years[0]);
  int* location = find (years, years + yearCount, 1972);

  cout << "Found 1972 at offset " << location - years << endl;

  return 0;
}
```

Found 1972 at offset 3

find_if

Synopsis:
Locate an item that satisfies a predicate in a range.

Declaration:
```
template< class InputIterator, class Predicate >
InputIterator find_if
   (
   InputIterator first,
   InputIterator last,
   Predicate pred
   )
```

Description:
Return an input iterator positioned at the first element in the range [first, last) that causes predicate to return true. If no such element exists, return last.

Complexity:
Time Complexity: is linear, as a maximum of (last - first) comparisons are performed.
Space Complexity: is constant.

Helper:
```
void os_find_if( Container& c, Predicate pred, T*& result )
```

Example <ospace/stl/examples/findif0.cpp>

```
#include <stl.h>
#include <iostream.h>

bool odd (int a)
{
  return a % 2;
}

int numbers[6] = { 2, 4, 8, 15, 32, 64 };

int main ()
{
  int* location = find_if (numbers, numbers + 6, odd);

  if (location != numbers + 6)
    cout
      << "Value "
      << *location
      << " at offset "
      << location - numbers
      << " is odd"
      << endl;
  return 0;
}
```

Value 15 at offset 3 is odd

Example <ospace/stl/examples/findif1.cpp>

```
#include <stl.h>
#include <iostream.h>

bool div_3 (int a)
{
  return a % 3 ? 0 : 1;
}

int main ()
{
  typedef vector <int> IntVec;
  IntVec v (10);
  for (int i = 0; i < v.size (); i++)
    v[i] = (i + 1) * (i + 1);

  IntVec::iterator iter;
  iter = find_if (v.begin (), v.end (), div_3);

  if (iter != v.end ())
    cout
      << "Value "
      << *iter
      << " at offset "
      << iter - v.begin ()
      << " is divisible by 3"
      << endl;
  return 0,
}
```

Value 9 at offset 2 is divisible by 3

for_each

Synopsis:

Apply a function to every item in a range.

Declaration:

```
template< class InputIterator, class Function >
Function for_each
  (
  InputIterator first,
  InputIterator last,
  Function f
  )
```

Description:

Apply `f` to every element in the range `[first, last)` and return the input parameter `f`.

Complexity:

Time Complexity: is linear, as `function` is called `(last - first)` times. Space Complexity: is constant.

Helper:

Function `os_for_each( Container& c, Function f )`

Example <ospace/stl/examples/foreach0.cpp>

```
#include <stl.h>
#include <iostream.h>

void print (int a)
{
  cout << a << ' ';
}

int numbers[10] = { 1, 1, 2, 3, 5, 8, 13, 21, 34, 55 };

int main ()
{
  for_each (numbers, numbers + 10, print);
  cout << endl;
  return 0;
}

1 1 2 3 5 8 13 21 34 55
```

Example <ospace/stl/examples/foreach1.cpp>

```cpp
#include <stl.h>
#include <iostream.h>

void print_sqr (int a)
{
  cout << a * a << " ";
}

int main ()
{
  vector <int> v1 (10);
  for (int i = 0; i < v1.size (); i++)
    v1[i] = i;

  for_each (v1.begin (), v1.end (), print_sqr);

  return 0;
}
```

0 1 4 9 16 25 36 49 64 81

generate

Synopsis:

Fill a sequence using a generator function.

Declaration:

```
template< class ForwardIterator, class Generator >
void generate
  (
  ForwardIterator first,
  ForwardIterator last,
  Generator gen
  )
```

Description:

Traverse the sequence [first..last), assigning to each element the result of executing
gen().

Complexity:

Time Complexity: is linear, as gen is executed (last - first) times. Space Complexity:
is constant.

Example <ospace/stl/examples/gener1.cpp>

```
#include <stl.h>
#include <iostream.h>
#include <stdlib.h>

int main ()
{
  int numbers[10];

  generate (numbers, numbers + 10, rand);

  for (int i = 0; i < 10; i++)
    cout << numbers[i] << ' ';
  cout << endl;
  return 0;
}

346 130 10982 1090 11656 7117 17595 6415 22948 31126
```

Example <ospace/stl/examples/gener2.cpp>

```
#include <stl.h>
#include <iostream.h>
#include <stdlib.h>

class Fibonacci
{
  public:
    Fibonacci () : v1 (0), v2 (1) {}
    int operator () ();
  private:
    int v1;
    int v2;
};

int
Fibonacci::operator () ()
{
  int r = v1 + v2;
  v1 = v2;
  v2 = r;
  return v1;
}

int main ()
{
  vector <int> v1 (10);
  Fibonacci generator;

  generate (v1.begin (), v1.end (), generator);

  ostream_iterator<int> iter (cout, " ");
  copy (v1.begin (), v1.end (), iter);
  return 0;
}

1 1 2 3 5 8 13 21 34 55
```

generate_n

Synopsis:

Generate a specified number of items.

Declaration:

```
template< class OutputIterator, class Size, class Generator >
void generate_n( OutputIterator first, Size n, Generator gen )
```

Description:

Traverse the sequence [first..first + n), assigning to each element the result of executing gen_().

Complexity:

Time Complexity: is linear, as gen is executed n times. Space Complexity: is constant.

Example <ospace/stl/examples/genern1.cpp>

```
#include <stl.h>
#include <iostream.h>
#include <stdlib.h>

int main ()
{
  vector <int> v1 (10);

  generate_n (v1.begin (), v1.size (), rand);

  for (int i = 0; i < 10; i++)
    cout << v1[i] << ' ';
  return 0;
}

346 130 10982 1090 11656 7117 17595 6415 22948 31126
```

Example <ospace/stl/examples/genern2.cpp>

```cpp
#include <stl.h>
#include <iostream.h>
#include <stdlib.h>

class Fibonacci
{
  public:
    Fibonacci () : v1 (0), v2 (1) {}
    int operator () ();
  private:
    int v1;
    int v2;
};

int
Fibonacci::operator () ()
{
  int r = v1 + v2;
  v1 = v2;
  v2 = r;
  return v1;
}

int main ()
{
  vector <int> v1 (10);
  Fibonacci generator;

  generate_n (v1.begin (), v1.size (), generator);

  ostream_iterator<int> iter (cout, " ");
  copy (v1.begin (), v1.end (), iter);
  return 0;
}
```

1 1 2 3 5 8 13 21 34 55

includes

Synopsis:
Search for one sequence in another sequence.

Declaration:
```
template< class InputIterator1, class InputIterator2 >
bool includes
  (
  InputIterator1 first1,
  InputIterator1 last1,
  InputIterator2 first2,
  InputIterator2 last2
  )

template< class InputIterator1, class InputIterator2, class Compare >
bool includes
  (
  InputIterator1 first1,
  InputIterator1 last1,
  InputIterator2 first2,
  InputIterator2 last2,
  Compare compare
  )
```

Description:
Search for one sequence of values in another sequence of values. Return `true` if every element in `[first2..last2)` is in the sequence `[first1..last1)`. The first version assumes that both sequences are already sorted using operator<. The second version assumes that both sequences are already sorted using `compare`.

Complexity:
Time Complexity: is linear. Space Complexity: is constant.

Helper:
```
bool os_includes( const Container& c1, const Container& c2 )
bool os_includes
  (
  const Container& c1,
  const Container& c2,
  Compare compare
  )
```

Example <ospace/stl/examples/incl0.cpp>

```
#include <stl.h>
#include <iostream.h>

int numbers1[5] = { 1, 2, 3, 4, 5 };
int numbers2[5] = { 1, 2, 4, 8, 16 };
int numbers3[2] = { 4, 8 };

int main ()
{
  if (includes (numbers1, numbers1 + 5, numbers3, numbers3 + 2))
    cout << "numbers1 includes numbers3" << endl;
  else
    cout << "numbers1 does not include numbers3" << endl;

  if (includes (numbers2, numbers2 + 5, numbers3, numbers3 + 2))
    cout << "numbers2 includes numbers3" << endl;
  else
    cout << "numbers2 does not include numbers3" << endl;


  return 0;
}
```

numbers1 does not include numbers3
numbers2 includes numbers3

Example <ospace/stl/examples/incl1.cpp>

```cpp
#include <stl.h>
#include <iostream.h>

int main ()
{
  vector<int> v1(10);
  vector<int> v2(3);
  for (int i = 0; i < v1.size (); i++)
  {
    v1[i] = i;
  }

  if (includes (v1.begin (), v1.end (), v2.begin (), v2.end ()))
    cout << "v1 includes v2" << endl;
  else
    cout << "v1 does not include v2" << endl;

  for (i = 0; i < v2.size (); i++)
    v2[i] = i + 3;

  if (includes (v1.begin (), v1.end (), v2.begin (), v2.end ()))
    cout << "v1 includes v2" << endl;
  else
    cout << "v1 does not include v2" << endl;
  return 0;
}
```

v1 does not include v2
v1 includes v2

Example <ospace/stl/examples/incl2.cpp>

```
#include <stl.h>
#include <iostream.h>
#include <string.h>

bool compare_strings (const char* s1, const char* s2)
{
  return ::strcmp (s1, s2) < 0 ? 1 : 0;
}

char* names[] = {  "Todd", "Mike", "Graham", "Jack", "Brett"};

int main ()
{
  const unsigned nameSize = sizeof (names)/sizeof (names[0]);

  vector <char*> v1(nameSize);
  for (int i = 0; i < v1.size (); i++)
  {
    v1[i] = names[i];
  }
  vector <char*> v2 (2);
  v2[0] = "foo";
  v2[1] = "bar";
  sort (v1.begin (), v1.end (), compare_strings);
  sort (v2.begin (), v2.end (), compare_strings);

  bool inc = includes (v1.begin (), v1.end (),
                        v2.begin (), v2.end (),
                        compare_strings);

  if (inc)
    cout << "v1 includes v2" << endl;
  else
    cout << "v1 does not include v2" << endl;

  v2[0] = "Brett";
  v2[1] = "Todd";

  inc = includes (v1.begin (), v1.end (),
                  v2.begin (), v2.end (),
                  compare_strings);

  if (inc)
    cout << "v1 includes v2" << endl;
  else
    cout << "v1 does not include v2" << endl;
  return 0;
}
```

v1 does not include v2
v1 includes v2

inner_product

Synopsis:
Calculate the inner product of two sequences.

Declaration:
```
template< class InputIterator1, class InputIterator2, class T >
T inner_product
   (
   InputIterator1 first1,
   InputIterator1 last1,
   InputIterator2 first2,
   T init
   )

template
   <
   class InputIterator1,
   class InputIterator2,
   class T,
   class BinaryOperation1,
   class BinaryOperation2
   >
T inner_product
   (
   InputIterator1 first1,
   InputIterator1 last1,
   InputIterator2 first2,
   T init,
   BinaryOperation1 binary_op1,
   BinaryOperation2 binary_op2
   )
```

Description:
Use a pair of iterators `i` and `j` to traverse the two sequences `[first1..last1)` and `[first2..first2_+(last1_-first1))`. Apply the formula `init = init op1 (*i op2 *j)` and return the final value of `init`. Note that `init` is not automatically initialized to zero prior to this operation. The first version automatically sets `op1` to `operator+` and `op2` to `operator*`.

Complexity:
Time Complexity: is linear. Space Complexity: is constant.

Example <ospace/stl/examples/inrprod0.cpp>

```
#include <stl.h>
#include <iostream.h>
#include <string.h>

int vector1[5] = { 1, 2, 3, 4, 5 };
int vector2[5] = { 1, 2, 3, 4, 5 };

int main ()
{
  int result;
  result = inner_product (vector1, vector1 + 5, vector2, 0);

  cout << "Inner product = " << result << endl;
  return 0;
}
```

Inner product = 55

Example <ospace/stl/examples/inrprod1.cpp>

```cpp
#include <stl.h>
#include <iostream.h>
#include <string.h>

int main ()
{
  vector <int> v1 (3);
  vector <int> v2 (v1.size ());

  for (int i = 0; i < v1.size (); i++)
  {
    v1[i] = i + 1;
    v2[i] = v1.size () - i;
  }

  ostream_iterator<int> iter (cout, " ");
  cout << "Inner product (sum of products) of:\n\t";
  copy (v1.begin (), v1.end (), iter);
  cout << "\n\t";
  copy (v2.begin (), v2.end (), iter);

  int result
    = inner_product (v1.begin (), v1.end (), v2.begin (), 0);

  cout << "\nis: " << result << endl;
  return 0;
}
```

```
Inner product (sum of products) of:
        1 2 3
        3 2 1
is: 10
```

Example <ospace/stl/examples/inrprod2.cpp>

```cpp
#include <stl.h>
#include <iostream.h>
#include <string.h>

int add (int a, int b)
{
  return a + b;
}

int mult (int a, int b)
{
  return a * b;
}

int main ()
{
  vector <int> v1 (3);
  vector <int> v2 (v1.size ());

  for (int i = 0; i < v1.size (); i++)
  {
    v1[i] = i + 1;
    v2[i] = v1.size () - i;
  }

  ostream_iterator<int> iter (cout, " ");
  cout << "Inner product (product of sums):\n\t";
  copy (v1.begin (), v1.end (), iter);
  cout << "\n\t";
  copy (v2.begin (), v2.end (), iter);

  int result =
    inner_product (v1.begin (), v1.end (),
                   v2.begin (),
                   1,
                   mult, add);

  cout << "\nis: " << result << endl;
  return 0;
}
```

Inner product (product of sums) of:
         1 2 3
         3 2 1
is: 64

inplace_merge

Synopsis:

Merge two sorted lists in place into a single sorted list.

Declaration:

```
template< class BidirectionalIterator >
void inplace_merge
  (
  BidirectionalIterator first,
  BidirectionalIterator middle,
  BidirectionalIterator last
  )

template< class BidirectionalIterator, class Compare >
void inplace_merge
  (
  BidirectionalIterator first,
  BidirectionalIterator middle,
  BidirectionalIterator last,
  Compare compare
  )
```

Description:

Given two sorted sub-sequences [first..middle) and [middle..last) within the range
[first..last), merge the two sub-sequence into one sorted sequence from
[first..last). This merge is stable in the sense that if both ranges contain equal values,
the value from the first range will be stored first. The first version assumes that the ranges
[first..middle) and [middle..last) are sorted using operator<.

Complexity:

Given enough memory, this algorithm's time Complexity: is linear and its space Complexity:
is (last - first). If enough memory is not available, the time Complexity: becomes N *
log(N) and the space Complexity: becomes constant.

Example <ospace/stl/examples/inplmrg1.cpp>

```cpp
#include <stl.h>
#include <iostream.h>

int numbers[6] = { 1, 10, 42, 3, 16, 32 };

int main ()
{
  for (int i = 0; i < 6; i++)
    cout << numbers[i] << ' ';
  cout << endl;

  inplace_merge (numbers, numbers + 3, numbers + 6);

  for (i = 0; i < 6; i++)
    cout << numbers[i] << ' ';
  cout << endl;
  return 0;
}
```

```
1 10 42 3 16 32
1 3 10 16 32 42
```

Example <ospace/stl/examples/inplmrg2.cpp>

```cpp
#include <stl.h>
#include <iostream.h>

int main ()
{
  vector <int> v1(10);
  for (int i = 0; i < v1.size (); i++)
    v1[i] = (v1.size () - i - 1) % 5;
  ostream_iterator <int> iter (cout, " ");
  copy (v1.begin (), v1.end (), iter);
  cout << endl;

  inplace_merge (v1.begin (), v1.begin () + 5,
                 v1.end (),
                 greater<int>());

  copy (v1.begin (), v1.end (), iter);
  cout << endl;
  return 0;
}
```

```
4 3 2 1 0 4 3 2 1 0
4 4 3 3 2 2 1 1 0 0
```

iota

Synopsis:
Fill a range with ascending values.

Declaration:
```
template< class ForwardIterator, class T >
void iota( ForwardIterator first, ForwardIterator last, T value )
```

Description:
Assign `value` to each element in the range `[first..last)`, incrementing `value` using `operator++` after each assignment.

Complexity:
Time Complexity: is linear, as `(last - first)` assignments are performed. Space Complexity: is constant.

Example <ospace/stl/examples/iota1.cpp>
```
#include <stl.h>
#include <iostream.h>

int main ()
{
  int numbers[10];
  iota (numbers, numbers + 10, 42);
  for (int i = 0; i < 10; i++)
    cout << numbers[i] << ' ';
  cout << endl;
  return 0;
}
```
```
42 43 44 45 46 47 48 49 50 51
```

iter_swap

Synopsis:

Swap the two elements indicated by two iterators.

Declaration:

```
template< class ForwardIterator1, class ForwardIterator2 >
void iter_swap( ForwardIterator1 a, ForwardIterator2 b )
```

Description:

Swap the two elements referenced by `a` and `b`.

Complexity:

Time and space Complexity: are both constant.

Example <ospace/stl/examples/iterswp0.cpp>

```cpp
#include <stl.h>
#include <iostream.h>

int numbers[6] = { 0, 1, 2, 3, 4, 5 };

int main ()
{
  iter_swap (numbers, numbers + 3);
  for (int i = 0; i < 6; i++)
    cout << numbers[i] << ' ';
  cout << endl;
  return 0;
}

3 1 2 0 4 5
```

Example <ospace/stl/examples/iterswp1.cpp>

```
#include <stl.h>
#include <iostream.h>

int main ()
{
  vector <int> v1 (6);
  iota (v1.begin (), v1.end (), 0);
  iter_swap (v1.begin (), v1.begin () + 3);
  ostream_iterator <int> iter (cout, " ");
  copy (v1.begin (), v1.end (), iter);
  cout << endl;
  return 0;
}
```

3 1 2 0 4 5

lexicographical_compare

Synopsis:
Lexicographically compare two sequences.

Declaration:
```
template< class InputIterator1, class InputIterator2 >
bool lexicographical_compare
  (
  InputIterator1 first1,
  InputIterator1 last1,
  InputIterator2 first2,
  InputIterator2 last2
  )

template< class InputIterator1, class InputIterator2, class Compare >
bool lexicographical_compare
  (
  InputIterator1 first1,
  InputIterator1 last1,
  InputIterator2 first2,
  InputIterator2 last2,
  Compare compare
  )
```

Description:
Use a pair of iterators `i` and `j` to traverse two sequences, starting at `first1` and `first2`, respectively. While traversing the sequences, if `*i` is less than `*j`, immediately return `true`. Similarly, if `*j < *i`, immediately return `false`. If the end of the first sequence is reached before the end of the second sequence, return `true`, otherwise return `false`. The first version uses `operator<` to perform the comparison, whereas the second version uses `compare`.

Complexity:
Time Complexity: is linear, as at most `(last1 - first1)` comparisons are performed.
Space Complexity: is constant.

Example <ospace/stl/examples/lexcmp1.cpp>

```cpp
#include <stl.h>
#include <iostream.h>

int main ()
{
  const unsigned size = 6;
  char n1[size] = "shoe";
  char n2[size] = "shine";

  bool before
    = lexicographical_compare (n1, n1 + size, n2, n2 + size);

  if (before)
    cout << n1 << " is before " << n2 << endl;
  else
    cout << n2 << " is before " << n1 << endl;

  return 0;
}
```

shine is before shoe

Example <ospace/stl/examples/lexcmp2.cpp>

```
#include <stl.h>
#include <iostream.h>

int main ()
{
  const unsigned size = 6;
  char n1[size] = "shoe";
  char n2[size] = "shine";

  bool before =
    lexicographical_compare (n1, n1 + size,
                             n2, n2 + size,
                             greater<char>());

  if (before)
    cout << n1 << " is after " << n2 << endl;
  else
    cout << n2 << " is after " << n1 << endl;

  return 0;
}
```

shoe is after shine

lower_bound

Synopsis:

Return the lower bound within a range.

Declaration:
```
template< class ForwardIterator, class T >
ForwardIterator lower_bound
   (
   ForwardIterator first,
   ForwardIterator last,
   const T& value
   )

template< class ForwardIterator, class T, class Compare >
ForwardIterator lower_bound
   (
   ForwardIterator first,
   ForwardIterator last,
   const T& value,
   Compare compare
   )
```

Description:

Return an iterator positioned at the first position in the range [first..last) that value can be inserted without violating the order of the collection. If no such position exists, return last. The first version assumes that the elements are already sorted using operator<, whereas the second version assumes that the elements are already sorted using the binary function compare.

Complexity:

Time Complexity: is O(log(N)) for random access iterators and O(N) for all other iterators.
Space Complexity: is constant.

Example <ospace/stl/examples/lwrbnd1.cpp>

```cpp
#include <stl.h>
#include <iostream.h>

int main ()
{
  vector <int> v1 (20);
  for (int i = 0; i < v1.size (); i++)
  {
    v1[i] = i/4;
    cout << v1[i] << ' ';
  }

  int* location = lower_bound (v1.begin (), v1.end (), 3);

  cout
    << "\n3 can be inserted at index: "
    << location - v1.begin ()
    << endl;

  return 0;
}

0 0 0 0 1 1 1 1 2 2 2 2 3 3 3 3 4 4 4 4
3 can be inserted at index: 12
```

Example <ospace/stl/examples/lwrbnd2.cpp>

```
#include <stl.h>
#include <iostream.h>
#include <string.h>

bool char_str_less (const char* a, const char* b)
{
  return ::strcmp (a, b) < 0 ? 1 : 0;
}

char* str [] = { "a", "a", "b", "b", "q", "w", "z" };

int main ()
{
  const unsigned count = sizeof (str) /sizeof (str[0]);

  cout
    << "d can be inserted at index: "
    << lower_bound (str,  str + count, "d", char_str_less) - str
    << endl;

  return 0;
}
```

d can be inserted at index: 4

make_heap

Synopsis:

Make a sequence into a heap

Declaration:

```
template< class RandomAccessIterator >
void make_heap
  (
  RandomAccessIterator first,
  RandomAccessIterator last
  )

template< class RandomAccessIterator, class Compare >
void make_heap
  (
  RandomAccessIterator first,
  RandomAccessIterator last,
  Compare compare
  )
```

Description:

Arrange the elements in the range `[first..last)` into a heap. The first version uses `operator<` to perform the comparisons, whereas the second version uses the binary function `compare`.

Complexity:

Time Complexity: is linear. Space Complexity: is constant.

Example <ospace/stl/examples/mkheap0.cpp>

```
#include <stl.h>
#include <iostream.h>

int numbers[6] = { 5, 10, 4, 13, 11, 19 };

int main ()
{
  make_heap (numbers, numbers + 6);
  for (int i = 6; i >= 1; i--)
  {
    cout << numbers[0] << endl;
    pop_heap (numbers, numbers + i);
  }
  return 0;
}
```

```
19
13
11
10
5
4
```

Example <ospace/stl/examples/mkheap1.cpp>

```
#include <stl.h>
#include <iostream.h>

int numbers[6] = { 5, 10, 4, 13, 11, 19 };

int main ()
{
  make_heap (numbers, numbers + 6, greater<int> ());
  for (int i = 6; i >= 1; i--)
  {
    cout << numbers[0] << endl;
    pop_heap (numbers, numbers + i, greater<int> ());
  }
  return 0;
}
```

```
4
5
10
11
13
19
```

max

Synopsis:

Return the maximum of two items.

Declaration:

```
template< class T >
const T& max( const T& a, const T& b )

template< class T, class Compare >
const T& max( const T& a, const T& b, Compare compare )
```

Description:

Return a reference to the larger of `a` and `b`, or `a` if `a` and `b` are equal. The first version uses `operator<` to perform the comparison, whereas the second version uses the binary function `compare.` using either `operator<` or `compare.`

Complexity:

Time and space Complexity: are constant.

Example <ospace/stl/examples/max1.cpp>

```
#include <stl.h>
#include <iostream.h>

int main ()
{
  cout << max (42, 100) << endl;
  return 0;
}
```

100

Example <ospace/stl/examples/max2.cpp>

```
#include <stl.h>
#include <iostream.h>
#include <string.h>

bool str_compare (const char* a, const char* b)
{
  return ::strcmp (a, b) < 0 ? 1 : 0;
}

int main ()
{
  cout << max ("shoe", "shine", str_compare) << endl;
  return 0;
}
```

shoe

max_element

Synopsis:

Return the maximum element within a range.

Declaration:
```
template< class InputIterator >
InputIterator max_element( InputIterator first, InputIterator last )

template< class InputIterator, class Compare >
InputIterator max_element
  (
  InputIterator first,
  InputIterator last,
  Compare compare
  )
```

Description:

Return an iterator positioned at the maximum element in the range [first, last). The first version uses operator< to perform the comparisons, whereas the second version uses the binary function compare.

Complexity:

Time Complexity: is linear, as (last - first) comparisons are performed. Space Complexity: is constant.

Helper:
```
void os_max_element( const Container& c, T*& t )
bool os_max_element_value( const Container& c, T& t )
```

Example <ospace/stl/examples/maxelem1.cpp>

```
#include <stl.h>
#include <iostream.h>

int numbers[6] = { 4, 10, 56, 11, -42, 19 };

int main ()
{
  cout
    << *max_element (numbers, numbers + 6)
    << endl;
  return 0;
}
```

56

Example <ospace/stl/examples/maxelem2.cpp>

```
#include <stl.h>
#include <iostream.h>
#include <string.h>

bool str_compare (const char* a, const char* b)
{
  return ::strcmp (a, b) < 0 ? 1 : 0;
}

char* names[] = { "Brett", "Graham", "Jack", "Mike", "Todd" };

int main ()
{
  const unsigned namesCt = sizeof (names)/sizeof (names[0]);
  cout
    << *max_element (names, names + namesCt, str_compare)
    << endl;
  return 0;
}
```

Todd

merge

Synopsis:

Merge two sorted lists into a single sorted list.

Declaration:

```
template
  <
  class InputIterator1,
  class InputIterator2,
  class OutputIterator
  >
OutputIterator merge
  (
  InputIterator1 first1,
  InputIterator1 last1,
  InputIterator2 first2,
  InputIterator2 last2,
  OutputIterator result
  )

template
  <
  class InputIterator1,
  class InputIterator2,
  class OutputIterator,
  class Compare
  >
OutputIterator merge
  (
  InputIterator1 first1,
  InputIterator1 last1,
  InputIterator2 first2,
  InputIterator2 last2,
  OutputIterator result,
  Compare compare
  )
```

Description:

Merge two sorted ranges into one sorted range, `result`. Return an iterator equal to `result` + n where n = `(last1 - first1) + (last2 - first2)`. The merge is stable in the sense that if both ranges contain equivalent values, the first ranges' value will be put in `result` before the values in the second range. The result of merging overlapping ranges is undefined. The first version assumes that both ranges are already sorted using `operator<`, whereas the second version assumes that both ranges are already sorted using the binary function `compare`.

Complexity:

Time Complexity: is O(N) where N = $(last1 - first1) + (last2 - first2)$. Space Complexity: is constant.

Example <ospace/stl/examples/merge0.cpp>

```
#include <stl.h>
#include <iostream.h>

int numbers1[5] = { 1, 6, 13, 25, 101 };
int numbers2[5] = {-5, 26, 36, 46, 99 };

int main ()
{
  int result[10];
  merge (numbers1, numbers1 + 5,
         numbers2, numbers2 + 5,
         result);
  for (int i = 0; i < 10; i++)
    cout << result[i] << ' ';
  cout << endl;
  return 0;
}

-5 1 6 13 25 26 36 46 99 101
```

Example <ospace/stl/examples/merge1.cpp>

```
#include <stl.h>
#include <iostream.h>

int main ()
{
  vector <int> v1 (5);
  vector <int> v2 (v1.size ());

  iota (v1.begin (), v1.end (), 0);
  iota (v2.begin (), v2.end (), 3);

  vector <int> result (v1.size () + v2.size ());

  merge (v1.begin (), v1.end (),
         v2.begin (), v2.end (),
         result.begin ());

  ostream_iterator <int> iter (cout, " ");
  copy (v1.begin (), v1.end (), iter);
  cout << endl;
  copy (v2.begin (), v2.end (), iter);
  cout << endl;
  copy (result.begin (), result.end (), iter);
  cout << endl;
  return 0;
}

0 1 2 3 4
3 4 5 6 7
0 1 2 3 3 4 4 5 6 7
```

Example <ospace/stl/examples/merge2.cpp>

```cpp
#include <stl.h>
#include <iostream.h>

int main ()
{
  vector <int> v1 (5);
  vector <int> v2 (v1.size ());

  for (int i = 0; i < v1.size (); i++)
  {
    v1[i] = 10 - i;
    v2[i] =  7 - i;
  }

  vector <int> result (v1.size () + v2.size ());

  merge (v1.begin (), v1.end (),
         v2.begin (), v2.end (),
         result.begin (),
         greater<int>() );

  ostream_iterator <int> iter (cout, " ");
  copy (v1.begin (), v1.end (), iter);
  cout << endl;
  copy (v2.begin (), v2.end (), iter);
  cout << endl;
  copy (result.begin (), result.end (), iter);
  cout << endl;
  return 0;
}
```

```
10 9 8 7 6
7 6 5 4 3
10 9 8 7 7 6 6 5 4 3
```

min

Synopsis:

Return the minimum of two items.

Declaration:

```
template< class T >
const T& min( const T& a, const T& b )

template< class T, class Compare >
const T& min( const T& a, const T& b, Compare compare )
```

Description:

Return the smaller of a and b, or a if a and b are equal. The first version uses `operator<` to perform the comparison, whereas the second version uses the binary function `compare`.

Complexity:

Space and time Complexity: are constant.

Example <ospace/stl/examples/min1.cpp>

```
#include <stl.h>
#include <iostream.h>

int main ()
{
  cout << min (42, 100) << endl;
  return 0;
}
```

```
42
```

Example <ospace/stl/examples/min2.cpp>

```
#include <stl.h>
#include <iostream.h>
#include <string.h>

bool str_compare (const char* a, const char* b)
{
  return ::strcmp (a, b) < 0 ? 1 : 0;
}

int main ()
{
  cout << min ("shoe", "shine", str_compare) << endl;
  return 0;
}
```

shine

min_element

Synopsis:
Return the minimum item within a range.

Declaration:
```
template< class InputIterator >
InputIterator min_element( InputIterator first, InputIterator last )

template< class InputIterator, class Compare >
InputIterator min_element
  (
  InputIterator first,
  InputIterator last,
  Compare compare
  )
```

Description:
Return an iterator positioned at the minimum element in the range [first, last). The first version uses operator< to perform the comparisons, whereas the second version uses the binary function compare .

Complexity:
Time Complexity: is linear, as (last   first) comparisons are performed. Space Complexity: is constant.

Helper:
```
void os_min_element( const Container& c, T*& t )
bool os_min_element_value( const Container& c, T& t )
```

Example <ospace/stl/examples/minelem1.cpp>

```cpp
#include <stl.h>
#include <iostream.h>

int numbers[6] = { -10, 15, -100, 36, -242, 42 };

int main ()
{
  cout
    << *min_element (numbers, numbers + 6)
    << endl;
  return 0;
}
```

```
-242
```

Example <ospace/stl/examples/minelem2.cpp>

```
#include <stl.h>
#include <iostream.h>
#include <string.h>

bool str_compare (const char* a, const char* b)
{
   return ::strcmp (a, b) < 0 ? 1 : 0;
}

char* names[] = { "Brett", "Graham", "Jack", "Mike", "Todd" };

int main ()
{
   const unsigned namesCt = sizeof (names)/sizeof (names[0]);
   cout
      << *min_element (names, names + namesCt, str_compare)
      << endl;
   return 0;
}
```

Brett

mismatch

Synopsis:

Search two sequences for a mismatched item.

Declaration:
```
template< class InputIterator1, class InputIterator2 >
pair< InputIterator1, InputIterator2 > mismatch
  (
  InputIterator1 first1,
  InputIterator1 last1,
  InputIterator2 first2
  )

template
  <
  class InputIterator1,
  class InputIterator2,
  class BinaryPredicate
  >
pair< InputIterator1, InputIterator2 > mismatch
  (
  InputIterator1 first1,
  InputIterator1 last1,
  InputIterator2 first2,
  BinaryPredicate binary_pred
  )
```

Description:

Use a pair of iterators i and j to traverse two sequences, starting at first1 and first2, respectively. Return the iterator pair (i, j) when either their respective elements mismatch or when i reaches last1. The first version uses operator== to perform the comparisons, whereas the second version uses binary_pred.

Complexity:

Time Complexity: is linear, as at most (last1 - first1) comparisons are performed.
Space Complexity: is constant.

Example <ospace/stl/examples/mismtch0.cpp>

```cpp
#include <stl.h>
#include <iostream.h>

int n1[5] = { 1, 2, 3, 4, 5 };
int n2[5] = { 1, 2, 3, 4, 5 };
int n3[5] = { 1, 2, 3, 2, 1 };

int main ()
{
  pair <int*, int*> result;
  result = mismatch (n1, n1 + 5, n2);
  if (result.first == (n1 + 5) && result.second == (n2 + 5))
    cout << "n1 and n2 are the same" << endl;
  else
    cout << "Mismatch at offset: " << result.first - n1 << endl;
  result = mismatch (n1, n1 + 5, n3);
  if (result.first == (n1 + 5) && result.second == (n3 + 5))
    cout << "n1 and n3 are the same" << endl;
  else
    cout << "Mismatch at offset: " << result.first - n1 << endl;
  return 0;
}
```

n1 and n2 are the same
Mismatch at offset: 3

Example <ospace/stl/examples/mismtch1.cpp>

```cpp
#include <stl.h>
#include <iostream.h>

int main ()
{
  typedef vector <int> IntVec;
  IntVec v1 (10);
  IntVec v2 (v1.size ());
  iota (v1.begin (), v1.end (), 0);
  iota (v2.begin (), v2.end (), 0);
  pair <IntVec::iterator, IntVec::iterator> result;
  result = mismatch (v1.begin (), v1.end (), v2.begin ());
  if (result.first == v1.end () && result.second == v2.end ())
    cout << "v1 and v2 are the same" << endl;
  else
    cout << "mismatch at index: " << result.first - v1.begin ()
         << endl;
  v2[v2.size()/2] = 42;
  result = mismatch (v1.begin (), v1.end (), v2.begin ());
  if (result.first == v1.end () && result.second == v2.end ())
    cout << "v1 and v2 are the same" << endl;
  else
    cout << "mismatch at index: " << result.first - v1.begin ()
         << endl;
  return 0;
}
```

```
v1 and v2 are the same
mismatch at index: 5
```

Example <ospace/stl/examples/mismtch2.cpp>

```
#include <stl.h>
#include <iostream.h>
#include <string.h>

bool str_equal (const char* a, const char* b)
{
  return ::strcmp (a, b) == 0 ? 1 : 0;
}

char* n1[size] = { "Brett", "Graham", "Jack", "Mike", "Todd" };

int main ()
{
  const unsigned size = 5;
  char* n2[size];
  copy (n1, n1 + 5, n2);
  pair <char**, char**> result;
  result = mismatch (n1, n1+ size, n2, str_equal);
  if (result.first == n1 + size && result.second == n2 + size)
    cout << "n1 and n2 are the same" << endl;
  else
    cout << "mismatch at index: " << result.first - n1 << endl;
  n2[2] = "QED";
  result = mismatch (n1, n1 + size, n2, str_equal);
  if (result.first == n2 + size && result.second == n2 + size)
    cout << "n1 and n2 are the same" << endl;
  else
    cout << "mismatch at index: " << result.first - n1 << endl;
  return 0;
}
```

n1 and n2 are the same
mismatch at index: 2

next_permutation

Synopsis:

Change sequence to next lexicographic permutation.

Declaration:
```
template< class BidirectionalIterator >
bool next_permutation
  (
  BidirectionalIterator first,
  BidirectionalIterator last
  )

template< class BidirectionalIterator, class Compare >
bool next_permutation
  (
  BidirectionalIterator first,
  BidirectionalIterator last,
  Compare compare
  )
```

Description:

Arrange the sequence `[first..last)` to be its next permutation and return `true`. If there is no next permutation, arrange the sequence to be the first permutation and return `false`. The first version orders the permutations using `operator<`, whereas the second version uses the binary function `compare`.

Complexity:

Time Complexity: is linear. Space Complexity: is constant.

Example <ospace/stl/examples/nextprm0.cpp>

```cpp
#include <stl.h>
#include <iostream.h>

int v1[3] = { 0, 1, 2 };

int main ()
{
  next_permutation (v1, v1 + 3);
  for (int i = 0; i < 3; i++)
    cout << v1[i] << ' ';
  cout << endl;
  return 0;
}
```

0 2 1

Example <ospace/stl/examples/nextprm1.cpp>

```cpp
#include <stl.h>
#include <iostream.h>

int main ()
{
  vector <int> v1 (3);
  iota (v1.begin (), v1.end (), 0);
  ostream_iterator<int> iter (cout, " ");
  copy (v1.begin (), v1.end (), iter);
  cout << endl;
  for (int i = 0; i < 9; i++)
  {
    next_permutation (v1.begin (), v1.end ());
    copy (v1.begin (), v1.end (), iter);
    cout << endl;
  }
  return 0;
}
```

0 1 2
0 2 1
1 0 2
1 2 0
2 0 1
2 1 0
0 1 2
0 2 1
1 0 2
1 2 0

Example <ospace/stl/examples/nextprm2.cpp>

```
#include <stl.h>
#include <iostream.h>

int main ()
{
  vector <char> v1 (3);
  iota (v1.begin (), v1.end (), 'A');
  ostream_iterator<char> iter (cout);
  copy (v1.begin (), v1.end (), iter);
  cout << endl;
  for (int i = 0; i < 9; i++)
  {
    next_permutation (v1.begin (), v1.end (), less<char>());
    copy (v1.begin (), v1.end (), iter);
    cout << endl;
  }
  return 0;
}
```

ABC
ACB
BAC
BCA
CAB
CBA
ABC
ACB
BAC
BCA

nth_element

Synopsis:

Partition a range by its nth element.

Declaration:

```
template< class RandomAccessIterator >
void nth_element
  (
  RandomAccessIterator first,
  RandomAccessIterator nth,
  RandomAccessIterator last
  )


template< class RandomAccessIterator, class Compare >
void nth_element
  (
  RandomAccessIterator first,
  RandomAccessIterator nth,
  RandomAccessIterator last,
  Compare compare
  )
```

Description:

If the value referenced by `nth` is `value`, partition the sequence `[first..last)` so that all elements to the left of `value` are less than or equal to `value`, and all elements to the right of `value` are greater than or equal to `value`. The first version uses `operator<` to perform the comparisons, whereas the second version uses the binary function `compare`.

Complexity:

Time Complexity: is O(N), where N is `(last - first)`. Space Complexity: is constant.

Example <ospace/stl/examples/nthelem0.cpp>

```
#include <stl.h>
#include <iostream.h>

int numbers[6] = { 5, 2, 4, 1, 0, 3 };

int main ()
{
  nth_element (numbers, numbers + 3, numbers + 6);
  for (int i = 0; i < 6; i++)
    cout << numbers[i] << ' ';
  cout << endl;
  return 0;
}
```

```
1 0 2 3 4 5
```

Example <ospace/stl/examples/nthelem1.cpp>

```
#include <stl.h>
#include <iostream.h>

int main ()
{
  vector <int> v1 (10);
  for (int i = 0; i < v1.size (); i++)
    v1[i] = rand () % 10;
  ostream_iterator<int> iter (cout, " ");
  copy (v1.begin (), v1.end (), iter);
  cout << endl;
  nth_element (v1.begin (),
               v1.begin () + v1.size () / 2,
               v1.end ());
  copy (v1.begin (), v1.end (), iter);
  cout << endl;
  return 0;
}
```

```
6 0 2 0 6 7 5 5 8 6
5 0 2 0 5 6 7 6 8 6
```

Example <ospace/stl/examples/nthelem2.cpp>

```
#include <stl.h>
#include <iostream.h>

int main ()
{
  vector <int> v1 (10);
  for (int i = 0; i < v1.size (); i++)
    v1[i] = rand () % 10;
  ostream_iterator<int> iter (cout, " ");
  copy (v1.begin (), v1.end (), iter);
  cout << endl;
  nth_element (v1.begin (),
               v1.begin () + v1.size () / 2,
               v1.end (),
               greater<int>());
  copy (v1.begin (), v1.end (), iter);
  cout << endl;
  return 0;
}

6 0 2 0 6 7 5 5 8 6
6 8 7 6 6 5 5 2 0 0
```

os_binary_search

Synopsis:
Locate an item in a sorted container.

Declaration:
```
template< class Container, class T >
bool os_binary_search( const Container& c, const T& value )
```

Description:
A helper algorithm for `binary_search()`. Return `true` if `value` is in the container `c`. This algorithm assumes that the elements in the container are already sorted using `operator<`.

Complexity:
See `binary_search()`.

Example <ospace/stl/examples/obinsch0.cpp>

```
#include <stl.h>
#include <iostream.h>

int main ()
{
  vector<int> v;
  for (int i = 0; i < 100; i++)
    v.push_back (i);
  if (os_binary_search (v, 42))
    cout << "found 42" << endl;
  else
    cout << "did not find 42" << endl;
  return 0;
}
```

found 42

os_count

Synopsis:

Count items in a container that match a value.

Declaration:
```
template< class Container, class T >
int os_count( const Container& c, const T& value )
```

Description:

A helper algorithm for `count()`. Return the number of elements in the container `c` that match `value` using `operator==`.

Complexity:

See `count()`.

Example <ospace/stl/examples/ocount0.cpp>
```
#include <stl.h>
#include <iostream.h>

int numbers[10] = { 1, 2, 4, 1, 2, 4, 1, 2, 4, 1 };

int main ()
{
  vector<int> v (numbers, numbers + 10 );
  int result = os_count (v, 1);
  cout << "Found " << result << " 1's." << endl;
  return 0;
}
```

```
Found 4 1's.
```

os_count_if

Synopsis:

Count items in a container that satisfy a predicate.

Declaration:

```
template< class Container, class Predicate >
int os_count_if( const Container& c, Predicate pred )
```

Description:

A helper algorithm for count_if(). Return the number of elements in container c that cause predicate pred to return true.

Complexity:

See count_if().

Example <ospace/stl/examples/ocntif0.cpp>

```
#include <stl.h>
#include <iostream.h>

int odd (int a)
{
  return a % 2;
}

int main ()
{
#ifdef OS_NO_FN_WITH_ARG_IN_TEMPLATE
  cout << "your compiler cannot compile this example" << endl;
#else
  vector <int> numbers(100);
  for (int i = 0; i < 100; i++)
    numbers[i] = i % 3;
  int elements = os_count_if (numbers, odd);
  cout << "Found " << elements << " odd elements." << endl;
#endif
  return 0;
}
```

Found 33 odd elements.

os_erase

Synopsis:
Erases all matching items from a container.

Declaration:
```
template< class Container, class T >
void os_erase( Container& c, const T& value )
```

Description:
A helper algorithm for remove(). Erase all occurrences of value from the container c.
Unlike remove(), the size of the container decreases by the number of items that are erased.

Complexity:
See remove().

Example <ospace/stl/examples/remove1.cpp>
```
#include <stl.h>
#include <iostream.h>

int numbers[6] = { 1, 2, 3, 1, 2, 3 };

int main ()
{
  vector<int> v (numbers, numbers + 6);
  os_erase (v, 1);
  vector<int>::iterator i;
  for (i = v.begin(); i != v.end(); i++)
    cout << *i << ' ';
  cout << endl;
  return 0;
}

2 3 2 3 2 3
```

os_erase_if

Synopsis:
Erases items from a container that satisfy a predicate.

Declaration:
```
template< class Container, class Predicate >
void os_erase_if( Container& c, Predicate pred )
```

Description:
A helper algorithm for `remove_if()`. Erase all elements that satisfy `pred` from the container `c`. Unlike `remove_if()`, the size of the container decreases by the number of elements that are erased.

Complexity:
See `remove_if()`.

Example <ospace/stl/examples/remif1.cpp>
```
#include <stl.h>
#include <iostream.h>

bool odd (int a)
{
  return a % 2;
}

int numbers[6] = { 0, 0, 1, 1, 2, 2 };

int main ()
{
#ifdef OS_NO_FN_WITH_ARG_IN_TEMPLATE
  cout << "your compiler cannot compile this example" << endl;
#else
  vector<int> v (numbers, numbers + 6);
  os_erase_if (v, odd);
  vector<int>::iterator i;
  for (i = v.begin(); i != v.end(); i++)
    cout << *i << ' ';
  cout << endl;
#endif
  return 0;
}

0 0 2 2 2 2
```

os_find

Synopsis:
Locate an item in a container.

Declaration:
```
template <class Container, class T>
void os_find( Container& c, const T& value, T*& result )
```

Description:
A helper algorithm for `find()`. Searches for an element in `c` that matches `value` using `operator==`. Sets `result` to point to the first matching element, or 0 if no match is found.

Complexity:
See `find()`.

Example <ospace/stl/examples/ofind0.cpp>
```
#include <stl.h>
#include <iostream.h>

int numbers[9] = { 0, 1, 4, 9, 16, 25, 36, 49, 64 };

int main ()
{
  vector<int> v (numbers, numbers + 9);
  int* location = 0;
  os_find (v, 25, location);
  if (location)
    cout << "Found " << *location << endl;
  return 0;
}
```

```
Found 25
```

os_find_if

Synopsis:
Locate an item that satisfies a predicate in a container.

Declaration:
```
template< class Container, class Predicate, class T >
void os_find_if( Container& c, Predicate pred, T*& result )
```

Description:
A helper algorithm for `find_if()`. Set `result` to point to the first element in `c` that causes `pred` to return `true`, or 0 if no such element exists.

Complexity:
See `find_if()`.

Example <ospace/stl/examples/ofindif0.cpp>

```
#include <stl.h>
#include <iostream.h>

bool odd (int a)
{
  return a % 2;
}

int numbers[6] = { 2, 4, 8, 15, 32, 64 };

int main ()
{
#ifdef OS_NO_FN_WITH_ARG_IN_TEMPLATE
  cout << "your compiler cannot compile this example" << endl;
#else
  vector<int> v (numbers, numbers + 6);
  int* location = 0;
  os_find_if (v, odd, location);
  if (location)
    cout << "Found " << *location << endl;
#endif
  return 0;
}
```

```
Found 15
```

os_for_each

Synopsis:
Apply a function to every item in a container.

Declaration:
```
template< class Container, class Function >
Function os_for_each( Container& c, Function f )
```

Description:
A helper algorithm for `for_each()`. Apply `f` to every element in `c` and return the input parameter `f`.

Complexity:
See `for_each()`.

Example <ospace/stl/examples/oforech0.cpp>
```
#include <stl.h>
#include <iostream.h>

void print (int a)
{
  cout << a << ' ';
}

int numbers[10] = { 1, 1, 2, 3, 5, 8, 13, 21, 34, 55 };

int main ()
{
#ifdef OS_NO_FN_WITH_ARG_IN_TEMPLATE
  cout << "your compiler cannot compile this example" << endl;
#else
  vector<int> v (numbers, numbers + 10);
  os_for_each (v, print);
  cout << endl;
#endif
  return 0;
}

1 1 2 3 5 8 13 21 34 55
```

os_includes

Synopsis:

Search for one container in another container.

Declaration:

```
template< class Container >
bool os_includes( const Container& c1, const Container& c2 )

template< class Container, class Compare >
bool os_includes
  (
  const Container& c1,
  const Container& c2,
  Compare compare
  )
```

Description:

A helper algorithm for `includes()`. Search for one container in another container. Return `true` if the container `c1` is embedded in container `c2`. The first version assumes that both sequences are already sorted using `operator<`. The second version assumes that both sequences are already sorted using `compare`.

Complexity:

See `includes()`.

Example <ospace/stl/examples/oincl0.cpp>

```cpp
#include <stl.h>
#include <iostream.h>

int numbers1[5] = { 1, 2, 3, 4, 5 };
int numbers2[5] = { 1, 2, 4, 8, 16 };
int numbers3[2] = { 4, 8 };

int main ()
{
  vector<int> v1 (numbers1, numbers1 + 5 );
  vector<int> v2 (numbers2, numbers2 + 5 );
  vector<int> v3 (numbers3, numbers3 + 2 );
  if (os_includes (v1, v3))
    cout << "numbers1 includes numbers3" << endl;
  else
    cout << "numbers1 does not include numbers3" << endl;
  if (os_includes (v2, v3))
    cout << "numbers2 includes numbers3" << endl;
  else
    cout << "numbers2 does not include numbers3" << endl;
  return 0;
}
```

```
numbers1 does not include numbers3
numbers2 includes numbers3
```

os_max_element, os_max_element_value

Synopsis:
Find the maximum element in a container.

Declaration:
```
template< class Container, class T >
void os_max_element( const Container& c, T*& t )

template< class Container, class T >
bool os_max_element_value( const Container& c, T& t )
```

Description:
Helper algorithms for max_element (). The first version sets t to point to the maximum element of c, or 0 if c is empty. If c is not empty, the second version sets t to the maximum element of c and returns true, otherwise it returns false.

Complexity:
See max_element ().

Example <ospace/stl/examples/omaxelm0.cpp>

```
#include <stl.h>
#include <iostream.h>

int numbers[6] = { -10, 15, -100, 36, -242, 42 };

int main ()
{
  vector<int> v (numbers, numbers + 6);
  int* ptr;
  os_max_element (v, ptr);
  if (ptr)
    cout << "maximum = " << *ptr << endl;;
  int value;
  bool result = os_max_element_value (v, value);
  if (result)
    cout << "maximum = " << value << endl;
  return 0;
}

maximum 42
maximum 42
```

os_min_element, os_min_element_value

Synopsis:

Find the minimum item in a container.

Declaration:
```
template< class Container, class T >
void os_min_element( const Container& c, T*& t )

template< class Container, class T >
bool os_min_element_value( const Container& c, T& t )
```

Description:

Helper algorithms for `min_element()`. The first version sets `t` to point to the minimum element of `c`, or 0 if `c` is empty. If `c` is not empty, the second version sets `t` to the minimum element of `c` and returns `true`, otherwise it returns `false`.

Complexity:

See `min_element()`.

Example <ospace/stl/examples/ominelm0.cpp>
```
#include <stl.h>
#include <iostream.h>

int numbers[6] = { -10, 15, -100, 36, -242, 42 };

int main ()
{
  vector<int> v (numbers, numbers + 6);
  int* ptr;
  os_min_element (v, ptr);
  if (ptr)
    cout << "minimum = " << *ptr << endl;;
  int value;
  bool result = os_min_element_value (v, value);
  if (result)
    cout << "minimum = " << value << endl;
  return 0;
}

minimum = -242
minimum = -242
```

os_random_shuffle

Synopsis:
Randomize a container using random shuffles.

Declaration:
```
template< class Container >
void os_random_shuffle( Container& c )
```

Description:
A helper algorithm for `random_shuffle()`. Shuffle all elements in the container `c` using uniformly selected random swaps. Use `operator=` to perform the swaps.

Complexity:
See `random_shuffle()`.

Example <ospace/stl/examples/orndshf0.cpp>

```
#include <stl.h>
#include <iostream.h>

int numbers[6] = { 1, 2, 3, 4, 5, 6 };

int main ()
{
  vector<int> v (numbers, numbers + 6);
  os_random_shuffle (v);
  for (int i = 0; i < v.size(); i++)
    cout << v[i] << ' ';
  cout << endl;
  return 0;
}

3 1 6 2 4 5
```

os_release

Synopsis:

Deletes a container of heap-based objects.

Declaration:
```
template< class Container >
void os_release( Container& c )
```

Description:

Calls operator `delete` on every item in the container. Assume that each item is a pointer to a heap-based object. If more than one item points to the same heap-based object, an error will most probably occur.

Complexity:

Time Complexity: is linear. Space Complexity: is constant.

Example <ospace/stl/examples/oreleas0.cpp>

```
#include <stl.h>
#include <iostream.h>

class X
{
  public:
    X (int i) : i (i) {}
    ~X () { cout << "Delete X(" << i << ")" << endl; }
    int i;
};

ostream& operator<< (ostream& stream, const X& x)
{
  return stream << "X(" << x.i << ")";
}

int main ()
{
  vector<X*> v;
  v.push_back (new X (2));
  v.push_back (new X (1));
  v.push_back (new X (4));
  vector<X*>::iterator i;
  for (i = v.begin (); i != v.end (); i++)
    cout << *(*i) << endl;
  os_release (v); // Delete all heap-based objects in container.
  return 0;
}
```

X(2)
X(1)
X(4)
Delete X(2)
Delete X(1)
Delete X(4)

os_replace

Synopsis:
Replace a specified value in a sequence with another value.

Declaration:
```
template< class Container, class T >
void os_replace( Container& c, const T& old, const T& new )
```

Description:
A helper algorithm for `replace()`. Replaces every occurrence of `old` in the container `c` with `new`.

Complexity:
See `replace()`.

Example <ospace/stl/examples/oreplac0.cpp>
```
#include <stl.h>
#include <iostream.h>

int numbers[6] = { 0, 1, 2, 0, 1, 2 };

int main ()
{
  vector<int> v (numbers, numbers + 6);
  os_replace (v, 2, 42);
  vector<int>::iterator i;
  for (i = v.begin(); i != v.end(); i++)
    cout << *i << ' ';
  cout << endl;
  return 0;
}

0 1 42 0 1 42
```

os_replace_if

Synopsis:
Replace specified values that satisfy a predicate.

Declaration:
```
template< class Container, class Predicate, class T >
void os_replace_if( Container& c, Predicate pred, const T& value )
```

Description:
A helper algorithm for `replace_if()`. Replaces every element in the container `c` that satisfies `pred` with `new_value`.

Complexity:
See `replace_if()`.

Example <ospace/stl/examples/oreplif1.cpp>
```
#include <stl.h>

bool odd (int a)
{
  return a % 2;
}

int main ()
{
#ifdef OS_NO_FN_WITH_ARG_IN_TEMPLATE
  cout << "your compiler cannot compile this example" << endl;
#else
  vector<int> v1 (10);
  for (int i = 0; i < v1.size (); i++)
  {
    v1[i] = i % 5;
    cout << v1[i] << ' ';
  }
  cout << endl;
  os_replace_if (v1, odd, 42);
  for (i = 0; i < v1.size (); i++)
    cout << v1[i] << ' ';
  cout << endl;
#endif
  return 0;
}

0 1 2 3 4 0 1 2 3 4
0 42 2 42 4 0 42 2 42 4
```

os_rotate

Synopsis:
Rotate a sequence by n positions.

Declaration:
```
template< class Container >
void os_rotate( Container& c, int n )
```

Description:
A helper algorithm for `rotate()`. If n is positive, rotate the container to the right by n positions, otherwise rotate the container to the left by n positions.

Complexity:
See `rotate()`.

Example <ospace/stl/examples/orotate0.cpp>

```
#include <stl.h>
#include <iostream.h>

int numbers[6] = { 0, 1, 2, 3, 4, 5 };

int main ()
{
  vector<int> v (numbers, numbers + 6);
  os_rotate (v, 3);
  vector<int>::iterator i;
  for (i = v.begin(); i != v.end(); i++)
    cout << *i << ' ';
  cout << endl;
  return 0;
}
```

```
3 4 5 0 1 2
```

os_sort

Synopsis:
Sort a sequence

Declaration:
```
template< class Container >
void os_sort( Container& c )

template< class Container, class Compare >
void os_sort( Container& c, Compare compare )
```

Description:
Helper algorithms for sort(). Sort all elements in the container c into ascending order. The first version uses operator< to compare elements, whereas the second version uses the binary function compare.

Complexity:
See sort().

Example <ospace/stl/examples/osort0.cpp>
```
#include <stl.h>
#include <iostream.h>

int array[6] = { 1, 50, -10, 11, 42, 19 };

int main ()
{
  vector<int> v (array, array + 6);
  os_sort (v);
  for (int i = 0; i < v.size(); i++)
    cout << v[i] << ' ';
  cout << endl;
  return 0;
}
```

-10 1 11 19 42 50

Example <ospace/stl/examples/osort1.cpp>
```
#include <stl.h>
#include <iostream.h>

int array[] = { 1, 50, -10, 11, 42, 19 };

int main ()
```

```
{
  vector<int> v (array, array + 6);
  os_sort (v, greater<int> ());
  for (int i = 0; i < v.size(); i++)
    cout << v[i] << ' ';
  cout << endl;
  return 0;
}
```

50 42 19 11 1 -10

partial_sort

Synopsis:

Sort the smallest N elements of a sequence.

Declaration:

```
template< class RandomAccessIterator >
void partial_sort
   (
   RandomAccessIterator first,
   RandomAccessIterator middle,
   RandomAccessIterator last
   )

template< class RandomAccessIterator, class Compare >
void partial_sort
   (
   RandomAccessIterator first,
   RandomAccessIterator middle,
   RandomAccessIterator last,
   Compare compare
   )
```

Description:

Sort the first N elements in the range `[first..last)` where N = `middle - first`. The remaining elements in the range `[first..last)` end up in an undefined order in the range `[middle..last)`. The first version performs the sort using `operator<`, whereas the second version uses the binary function `compare`.

Complexity:

Time Complexity: is `(last - first) * log(N)`. Space Complexity: is constant.

Example <ospace/stl/examples/parsrt0.cpp>

```
#include <stl.h>
#include <iostream.h>

int numbers[6] = { 5, 2, 4, 3, 1, 6 };

int main ()
{
  partial_sort (numbers, numbers + 3, numbers + 6);
  for (int i = 0; i < 6; i++)
    cout << numbers[i] << ' ';
  cout << endl;
  return 0;
}
```

```
1 2 3 5 4 6
```

Example <ospace/stl/examples/parsrt1.cpp>

```
#include <stl.h>
#include <iostream.h>

int main ()
{
  vector <int> v1 (10);
  for (int i = 0; i < v1.size (); i++)
    v1[i] = rand () % 10;
  ostream_iterator<int> iter (cout, " ");
  copy (v1.begin (), v1.end (), iter);
  cout << endl;
  partial_sort (v1.begin (),
                v1.begin () + v1.size () / 2,
                v1.end ());
  copy (v1.begin (), v1.end (), iter);
  cout << endl;
  return 0;
}
```

```
6 0 2 0 6 7 5 5 8 6
0 0 2 5 5 7 6 6 8 6
```

Example <ospace/stl/examples/parsrt2.cpp>

```
#include <stl.h>
#include <iostream.h>
#include <string.h>

bool str_compare (const char* a, const char* b)
{
  return ::strcmp (a, b) < 0 ? 1 : 0;
}

char* names[] = { "aa", "ff", "dd", "ee", "cc", "bb" };

int main ()
{
  const unsigned nameSize = sizeof (names) / sizeof (names[0]);
  vector <char*> v1 (nameSize);
  for (int i = 0; i < v1.size (); i++)
    v1[i] = names[i];
  ostream_iterator<char*> iter (cout, " ");
  copy (v1.begin (), v1.end (), iter);
  cout << endl;
  partial_sort (v1.begin (),
                v1.begin () + nameSize / 2,
                v1.end (),
                str_compare);
  copy (v1.begin (), v1.end (), iter);
  cout << endl;
  return 0;
}
```

aa ff dd ee cc bb
aa dd ff ee cc bb

partial_sort_copy

Synopsis:
   Sort the smallest N elements of a sequence and copy the result.

Declaration:
```
template< class InputIterator, class RandomAccessIterator >
RandomAccessIterator partial_sort_copy
   (
   InputIterator first,
   InputIterator last,
   RandomAccessIterator result_first,
   RandomAccessIterator result_last
   )

template
   <
   class InputIterator,
   class RandomAccessIterator,
   class Compare
   >
RandomAccessIterator partial_sort_copy
   (
   InputIterator first,
   InputIterator last,
   RandomAccessIterator result_first,
   RandomAccessIterator result_last,
   Compare compare
   )
```

Description:
   Sort the first N elements of `[first..last)` where `N = min((last - first),`
   `(result_last - result_first))` and place the result into
   `[result_first..result_first + N)`. Return the smaller of `result_last` or
   `result_first + n` where `n = last - first`. The first version sorts the elements using
   `operator<`, whereas the second version uses the binary function `compare`.

Complexity:
   Time Complexity: is `(last - first) * log(N)`. Space Complexity: is constant.

partial_sort_copy

Example <ospace/stl/examples/parsrtc0.cpp>

```
#include <stl.h>
#include <iostream.h>

int numbers[6] = { 5, 2, 4, 3, 1, 6 };

int main ()
{
  int result[3];
  partial_sort_copy (numbers, numbers + 6, result, result + 3);
  for (int i = 0; i < 3; i++)
    cout << result[i] << ' ';
  cout << endl;
  return 0;
}
```

1 2 3

Example <ospace/stl/examples/parsrtc1.cpp>

```
#include <stl.h>
#include <iostream.h>

int main ()
{
  vector <int> v1 (10);
  for (int i = 0; i < v1.size (); i++)
    v1[i] = rand () % 10;
  vector <int> result (5);
  ostream_iterator<int> iter (cout, " ");
  copy (v1.begin (), v1.end (), iter);
  cout << endl;
  partial_sort_copy (v1.begin (),
                     v1.end (),
                     result.begin (),
                     result.end ());
  copy (result.begin (), result.end (), iter);
  cout << endl;
  return 0;
}
```

6 0 2 0 6 7 5 5 8 6
0 0 2 5 5

Example <ospace/stl/examples/parsrtc2.cpp>

```
#include <stl.h>
#include <iostream.h>
#include <string.h>

bool str_compare (const char* a, const char* b)
{
  return ::strcmp (a, b) < 0 ? 1 : 0;
}

char* names[] = { "aa", "ff", "dd", "ee", "cc", "bb" };

int main ()
{
  const unsigned nameSize = sizeof (names) / sizeof (names[0]);
  vector <char*> v1 (nameSize);
  for (int i = 0; i < v1.size (); i++)
    v1[i] = names[i];
  ostream_iterator<char*> iter (cout, " ");
  copy (v1.begin (), v1.end (), iter);
  cout << endl;
  vector <char*> result (5);
  partial_sort_copy (v1.begin (),
                     v1.end (),
                     result.begin (),
                     result.end (),
                     str_compare);
  copy (v1.begin (), v1.end (), iter);
  cout << endl;
  return 0;
}
```

aa ff dd ee cc bb
aa ff dd ee cc bb

partial_sum

Synopsis:

Fill a range with a running total.

Declaration:
```
template< class InputIterator, class OutputIterator >
OutputIterator partial_sum
  (
  InputIterator first,
  InputIterator last,
  OutputIterator result
  )

template
  <
  class InputIterator,
  class OutputIterator,
  class BinaryOperation
  >
OutputIterator partial_sum
  (
  InputIterator first,
  InputIterator last,
  OutputIterator result,
  BinaryOperation binary_op
  )
```

Description:

Assign to `(result + N)` the running total `first..(first + N)`, where `N = (last - first)`, and return an iterator positioned immediately after the last element in `result`. The first version uses `operator+` to perform the summation, whereas the second version uses the binary function `binary_op`.

Complexity:

Space Complexity: is constant. Time Complexity: is linear as `(last - first)` applications of either `operator+` or `binary_op` are performed.

Example <ospace/stl/examples/partsum0.cpp>

```
#include <stl.h>
#include <iostream.h>

int numbers[6] = { 1, 2, 3, 4, 5, 6 };

int main ()
{
  int result[6];
  partial_sum (numbers, numbers + 6, result);
  for (int i = 0; i < 6; i ++)
    cout << result[i] << ' ';
  cout << endl;
  return 0;
}
```

1 3 6 10 15 21

Example <ospace/stl/examples/partsum1.cpp>

```
#include <stl.h>
#include <iostream.h>

int main ()
{
  vector <int> v1 (10);
  iota (v1.begin (), v1.end (), 0);
  vector <int> v2 (v1.size());
  partial_sum (v1.begin (), v1.end (), v2.begin ());
  ostream_iterator <int> iter (cout, " ");
  copy (v1.begin (), v1.end (), iter);
  cout << endl;
  copy (v2.begin (), v2.end (), iter);
  cout << endl;
  return 0;
}
```

0 1 2 3 4 5 6 7 8 9
0 1 3 6 10 15 21 28 36 45

Example <ospace/stl/examples/partsum2.cpp>

```
#include <stl.h>
#include <iostream.h>

int main ()
{
  vector <int> v1 (5);
  iota (v1.begin (), v1.end (), 1);
  vector <int> v2 (v1.size());
  partial_sum (v1.begin (), v1.end (), v2.begin (), times<int>());
  ostream_iterator <int> iter (cout, " ");
  copy (v1.begin (), v1.end (), iter);
  cout << endl;
  copy (v2.begin (), v2.end (), iter);
  cout << endl;
  return 0;
}

1 2 3 4 5
1 2 6 24 120
```

partition

Synopsis:

Partition a range using a predicate.

Declaration:

```
template< class BidirectionalIterator, class Predicate >
BidirectionalIterator partition
  (
  BidirectionalIterator first,
  BidirectionalIterator last,
  Predicate pred
  )
```

Description:

Place all elements in the range `[first..last)` that make `pred` evaluate to `true` before all elements in the range that make `pred` evaluate to `false`. Return an iterator positioned at the first element of the second sequence.

Complexity:

Time Complexity: is O(N), where N = `(last - first)`, as `pred` will be evaluated N times and at most N / 2 swaps will be performed.

Example <ospace/stl/examples/ptition0.cpp>

```
#include <stl.h>
#include <iostream.h>

int less_10 (int a)
{
  return a < 10 ? 1 : 0;
}

int numbers[6] = { 6, 12, 3, 10, 1, 20 };

int main ()
{
  partition (numbers, numbers + 6, less_10);
  for (int i = 0; i < 6; i++)
    cout << numbers[i] << ' ';
  cout << endl;
  return 0;
}

6 1 3 10 12 20
```

partition

Example <ospace/stl/examples/ptition1.cpp>

```
#include <stl.h>
#include <iostream.h>

int main ()
{
  vector <int> v1 (10);
  for (int i = 0; i < v1.size (); i++)
    v1[i] = rand () % 20;
  ostream_iterator <int> iter (cout, " ");
  copy (v1.begin (), v1.end (), iter);
  cout << endl;
  partition (v1.begin (), v1.end (), bind2nd(less<int>(), 11));
  copy (v1.begin (), v1.end (), iter);
  cout << endl;
  return 0;
}

6 10 2 10 16 17 15 15 8 6
6 10 2 10 6 8 15 15 17 16
```

pop_heap

Synopsis:

Pop the top element from a heap.

Declaration:
```
template< class RandomAccessIterator >
void pop_heap
  (
  RandomAccessIterator first,
  RandomAccessIterator last
  )

template< class RandomAccessIterator, class Compare >
void pop_heap
  (
  RandomAccessIterator first,
  RandomAccessIterator last,
  Compare compare
  )
```

Description:

Starting with [first..last) as a heap, swap the first and last elements on the heap [first..last) and then make [first..(last - 1)) a heap. The first version uses operator< to perform the comparisons, whereas the second version uses the binary function compare.

Complexity:

Time Complexity: is 2 * log (last - first). Space Complexity: is constant.

Examples:

See make_heap().

prev_permutation

Synopsis:

Change a sequence to its previous lexicographical permutation.

Declaration:
```
template< class BidirectionalIterator >
bool prev_permutation
  (
  BidirectionalIterator first,
  BidirectionalIterator last
  )

template< class BidirectionalIterator, class Compare >
bool prev_permutation
  (
  BidirectionalIterator first,
  BidirectionalIterator last,
  Compare compare
  )
```

Description:

Arrange the sequence [first..last) to be its previous permutation and return `true`. If there is no previous permutation, arrange the sequence to be the last permutation and return `false`. The first version orders the permutations using `operator<`, whereas the second version uses the binary function `compare`.

Complexity:

Time Complexity: is linear. Space Complexity: is constant.

Example <ospace/stl/examples/prevprm0.cpp>

```
#include <stl.h>
#include <iostream.h>

int v1[3] = { 0, 1, 2 };

int main ()
{
  prev_permutation (v1, v1 + 3);
  for (int i = 0; i < 3; i++)
    cout << v1[i] << ' ';
  cout << endl;
  return 0;
}
```

```
2 1 0
```

Example <ospace/stl/examples/prevprm1.cpp>

```
#include <stl.h>
#include <iostream.h>

int main ()
{
  vector <int> v1 (3);
  iota (v1.begin (), v1.end (), 0);
  ostream_iterator<int> iter (cout, " ");
  copy (v1.begin (), v1.end (), iter);
  cout << endl;
  for (int i = 0; i < 9; i++)
  {
    prev_permutation (v1.begin (), v1.end ());
    copy (v1.begin (), v1.end (), iter);
    cout << endl;
  }
  return 0;
}
```

```
0 1 2
2 1 0
2 0 1
1 2 0
1 0 2
0 2 1
0 1 2
2 1 0
2 0 1
1 2 0
```

Example <ospace/stl/examples/prevprm2.cpp>

```cpp
#include <stl.h>
#include <iostream.h>

int main ()
{
  vector <int> v1 (3);
  iota (v1.begin (), v1.end (), 0);
  ostream_iterator<int> iter (cout, " ");
  copy (v1.begin (), v1.end (), iter);
  cout << endl;
  for (int i = 0; i < 9; i++)
  {
    prev_permutation (v1.begin (), v1.end (), greater<int>());
    copy (v1.begin (), v1.end (), iter);
    cout << endl;
  }
  return 0;
}
```

```
0 1 2
0 2 1
1 0 2
1 2 0
2 0 1
2 1 0
0 1 2
0 2 1
1 0 2
1 2 0
```

push_heap

Synopsis:

Place the last element into a heap.

Declaration:
```
template< class RandomAccessIterator >
void push_heap
  (
  RandomAccessIterator first,
  RandomAccessIterator last
  )

template< class RandomAccessIterator, class Compare >
void push_heap
  (
  RandomAccessIterator first,
  RandomAccessIterator last,
  Compare compare
  )
```

Description:

Starting with the heap `[first..(last_-1))`, insert the element referenced by `last` into the heap `[first..(last - 1)]` so that `[first..last)` is a heap. The first version uses `operator<` to perform comparisons, whereas the second version uses the binary function `compare`.

Complexity:

Time Complexity: is O(log(N)), where N is the size of the heap. Space Complexity: is constant.

Example <ospace/stl/examples/pheap1.cpp>

```
#include <stl.h>
#include <iostream.h>

int main ()
{
  vector<int> v;
  v.push_back (1);
  v.push_back (20);
  v.push_back (4);
  make_heap (v.begin (), v.end ());
  v.push_back (7);
  push_heap (v.begin (), v.end ());
  sort_heap (v.begin (), v.end ());
  ostream_iterator<int> iter (cout, " ");
  copy (v.begin (), v.end (), iter);
  cout << endl;
  return 0;
}
```

1 4 20
1 4 7 20

Examples <ospace/stl/examples/pheap2.cpp>

```
#include <stl.h>
#include <iostream.h>

int main ()
{
  vector<int> v;
  v.push_back (1);
  v.push_back (20);
  v.push_back (4);
  make_heap (v.begin (), v.end (), greater<int> ());
  v.push_back (7);
  push_heap (v.begin (), v.end (), greater<int> ());
  sort_heap (v.begin (), v.end (), greater<int> ());
  ostream_iterator<int> iter (cout, " ");
  copy (v.begin (), v.end (), iter);
  cout << endl;

  return 0;
}
```

20 7 4 1

random_shuffle

Synopsis:
Randomize a sequence using random shuffles.

Declaration:
```
template< class RandomAccessIterator >
void random_shuffle
  (
  RandomAccessIterator first,
  RandomAccessIterator last
  )

template< class RandomAccessIterator, class RandomNumberGenerator >
void random_shuffle
  (
  RandomAccessIterator first,
  RandomAccessIterator last,
  RandomNumberGenerator& rand
  )
```

Description:
Shuffle all elements in the sequence `[first..last)` using uniformly selected random swaps. Use `operator=` to perform the swaps. The first version uses an internal random number generator to generate the indices of the elements to swap, whereas the second version uses the random number generator `rand`. `rand` must be a random number generator that takes a parameter `n` and returns a integral random number between 0 and `(n - 1)`.

Complexity:
Time Complexity: is linear as `(last - first)` swaps are performed. Space Complexity: is constant.

Helper:
```
void os_random_shuffle( Container& c )
```

Example <ospace/stl/examples/rndshuf0.cpp>

```cpp
#include <stl.h>
#include <iostream.h>

int numbers[6] = { 1, 2, 3, 4, 5, 6 };

int main ()
{
  random_shuffle (numbers, numbers + 6);
  for (int i = 0; i < 6; i++)
    cout << numbers[i] << ' ';
  cout << endl;
  return 0;
}
```

3 1 6 2 4 5

Example <ospace/stl/examples/rndshuf1.cpp>

```cpp
#include <stl.h>
#include <iostream.h>

int main ()
{
  vector <int> v1(10);
  iota (v1.begin (), v1.end (), 0);
  ostream_iterator <int> iter (cout, " ");
  copy (v1.begin (), v1.end (), iter);
  cout << endl;
  for (int i = 0; i < 3; i++)
  {
    random_shuffle (v1.begin (), v1.end ());
    copy (v1.begin (), v1.end (), iter);
    cout << endl;
  }
  return 0;
}
```

```
0 1 2 3 4 5 6 7 8 9
2 8 9 1 3 4 0 7 6 5
2 5 3 1 4 8 7 6 0 9
8 1 3 6 7 9 2 5 0 4
```

Example <ospace/stl/examples/rndshuf2.cpp>

```cpp
#include <stl.h>
#include <iostream.h>

class MyRandomGenerator
{
  public:
    unsigned long operator () (unsigned long n);
};

unsigned long
MyRandomGenerator::operator () (unsigned long n)
{
  return time(0) % n;
}

int main ()
{
  vector <int> v1(10);
  iota (v1.begin (), v1.end (), 0);
  ostream_iterator <int> iter (cout, " ");
  copy (v1.begin (), v1.end (), iter);
  cout << endl;

  for (int i = 0; i < 3; i++)
  {
    random_shuffle (v1.begin (), v1.end (), MyRandomGenerator());
    copy (v1.begin (), v1.end (), iter);
    cout << endl;
  }

  return 0;
}
```

```
0 1 2 3 4 5 6 7 8 9
5 0 7 1 9 2 8 3 4 6
2 5 3 0 6 7 4 1 9 8
7 2 1 5 8 3 9 0 6 4
```

remove

Synopsis:
Remove all matching items from a sequence.

Declaration:
```
template< class ForwardIterator, class T >
ForwardIterator remove
  (
  ForwardIterator first,
  ForwardIterator last,
  const T& value
  )
```

Description:
Remove all occurrences of `value` from the sequence `[first..last)`. Return an iterator equal to `last - n` where n = number of elements removed. The size of the container is not altered; if n elements are removed, the last n elements of the sequence `[first..last)` will have undefined values.

Complexity:
Time Complexity: is linear, as `(last - first)` comparisons are performed. Space Complexity: is constant.

Helper:
```
void os_erase( Container& c, const T& t )
```

Example <ospace/stl/examples/remove1.cpp>
```
#include <stl.h>
#include <iostream.h>

int numbers[6] = { 1, 2, 3, 1, 2, 3 };

int main ()
{
  remove (numbers, numbers + 6, 1);
  for (int i = 0; i < 6; i++)
    cout << numbers[i] << ' ';
  cout << endl;
  return 0;
}

2 3 2 3 2 3
```

remove_copy

Synopsis:
Copy a sequence, removing all matching items.

Declaration:
```
template< class InputIterator, class OutputIterator, class T >
OutputIterator remove_copy
   (
   InputIterator first,
   InputIterator last,
   OutputIterator result,
   const T& value
   )
```

Description:
Copy the sequence [first..last) to a sequence starting at result, skipping any occurrences of value. Return an iterator positioned immediately after the last new element.

Complexity:
Time Complexity: is linear, as (last - first) comparisons are performed. Space Complexity: is constant.

Example <ospace/stl/examples/remcopy1.cpp>

```cpp
#include <stl.h>
#include <iostream.h>

int numbers[6] = { 1, 2, 3, 1, 2, 3 };
int result[6] = { 0, 0, 0, 0, 0, 0 };

int main ()
{
  remove_copy (numbers, numbers + 6, result, 2);
  for (int i = 0; i < 6; i++)
    cout << result[i] << ' ';
  cout << endl;
  return 0;
}
```

```
1 3 1 3 0 0
```

remove_copy_if

Synopsis:

Copy a sequence, removing all items that satisfy a predicate.

Declaration:
```
template< class InputIterator, class OutputIterator, class Predicate >
OutputIterator remove_copy_if
    (
    InputIterator first,
    InputIterator last,
    OutputIterator result,
    Predicate pred
    )
```

Description:

Copy the sequence `[first..last)` to a sequence starting at `result`, skipping any elements that satisfy `pred`. Return an iterator positioned immediately after the last new element.

Complexity:

Time Complexity: is linear, as `(last - first)` comparisons are performed. Space Complexity: is constant.

Example <ospace/stl/examples/remcpif1.cpp>

```cpp
#include <stl.h>
#include <iostream.h>

bool odd (int a)
{
  return a % 2;
}

int numbers[6] = { 1, 2, 3, 1, 2, 3 };
int result[6] = { 0, 0, 0, 0, 0, 0 };

int main ()
{
  remove_copy_if (numbers, numbers + 6, result, odd);
  for (int i = 0; i < 6; i++)
    cout << result[i] << ' ';
  cout << endl;
  return 0;
}
```

2 2 0 0 0 0

remove_if

Synopsis:

Remove items from a sequence that satisfy a predicate.

Declaration:
```
template< class ForwardIterator, class Predicate >
ForwardIterator remove_if
   (
   ForwardIterator first,
   ForwardIterator last,
   Predicate pred
   )
```

Description:

Remove all elements that satisfy `pred` from the sequence `[first..last)`. Return an iterator equal to `first + n` where n = number of elements removed. The size of the container is not altered; if n elements are removed, the last n elements of the sequence `[first..last)` will have undefined values.

Complexity:

Time Complexity: is linear, as `(last - first)` comparisons are performed. Space Complexity: is constant.

Helper:
```
void os_erase_if( Container& c, Predicate p )
```

Example <ospace/stl/examples/remif1.cpp>

```
#include <stl.h>
#include <iostream.h>

bool odd (int a)
{
  return a % 2;
}

int numbers[6] = { 0, 0, 1, 1, 2, 2 };

int main ()
{
  remove_if (numbers, numbers + 6, odd);
  for (int i = 0; i < 6; i++)
    cout << numbers[i] << ' ';
  cout << endl;
  return 0;
}

0 0 2 2 2 2
```

replace

Synopsis:

Replace a specified value in a sequence with another value.

Declaration:

```
template< class ForwardIterator, class T >
void replace
  (
  ForwardIterator first,
  ForwardIterator last,
  const T& old_value,
  const T& new_value
  )
```

Description:

Replace every occurrence of `old_value` in the range `[first..last)` with `new_value`.

Complexity:

Time Complexity: is linear, as `(last - first)` comparisons are performed. Space Complexity: is constant.

Helper:

```
void os_replace( Container& c, const T& old, const T& new )
```

Example <ospace/stl/examples/replace0.cpp>

```
#include <stl.h>
#include <iostream.h>

int numbers[6] = { 0, 1, 2, 0, 1, 2 };

int main ()
{
  replace (numbers, numbers + 6, 2, 42);
  for (int i = 0; i < 6; i++)
    cout << numbers[i] << ' ';
  cout << endl;
  return 0;
}
```

0 1 42 0 1 42

replace_copy

Synopsis:

Copy a sequence, replacing matching values.

Declaration:

```
template< class InputIterator, class OutputIterator, class T >
OutputIterator replace_copy
  (
  InputIterator first,
  InputIterator last,
  OutputIterator result,
  const T& old_value,
  const T& new_value
  )
```

Description:

Copy the sequence [first..last) to a sequence of the same size starting at result, replacing all occurrences of old_value with new_value. Return an iterator positioned immediately after the last new element.

Complexity:

Time Complexity: is linear, as (last - first) comparisons are performed. Space Complexity: is constant.

Example <ospace/stl/examples/replcpy1.cpp>

```
#include <stl.h>
#include <iostream.h>

int numbers [6] = { 0, 1, 2, 0, 1, 2 };
int result [6] = { 0, 0, 0, 0, 0, 0 };

int main ()
{
  replace_copy (numbers, numbers + 6, result, 2, 42);
  for (int i = 0; i < 6; i++)
    cout << result[i] << ' ';
  cout << endl;
  return 0;
}
```

```
0 1 42 0 1 42
```

replace_copy_if

Synopsis:

Copy a sequence, replacing values that satisfy a predicate.

Declaration:

```
template
  <
  class InputIterator,
  class OutputIterator,
  class Predicate,
  class T
  >
OutputIterator replace_copy_if
  (
  InputIterator first,
  InputIterator last,
  OutputIterator result,
  Predicate pred,
  const T& new_value
  )
```

Description:

Copy the sequence `[first..last)` to a sequence of the same size starting at `result`, replacing all elements that satisfy `pred` with `new_value`. Return an iterator positioned immediately after the last new element.

Complexity:

Time Complexity: is linear, as `(last - first)` comparisons are performed. Space Complexity: is constant.

Example <ospace/stl/examples/repcpif1.cpp>

```
#include <stl.h>
#include <iostream.h>

bool odd (int a)
{
  return a % 2;
}

int main ()
{
  vector <int> v1 (10);
  for (int i = 0; i < v1.size (); i++)
    v1[i] = i % 5;
  ostream_iterator <int> iter (cout, " ");
  copy (v1.begin (), v1.end (), iter);
  cout << endl;
  vector <int> v2 (v1.size ());
  replace_copy_if (v1.begin (), v1.end (), v2.begin (), odd, 42);
  copy (v1.begin (), v1.end (), iter);
  cout << endl;
  copy (v2.begin (), v2.end (), iter);
  cout << endl;
  return 0;
}

0 1 2 3 4 0 1 2 3 4
0 1 2 3 4 0 1 2 3 4
0 42 2 42 4 0 42 2 42 4
```

replace_if

Synopsis:
Replace specified values that satisfy a predicate.

Declaration:
```
template< class ForwardIterator, class Predicate, class T >
void replace_if
  (
  ForwardIterator first,
  ForwardIterator last,
  Predicate pred,
  const T& new_value
  )
```

Description:
Replace every element in the range [first..last) that satisfy pred with new_value.

Complexity:
Time Complexity: is linear, as (last - first) comparisons are performed. Space Complexity: is constant.

Helper:
```
void os_replace_if( Container& c, Predicate pred, const T& value )
```

Example <ospace/stl/examples/replif1.cpp>

```
#include <stl.h>
#include <iostream.h>

bool odd (int a)
{
  return a % 2;
}

int main ()
{
  vector <int> v1 (10);
  for (int i = 0; i < v1.size (); i++)
  {
    v1[i] = i % 5;
    cout << v1[i] << ' ';
  }
  cout << endl;
  replace_if (v1.begin (), v1.end (), odd, 42);
  for (i = 0; i < v1.size (); i++)
    cout << v1[i] << ' ';
  cout << endl;
  return 0;
}

0 1 2 3 4 0 1 2 3 4
0 42 2 42 4 0 42 2 42 4
```

reverse

Synopsis:
Reverse the items in a sequence.

Declaration:
```
template< class BidirectionalIterator >
void reverse
  (
  BidirectionalIterator first,
  BidirectionalIterator last
  )
```

Description:
Reverse the order of the elements in the range `[first, last)`.

Complexity:
Time Complexity: is linear, as `(last - first)` swaps are performed. Space Complexity: is constant.

Example <ospace/stl/examples/reverse1.cpp>

```
#include <stl.h>
#include <iostream.h>

int numbers[6] = { 0, 1, 2, 3, 4, 5 };

int main ()
{
  reverse (numbers, numbers + 6);
  for (int i = 0; i < 6; i++)
    cout << numbers[i] << ' ';
  cout << endl;
  return 0;
}

5 4 3 2 1 0
```

reverse_copy

Synopsis:

Create a reversed copy of a sequence.

Declaration:

```
template< class BidirectionalIterator, class OutputIterator >
OutputIterator reverse_copy
  (
  BidirectionalIterator first,
  BidirectionalIterator last,
  OutputIterator result
  )
```

Description:

Copy a reverse of the sequence [first..last) into a sequence of the same size, starting at result. Return an iterator positioned immediately after the last new element.

Complexity:

Time Complexity: is linear, as (last - first) assignments are performed. Space Complexity: is constant.

Example <ospace/stl/examples/revcopy1.cpp>

```
#include <stl.h>
#include <iostream.h>

int numbers[6] = { 0, 1, 2, 3, 4, 5 };

int main ()
{
  int result[6];
  reverse_copy (numbers, numbers + 6, result);
  for (int i = 0; i < 6; i++)
    cout << numbers[i] << ' ';
  cout << endl;
  for (i = 0; i < 6; i++)
    cout << result[i] << ' ';
  cout << endl;
  return 0;
}

0 1 2 3 4 5
5 4 3 2 1 0
```

rotate

Synopsis:

Rotate a sequence by n positions.

Declaration:

```
template< class ForwardIterator >
void rotate
  (
  ForwardIterator first,
  ForwardIterator middle,
  ForwardIterator last
  )
```

Description:

Rotate the sequence `[first..last)` to the left by `(middle - first)` positions.

Complexity:

Time Complexity: is linear. Space Complexity: is constant.

Helper:

```
void os_rotate( Container& c, int n )
```

Example <ospace/stl/examples/rotate0.cpp>

```
#include <stl.h>
#include <iostream.h>

int numbers[6] = { 0, 1, 2, 3, 4, 5 };

int main ()
{
  rotate (numbers, numbers + 3, numbers + 6);
  for (int i = 0; i < 6; i++)
    cout << numbers[i] << ' ';
  cout << endl;
  return 0;
}

3 4 5 0 1 2
```

Example <ospace/stl/examples/rotate1.cpp>

```cpp
#include <stl.h>
#include <iostream.h>

int main ()
{
  vector <int> v1 (10);
  iota (v1.begin (), v1.end (), 0);
  ostream_iterator <int> iter (cout, " ");
  copy (v1.begin (), v1.end (), iter);
  cout << endl;
  for (int i = 0; i < v1.size (); i++)
  {
    rotate (v1.begin (), v1.begin () + i, v1.end ());
    ostream_iterator <int> iter (cout, " ");
    copy (v1.begin (), v1.end (), iter);
    cout << endl;
  }
  cout << endl;
  return 0;
}
```

```
0 1 2 3 4 5 6 7 8 9
0 1 2 3 4 5 6 7 8 9
1 2 3 4 5 6 7 8 9 0
3 4 5 6 7 8 9 0 1 2
6 7 8 9 0 1 2 3 4 5
0 1 2 3 4 5 6 7 8 9
5 6 7 8 9 0 1 2 3 4
1 2 3 4 5 6 7 8 9 0
8 9 0 1 2 3 4 5 6 7
6 7 8 9 0 1 2 3 4 5
5 6 7 8 9 0 1 2 3 4
```

rotate_copy

Synopsis:

Copy a sequence, rotating it by n positions.

Declaration:
```
template< class ForwardIterator, class OutputIterator >
OutputIterator rotate_copy
  (
  ForwardIterator first,
  ForwardIterator middle,
  ForwardIterator last,
  OutputIterator result
  )
```

Description:

Perform the same operations as rotate `(first, middle, last)`, except that the result is placed into a sequence of the same size starting at `result`. Return an iterator positioned immediately after the last new element.

Complexity:

Time Complexity: is linear. Space Complexity: is constant.

Example <ospace/stl/examples/rotcopy0.cpp>

```
#include <stl.h>
#include <iostream.h>

int numbers[6] = { 0, 1, 2, 3, 4, 5 };

int main ()
{
  int result[6];
  rotate_copy (numbers, numbers + 3, numbers + 6, result);
  for (int i = 0; i < 6; i++)
    cout << result[i] << ' ';
  cout << endl;
  return 0;
}

3 4 5 0 1 2
```

Example <ospace/stl/examples/rotcopy1.cpp>

```cpp
#include <stl.h>
#include <iostream.h>

int main ()
{
  vector <int> v1 (10);
  iota (v1.begin (), v1.end (), 0);
  ostream_iterator <int> iter (cout, " ");
  copy (v1.begin (), v1.end (), iter);
  cout << endl;
  vector <int> v2 (v1.size ());
  for (int i = 0; i < v1.size (); i++)
  {
    rotate_copy (v1.begin (),
                 v1.begin () + i,
                 v1.end (),
                 v2.begin ());
    ostream_iterator <int> iter (cout, " ");
    copy (v2.begin (), v2.end (), iter);
    cout << endl;
  }
  cout << endl;
  return 0;
}
```

```
0 1 2 3 4 5 6 7 8 9
0 1 2 3 4 5 6 7 8 9
1 2 3 4 5 6 7 8 9 0
2 3 4 5 6 7 8 9 0 1
3 4 5 6 7 8 9 0 1 2
4 5 6 7 8 9 0 1 2 3
5 6 7 8 9 0 1 2 3 4
6 7 8 9 0 1 2 3 4 5
7 8 9 0 1 2 3 4 5 6
8 9 0 1 2 3 4 5 6 7
9 0 1 2 3 4 5 6 7 8
```

search

Synopsis:

Locate one sequence within another.

Declaration:
```
template< class ForwardIterator1, class ForwardIterator2 >
ForwardIterator1 search
  (
  ForwardIterator1 first1,
  ForwardIterator1 last1,
  ForwardIterator2 first2,
  ForwardIterator2 last2
  )

template
  <
  class ForwardIterator1,
  class ForwardIterator2,
  class BinaryPredicate
  >
ForwardIterator1 search
  (
  ForwardIterator1 first1,
  ForwardIterator1 last1,
  ForwardIterator2 first2,
  ForwardIterator2 last2,
  BinaryPredicate binary_pred
  )
```

Description:

Search for the sequence `[first2..last2)` within the sequence `[first1, last1)`. Return an iterator into `first1..last1` where the second sequence was found, or `last1` if the sequence was not found. The first version uses `operator==` to compare elements, whereas the second version uses the binary function `binary_pred`.

Complexity:

Time Complexity: is quadratic. Space Complexity: is constant.

Example <ospace/stl/examples/search0.cpp>

```
#include <stl.h>
#include <iostream.h>

int v1[6] = { 1, 1, 2, 3, 5, 8 };
int v2[6] = { 0, 1, 2, 3, 4, 5 };
int v3[2] = { 3, 4 };

int main ()
{
  int* location;
  location = search (v1, v1 + 6, v3, v3 + 2);
  if (location == v1 + 6)
    cout << "v3 not contained in v1" << endl;
  else
    cout
      << "Found v3 in v1 at offset: "
      << location - v1
      << endl;
  location = search (v2, v2 + 6, v3, v3 + 2);
  if (location == v2 + 6)
    cout << "v3 not contained in v2" << endl;
  else
    cout
      << "Found v3 in v2 at offset: "
      << location - v2
      << endl;
  return 0;
}
```

v3 not contained in v1
Found v2 in v2 at offset: 3

Example <ospace/stl/examples/search1.cpp>

```cpp
#include <stl.h>
#include <iostream.h>

int main ()
{
  typedef vector <int> IntVec;
  IntVec v1 (10);
  iota (v1.begin (), v1.end (), 0);
  IntVec v2 (3);
  iota (v2.begin (), v2.end (), 50);
  ostream_iterator <int> iter (cout, " ");
  cout << "v1: ";
  copy (v1.begin (), v1.end (), iter);
  cout << endl;
  cout << "v2: ";
  copy (v2.begin (), v2.end (), iter);
  cout << endl;
  IntVec::iterator location;
  location = search (v1.begin (), v1.end (), v2.begin (), v2.end ());
  if (location == v1.end ())
    cout << "v2 not contained in v1" << endl;
  else
    cout
      << "Found v2 in v1 at offset: "
      << location - v1.begin ()
      << endl;
  iota (v2.begin (), v2.end (), 4);
  cout << "v1: ";
  copy (v1.begin (), v1.end (), iter);
  cout << endl;
  cout << "v2: ";
  copy (v2.begin (), v2.end (), iter);
  cout << endl;
  location = search (v1.begin (), v1.end (), v2.begin (), v2.end ());
  if (location == v1.end ())
    cout << "v2 not contained in v1" << endl;
  else
    cout
      << "Found v2 in v1 at offset: "
      << location - v1.begin ()
      << endl;
  return 0;
}
```

```
v1: 0 1 2 3 4 5 6 7 8 9
v2: 50 51 52
v2 not contained in v1
v1: 0 1 2 3 4 5 6 7 8 9
v2: 4 5 6
Found v2 in v1 at offset: 4
```

Example <ospace/stl/examples/search2.cpp>

```
#include <stl.h>
#include <iostream.h>
#include <string.h>

bool str_equal (const char* a, const char* b)
{
  return ::strcmp (a, b) == 0 ? 1 : 0;
}

char* grades[] = { "A", "B", "C", "D", "F" };
char* letters[] = { "Q", "E", "D" };

int main ()
{
  const unsigned gradeCount = sizeof (grades) / sizeof (grades[0]);
  const unsigned letterCount = sizeof (letters) / sizeof(letters[0]);
  ostream_iterator <char*> iter (cout, " ");
  cout << "grades: ";
  copy (grades, grades + gradeCount, iter);
  cout << "\nletters:";
  copy (letters, letters + letterCount, iter);
  cout << endl;
  char** location =
    search (grades, grades + gradeCount,
            letters, letters + letterCount,
            str_equal);
  if (location == grades + gradeCount)
    cout << "letters not found in grades" << endl;
  else
    cout
      << "letters found in grades at offset: "
      << location - grades
      << endl;
  copy (grades + 1, grades + 1 + letterCount, letters);
  cout << "grades: ";
  copy (grades, grades + gradeCount, iter);
  cout << "\nletters:";
  copy (letters, letters + letterCount, iter);
  cout << endl;
  location = search (grades, grades + gradeCount,
                     letters, letters + letterCount,
                     str_equal);
  if (location == grades + gradeCount)
    cout << "letters not found in grades" << endl;
  else
    cout
      << "letters found in grades at offset: "
      << location - grades
      << endl;
  return 0;
}
```

```
grades: A B C D F
letters:Q E D
letters not found in grades
grades: A B C D F
letters:B C D
letters found in grades at offset: 1
```

set_difference

Synopsis:
Create set of elements in 1st sequence that are not in 2nd.

Declaration:
```
template
    <
    class InputIterator1,
    class InputIterator2,
    class OutputIterator
    >
OutputIterator set_difference
    (
    InputIterator1 first1,
    InputIterator1 last1,
    InputIterator2 first2,
    InputIterator2 last2,
    OutputIterator result
    )

template
    <
    class InputIterator1,
    class InputIterator2,
    class OutputIterator,
    class Compare
    >
OutputIterator set_difference
    (
    InputIterator1 first1,
    InputIterator1 last1,
    InputIterator2 first2,
    InputIterator2 last2,
    OutputIterator result,
    Compare compare
    )
```

Description:
Place the sorted difference of all the elements in the sequences [first1..last) and [first2..last2) into a sequence starting at result. The output sequence will contain all elements that are in the first sequence but not in the second. Return an iterator positioned immediately after the end of the new sequence. The result is undefined if the two input sequences overlap. The first version assumes that the elements were sorted using operator<, whereas the second version assumes that the elements were sorted using the binary function compare.

Complexity:
Time Complexity: is linear. Space Complexity: is constant.

Example <ospace/stl/examples/setdiff0.cpp>

```
#include <stl.h>
#include <iostream.h>

int v1[3] = { 13, 18, 23 };
int v2[4] = { 10, 13, 17, 23 };
int result[4] = { 0, 0, 0, 0 };

int main ()
{
  set_difference (v1, v1 + 3, v2, v2 + 4, result);
  for (int i = 0; i < 4; i++)
    cout << result[i] << ' ';
  cout << endl;
  set_difference (v2, v2 + 4, v1, v1 + 2, result);
  for (i = 0; i < 4; i++)
    cout << result[i] << ' ';
  cout << endl;
  return 0;
}

18 0 0 0
10 17 23 0
```

Example <ospace/stl/examples/setdiff1.cpp>

```
#include <stl.h>
#include <iostream.h>

int main ()
{
  vector <int> v1 (10);
  iota (v1.begin (), v1.end (), 0);
  vector <int> v2 (10);
  iota (v2.begin(), v2.end (), 7);
  ostream_iterator <int> iter (cout, " ");
  cout << "v1: ";
  copy (v1.begin (), v1.end (), iter);
  cout << "\nv2: ";
  copy (v2.begin (), v2.end (), iter);
  cout << endl;
  set_difference (v1.begin (), v1.end (),
                  v2.begin (), v2.end (),
                  iter);
  return 0;
}
```

```
v1: 0 1 2 3 4 5 6 7 8 9
v2: 7 8 9 10 11 12 13 14 15 16
0 1 2 3 4 5 6
```

Example <ospace/stl/examples/setdiff2.cpp>

```cpp
#include <stl.h>
#include <iostream.h>
#include <string.h>

char* word1 = "ABCDEFGHIJKLMNO";
char* word2 = "LMNOPQRSTUVWXYZ";

int main ()
{
  ostream_iterator <char> iter (cout, " ");
  cout << "word1: ";
  copy (word1, word1 + ::strlen (word1), iter);
  cout << "\nword2: ";
  copy (word2, word2 + ::strlen (word2), iter);
  cout << endl;
  set_difference (word1, word1 + ::strlen (word1),
                  word2, word2 + ::strlen (word2),
                  iter,
                  less<char>());
  return 0;
}
```

word1: A B C D E F G H I J K L M N O
word2: L M N O P Q R S T U V W X Y Z
A B C D E F G H I J K

set_intersection

Synopsis:

Create set of elements that are in both sequences.

Declaration:
```
template
  <
  class InputIterator1,
  class InputIterator2,
  class OutputIterator
  >
OutputIterator set_intersection
  (
  InputIterator1 first1,
  InputIterator1 last1,
  InputIterator2 first2,
  InputIterator2 last2,
  OutputIterator result
  )

template
  <
  class InputIterator1,
  class InputIterator2,
  class OutputIterator,
  class Compare
  >
OutputIterator set_intersection
  (
  InputIterator1 first1,
  InputIterator1 last1,
  InputIterator2 first2,
  InputIterator2 last2,
  OutputIterator result,
  Compare compare
  )
```

Description:

Place the sorted intersection of all the elements in the sequences [first1..last) and [first2..last2) into a sequence starting at `result`. Return an iterator positioned immediately after the end of the new sequence. The result is undefined if the two input sequences overlap. The first version assumes that both sequences are already sorted using `operator<`, whereas the second version assumes that both sequences are already sorted using the binary function `compare`.

Complexity:

Time Complexity: is linear. Space Complexity: is constant.

Example <ospace/stl/examples/setintr0.cpp>

```
#include <stl.h>
#include <iostream.h>

int v1[3] = { 13, 18, 23 };
int v2[4] = { 10, 13, 17, 23 };
int result[4] = { 0, 0, 0, 0 };

int main ()
{
  set_intersection (v1, v1 + 3, v2, v2 + 4, result);
  for (int i = 0; i < 4; i++)
    cout << result[i] << ' ';
  cout << endl;
  return 0;
}
```

13 23 0 0

Example <ospace/stl/examples/setintr1.cpp>

```
#include <stl.h>
#include <iostream.h>

int main ()
{
  vector <int> v1 (10);
  iota (v1.begin (), v1.end (), 0);
  vector <int> v2 (10);
  iota (v2.begin(), v2.end (), 7);
  ostream_iterator <int> iter (cout, " ");
  cout << "v1: ";
  copy (v1.begin (), v1.end (), iter);
  cout << "\nv2: ";
  copy (v2.begin (), v2.end (), iter);
  cout << endl;
  set_intersection (v1.begin (), v1.end (),
                    v2.begin (), v2.end (),
                    iter);
  return 0;
}
```

v1: 0 1 2 3 4 5 6 7 8 9
v2: 7 8 9 10 11 12 13 14 15 16
7 8 9

Example <ospace/stl/examples/setintr2.cpp>

```
#include <stl.h>
#include <iostream.h>
#include <string.h>

char* word1 = "ABCDEFGHIJKLMNO";
char* word2 = "LMNOPQRSTUVWXYZ";

int main ()
{
  ostream_iterator <char> iter (cout, " ");
  cout << "word1: ";
  copy (word1, word1 + ::strlen (word1), iter);
  cout << "\nword2: ";
  copy (word2, word2 + ::strlen (word2), iter);
  cout << endl;
  set_intersection (word1, word1 + ::strlen (word1),
                    word2, word2 + ::strlen (word2),
                    iter,
                    less<char>());
  return 0;
}
```

word1: A B C D E F G H I J K L M N O
word2: L M N O P Q R S T U V W X Y Z
L M N O

set_symmetric_difference

Synopsis:

Create set of elements that are not in both sequences.

Declaration:
```
template
  <
  class InputIterator1,
  class InputIterator2,
  class OutputIterator
  >
OutputIterator set_symmetric_difference
  (
  InputIterator1 first1,
  InputIterator1 last1,
  InputIterator2 first2,
  InputIterator2 last2,
  OutputIterator result
  )

template
  <
  class InputIterator1,
  class InputIterator2,
  class OutputIterator,
  class Compare
  >
OutputIterator set_symmetric_difference
  (
  InputIterator1 first1,
  InputIterator1 last1,
  InputIterator2 first2,
  InputIterator2 last2,
  OutputIterator result,
  Compare compare
  )
```

Description:

Place all elements that are not in both sequences into `result`, in their sorted order. Return an iterator positioned immediately after the end of the new sequence. The result is undefined if the two input sequences overlap. The first version assumes that both sequences are already sorted using `operator<`, whereas the second version assumes that both sequences are already sorted using the binary function `compare`.

Complexity:

Time Complexity: is linear. Space Complexity: is constant.

Example <ospace/stl/examples/setsymd0.cpp>

```
#include <stl.h>
#include <iostream.h>

int v1[3] = { 13, 18, 23 };
int v2[4] = { 10, 13, 17, 23 };
int result[4] = { 0, 0, 0, 0 };

int main ()
{
  set_symmetric_difference (v1, v1 + 3, v2, v2 + 4, result);
  for (int i = 0; i < 4; i++)
    cout << result[i] << ' ';
  cout << endl;
  return 0;
}
```

10 17 18 0

Example <ospace/stl/examples/setsymd1.cpp>

```
#include <stl.h>
#include <iostream.h>

int main ()
{
  vector <int> v1 (10);
  iota (v1.begin (), v1.end (), 0);
  vector <int> v2 (10);
  iota (v2.begin(), v2.end (), 7);
  ostream_iterator <int> iter (cout, " ");
  cout << "v1: ";
  copy (v1.begin (), v1.end (), iter);
  cout << "\nv2: ";
  copy (v2.begin (), v2.end (), iter);
  cout << endl;
  set_symmetric_difference (v1.begin (), v1.end (),
                            v2.begin (), v2.end (),
                            iter);
  return 0;
}
```

v1: 0 1 2 3 4 5 6 7 8 9
v2: 7 8 9 10 11 12 13 14 15 16
0 1 2 3 4 5 6 10 11 12 13 14 15 16

Example <ospace/stl/examples/setsymd2.cpp>

```cpp
#include <stl.h>
#include <iostream.h>
#include <string.h>

char* word1 = "ABCDEFGHIJKLMNO";
char* word2 = "LMNOPQRSTUVWXYZ";

int main ()
{
  ostream_iterator <char> iter (cout, " ");
  cout << "word1: ";
  copy (word1, word1 + ::strlen (word1), iter);
  cout << "\nword2: ";
  copy (word2, word2 + ::strlen (word2), iter);
  cout << endl;
  set_symmetric_difference (word1, word1 + ::strlen (word1),
                            word2, word2 + ::strlen (word2),
                            iter,
                            less<char>());
  return 0;
}
```

word1: A B C D E F G H I J K L M N O
word2: L M N O P Q R S T U V W X Y Z
A B C D E F G H I J K P Q R S T U V W X Y Z

set_union

Synopsis:

Create set of elements that are in either sequence.

Declaration:

```
template
    <
    class InputIterator1,
    class InputIterator2,
    class OutputIterator
    >
OutputIterator set_union
    (
    InputIterator1 first1,
    InputIterator1 last1,
    InputIterator2 first2,
    InputIterator2 last2,
    OutputIterator result
    )
template
    <
    class InputIterator1,
    class InputIterator2,
    class OutputIterator,
    class Compare
    >
OutputIterator set_union
    (
    InputIterator1 first1,
    InputIterator1 last1,
    InputIterator2 first2,
    InputIterator2 last2,
    OutputIterator result,
    Compare compare
    )
```

Description:

Place the sorted union of all the elements in the sequences [first1..last) and
[first2..last2) into a sequence starting at `result`. Return an iterator positioned
immediately after the end of the new sequence. The result is undefined if the two input
sequences overlap. If an element occurs in both sequences, the element from the first sequence
is copied into the result sequence. The first version assumes that both sequences were already
sorted using `operator<`, whereas the second version assumes that both sequences were
already sorted using the binary function `compare`.

Example <ospace/stl/examples/setunon0.cpp>

```
#include <stl.h>
#include <iostream.h>

int v1[3] = { 13, 18, 23 };
int v2[4] = { 10, 13, 17, 23 };
int result[7] = { 0, 0, 0, 0, 0, 0, 0 };

int main ()
{
  set_union (v1, v1 + 3, v2, v2 + 4, result);
  for (int i = 0; i < 7; i++)
    cout << result[i] << ' ';
  cout << endl;
  return 0;
}
```

10 13 17 18 23 0 0

Example <ospace/stl/examples/setunon1.cpp>

```
#include <stl.h>
#include <iostream.h>

int main ()
{
  vector <int> v1 (10);
  iota (v1.begin (), v1.end (), 0);
  vector <int> v2 (10);
  iota (v2.begin(), v2.end (), 7);
  ostream_iterator <int> iter (cout, " ");
  cout << "v1: ";
  copy (v1.begin (), v1.end (), iter);
  cout << "\nv2: ";
  copy (v2.begin (), v2.end (), iter);
  cout << endl;
  set_union (v1.begin (), v1.end (),
             v2.begin (), v2.end (),
             iter);
  return 0;
}
```

v1: 0 1 2 3 4 5 6 7 8
v2: 7 8 9 10 11 12 13 14 15 16
0 1 2 3 4 5 6 7 8 9 10 11 12 13 14 15 16

Example <ospace/stl/examples/setunon2.cpp>

```
#include <stl.h>
#include <iostream.h>
#include <string.h>

char* word1 = "ABCDEFGHIJKLMNO";
char* word2 = "LMNOPQRSTUVWXYZ";

int main ()
{
  ostream_iterator <char> iter (cout, " ");
  cout << "word1: ";
  copy (word1, word1 + ::strlen (word1), iter);
  cout << "\nword2: ";
  copy (word2, word2 + ::strlen (word2), iter);
  cout << endl;
  set_union (word1, word1 + ::strlen (word1),
             word2, word2 + ::strlen (word2),
             iter,
             less<char>());
  return 0;
}
```

word1: A B C D E F G H I J K L M N O
word2: L M N O P Q R S T U V W X Y Z
A B C D E F G H I J K L M N O P Q R S T U V W X Y Z

sort

Synopsis:
Sort a sequence

Declaration:
```
template< class RandomAccessIterator >
void sort( RandomAccessIterator first, RandomAccessIterator last )

template< class RandomAccessIterator, class Compare >
void sort
  (
  RandomAccessIterator first,
  RandomAccessIterator last,
  Compare compare
  )
```

Description:
Sort all elements in the range [`first..last`) into ascending order. The first version uses `operator<` to compare elements, whereas the second version uses the binary function `compare`.

Complexity:
Time Complexity: is O(N * log(N)). Space Complexity: is constant.

Helper:
```
void os_sort( Container& c )
void os_sort( Container& c, Compare compare )
```

Example <ospace/stl/examples/sort1.cpp>

```
#include <stl.h>
#include <iostream.h>

int vector[6] = { 1, 50, -10, 11, 42, 19 };

int main ()
{
  sort (vector, vector + 6);
  for (int i = 0; i < 6; i++)
    cout << vector[i] << ' ';
  cout << endl;
  return 0;
}
```

-10 1 11 19 42 50

Example <ospace/stl/examples/sort2.cpp>

```
#include <stl.h>
#include <iostream.h>

int vector[] = { 1, 50, -10, 11, 42, 19 };

int main ()
{
  int count = sizeof (vector) / sizeof (vector[0]);
  ostream_iterator <int> iter (cout, " ");
  cout << "before: ";
  copy (vector, vector + count, iter);
  cout << "\nafter: ";
  sort (vector, vector + count, greater<int>());
  copy (vector, vector + count, iter);
  return 0;
}
```

before: 1 50 -10 11 42 19
after: 50 42 19 11 1 -10

sort_heap

Synopsis:
Sort a heap

Declaration:
```
template< class RandomAccessIterator >
void sort_heap
  (
  RandomAccessIterator first,
  RandomAccessIterator last
  )

template<class RandomAccessIterator, class Compare>
void sort_heap
  (
  RandomAccessIterator first,
  RandomAccessIterator last,
  Compare compare
  )
```

Description:
Starting with a heap as an input sequence, produce a sorted collection. The first version uses `operator<` to compare elements, whereas the second version uses the binary function `compare`. *Note that a heap ceases to be a heap when it is sorted.*

Complexity:
Time Complexity: is N * log(N). Space Complexity: is constant.

Examples
See `push_heap`.

stable_partition

Synopsis:

Partition a range using a predicate.

Declaration:
```
template< class BidirectionalIterator, class Predicate >
BidirectionalIterator stable_partition
  (
  BidirectionalIterator first,
  BidirectionalIterator last,
  Predicate pred
  )
```

Description:

Place all elements in the range [first..last) that make pred evaluate to true before all elements in the range that make pred evaluate to false. Return an iterator i such that all elements in the range [first..i) make pred evaluate to true and all elements in the range [i..last) make pred evaluate to false. This algorithm is stable in the sense that elements which satisfy pred that were before other elements which also satisfied pred before the partition will remain in the same relative order after the partition.

Complexity:

Time Complexity: is O(N * log(N)), where N = (last - first), as pred will be evaluated N times and at most N * log(N) swaps are performed. If there is enough available memory, O(N) swaps be performed instead

stable_partition

Example <ospace/stl/examples/stblptn0.cpp>

```
#include <stl.h>
#include <iostream.h>

bool less_10 (int a)
{
  return a < 10 ? 1 : 0;
}

int numbers[6] = { 10, 5, 11, 20, 6, -2 };

int main ()
{
  stable_partition (numbers, numbers + 6, less_10);
  for (int i = 0; i < 6; i++)
    cout << numbers[i] << ' ';
  cout << endl;
  return 0;
}
```

5 6 -2 10 11 20

Example <ospace/stl/examples/stblptn1.cpp>

```
#include <stl.h>
#include <iostream.h>

int main ()
{
  vector <int> v1 (10);
  for (int i = 0; i < v1.size (); i++)
    v1[i] = rand () % 20;
  ostream_iterator <int> iter (cout, " ");
  copy (v1.begin (), v1.end (), iter);
  cout << endl;
  stable_partition (v1.begin (), v1.end (),
  bind2nd(less<int>(), 11));
  copy (v1.begin (), v1.end (), iter);
  cout << endl;
  return 0;
}
```

6 10 2 10 16 17 15 15 8 6
6 10 2 10 8 6 16 17 15 15

stable_sort

Synopsis:

Sort a sequence in ascending order.

Declaration:

```
template< class RandomAccessIterator >
void stable_sort
  (
  RandomAccessIterator first,
  RandomAccessIterator last
  )
template< class RandomAccessIterator, class Compare >
void stable_sort
  (
  RandomAccessIterator first,
  RandomAccessIterator last,
  Compare compare
  )
```

Description:

Sort all of elements in the range [first..last). The relative order of equal objects is preserved. The first version uses operator< to compare elements, whereas the second version uses the binary function compare.

Complexity:

Time Complexity: is $O(N(log(N))^2)$ where N = (last - first). If enough memory is available, time Complexity: becomes $O(N * log(N))$. Space Complexity: is N if enough memory is available, otherwise it is constant.

Example <ospace/stl/examples/stblsrt1.cpp>

```
#include <stl.h>
#include <iostream.h>

int vector[6] = { 1, 50, -10, 11, 42, 19 };

int main ()
{
  stable_sort (vector, vector + 6);
  for (int i = 0; i < 6; i++)
    cout << vector[i] << ' ';
  cout << endl;
  return 0;
}
```

-10 1 11 19 42 50

Example <ospace/stl/examples/stblsrt2.cpp>

```
#include <stl.h>
#include <iostream.h>
#include <string.h>

bool string_less (const char* a, const char* b)
{
  return ::strcmp (a, b) < 0 ? 1 : 0;
}

char* letters[6] = {"bb", "aa", "ll", "dd", "qq", "cc" };

int main ()
{
  stable_sort (letters, letters + 6, string_less);
  for (int i = 0; i < 6; i++)
    cout << letters[i] << ' ';
  cout << endl;
  return 0;
}
```

aa bb cc dd ll qq

swap

Synopsis:

Swap two values.

Declaration:
```
template< class T >
void swap( T& a, T& b )
```

Description:

Swap the elements `a` and `b`.

Complexity:

Time and space Complexity: are constant.

Example <ospace/stl/examples/swap1.cpp>

```
#include <stl.h>
#include <iostream.h>

int main ()
{
  int a = 42;
  int b = 19;
  cout << "a = " << a << " b = " << b << endl;

  swap (a, b);

  cout << "a = " << a << " b = " << b << endl;
  return 0;
}

a = 41 b = 19
a = 19 b = 42
```

swap_ranges

Synopsis:

Swap two ranges of items.

Declaration:

```
template< class ForwardIterator1, class ForwardIterator2 >
ForwardIterator2 swap_ranges
  (
  ForwardIterator1 first1,
  ForwardIterator1 last1,
  ForwardIterator2 first2
  )
```

Description:

Swap the elements in the range [first1, last1) with the elements in the range of the same size starting at first2. Return an iterator positioned immediately after the last element in the second range.

Complexity:

Time Complexity: is linear. Space Complexity: is constant.

Example <ospace/stl/examples/swprnge1.cpp>

```
#include <stl.h>
#include <iostream.h>
#include <string.h>

int main ()
{
  char* word1 = "World";
  char* word2 = "Hello";
  cout << word1 << " " << word2 << endl;
  swap_ranges (word1, word1 + ::strlen (word1), word2);
  cout << word1 << " " << word2 << endl;
  return 0;
}

World Hello
Hello World
```

transform

Synopsis:

Transform one sequence into another.

Declaration:

```
template
    <
    class InputIterator,
    class OutputIterator,
    class UnaryOperation
    >
OutputIterator transform
    (
    InputIterator first,
    InputIterator last,
    OutputIterator result,
    UnaryOperation op
    )

template
    <
    class InputIterator1,
    class InputIterator2,
    class OutputIterator,
    class BinaryOperation
    >
OutputIterator transform
    (
    InputIterator1 first1,
    InputIterator1 last1,
    InputIterator2 first2,
    OutputIterator result,
    BinaryOperation binary_op
    )
```

Description:

The first version traverses the sequence [first..last) and store the results of invoking op on each element into a sequence of the same size starting at result. The second version uses a pair of iterators i and j to traverse two sequences, starting at first1 and first2, respectively, until i reaches last1. The second version stores the results of invoking binary_op on the elements referenced by the iterator pair into a sequence of the same size starting at result. Both versions return an iterator positioned immediately after the last new element.

Complexity:

Time Complexity: is linear, as (last1 - first1) operations are performed. Space Complexity: is constant.

Example <ospace/stl/examples/trnsfrm1.cpp>

```
#include <stl.h>
#include <iostream.h>

int negate_int (int a)
{
  return -a;
}

int numbers[6] = { -5, -1, 0, 1, 6, 11 };

int main ()
{
  int result[6];
  transform (numbers, numbers + 6, result, negate_int);
  for (int i = 0; i < 6; i++)
    cout << result[i] << ' ';
  cout << endl;
  return 0;
}
```

5 1 0 -1 -6 -11

Example <ospace/stl/examples/trnsfrm2.cpp>

```
#include <stl.h>
#include <iostream.h>
#include <string.h>

char map_char (char a, int b)
{
  return char (a + b);
}

int trans[] = {-4, 4, -6, -6, -10, 0, 10, -6, 6, 0, -1, -77};

int main ()
{
  char n[] = "Larry Mullen";
  const unsigned count = ::strlen (n);
  ostream_iterator <char> iter (cout);
  transform (n, n + count, trans, iter, map_char);
  return 0;
}
```

Hello World!

unique

Synopsis:

Collapse all consecutive values in a sequence.

Declaration:

```
template< class ForwardIterator >
ForwardIterator unique
  (
  ForwardIterator first,
  ForwardIterator last
  )

template< class ForwardIterator, class BinaryPredicate >
ForwardIterator unique
  (
  ForwardIterator first,
  ForwardIterator last,
  BinaryPredicate binary_pred
  )
```

Description:

Replace all consecutive matching occurrences of a value in the range `[first..last)` by a single instance of that value. Return an iterator positioned immediately after the last element of the new sequence. The size of the container is not altered; if n elements are removed, the last n elements of the sequence `[first..last)` will have undefined values. The first version uses `operator==` to match values, whereas the second version uses the binary function `binary_pred`.

Complexity:

Time Complexity: is linear, as `(last - first)` comparisons are performed. Space Complexity: is constant.

unique

Example <ospace/stl/examples/unique1.cpp>

```
#include <stl.h>
#include <iostream.h>

int numbers[8] = { 0, 1, 1, 2, 2, 2, 3, 4 };

int main ()
{
  unique (numbers, numbers + 8);
  for (int i = 0; i < 8; i ++)
    cout << numbers[i] << ' ';
  cout << endl;
  return 0;
}
```

0 1 2 3 4 2 3 4

Example <ospace/stl/examples/unique2.cpp>

```
#include <stl.h>
#include <iostream.h>
#include <string.h>

bool str_equal (const char* a, const char* b)
{
  return ::strcmp (a, b) == 0 ? 1 : 0;
}

char* labels[] = { "Q","Q","W","W","E","E","R","T","T","Y","Y" };

int main ()
{
  const unsigned count = sizeof (labels) / sizeof (labels[0]);
  ostream_iterator <char*> iter (cout);
  copy (labels, labels + count, iter);
  cout << endl;
  unique (labels, labels + count, str_equal);
  copy (labels, labels + count, iter);
  cout << endl;
  return 0;
}
```

QQWWERRTTYY
QWERTYRTTYY

unique_copy

Synopsis:

Copy a sequence, collapsing consecutive values.

Declaration:
```
template< class InputIterator, class OutputIterator >
OutputIterator unique_copy
   (
   InputIterator first,
   InputIterator last,
   OutputIterator result
   )

template
   <
   class InputIterator,
   class OutputIterator,
   class BinaryPredicate
   >
OutputIterator unique_copy
   (
   InputIterator first,
   InputIterator last,
   OutputIterator result,
   BinaryPredicate binary_pred
   )
```

Description:

Copy the sequence [first..last) to a sequence starting at result, replacing all consecutive occurrences of a value by a single instance of that value. Return an iterator positioned immediately after the last element of new sequence. The first version uses operator== to determine equality, whereas the second version uses the binary function binary_pred.

Complexity:

Time Complexity: is linear, as (last - first) comparisons are performed. Space Complexity: is linear.

Example <ospace/stl/examples/uniqcpy1.cpp>

```
#include <stl.h>
#include <iostream.h>

int numbers[8] = { 0, 1, 1, 2, 2, 2, 3, 4 };
int result[8] = { 0, 0, 0, 0, 0, 0, 0, 0 };

int main ()
{
  unique_copy (numbers, numbers + 8, result);
  for (int i = 0; i < 8; i++)
    cout << result[i] << ' ';
  cout << endl;
  return 0;
}
```

0 1 2 3 4 0 0 0

Example <ospace/stl/examples/uniqcpy2.cpp>

```
#include <stl.h>
#include <iostream.h>
#include <string.h>

bool str_equal (const char* a, const char* b)
{
  return ::strcmp (a, b) == 0 ? 1 : 0;
}

char* labels[] = { "Q","Q","W","W","E","E","R","T","T","Y","Y" };

int main ()
{
  const unsigned count = sizeof (labels) / sizeof (labels[0]);
  ostream_iterator <char*> iter (cout);
  copy (labels, labels + count, iter);
  cout << endl;
  char* uCopy[count];
  fill (uCopy, uCopy + count, "");
  unique_copy (labels, labels + count, uCopy, str_equal);
  copy (labels, labels + count, iter);
  cout << endl;
  copy (uCopy, uCopy + count, iter);
  cout << endl;
  return 0;
}
```

QQWWEERRTTYY
QQWWEERRTTYY
QWERTY

upper_bound

Synopsis:

Return the upper bound within a range.

Declaration:
```
template< class ForwardIterator, class T >
ForwardIterator upper_bound
    (
    ForwardIterator first,
    ForwardIterator last,
    const T& value
    )

template< class ForwardIterator, class T, class Compare >
ForwardIterator upper_bound
    (
    ForwardIterator first,
    ForwardIterator last,
    const T& value,
    Compare compare
    )
```

Description:

Return the last position in the range `[first..last)` that `value` can be inserted without violating the order of the collection. The first version uses `operator<` for comparison, whereas the second version uses the binary function `compare`.

Complexity:

Time Complexity: is O(log(N)) for random access iterators, O(N) for all other iterators. Space Complexity: is constant.

Example <ospace/stl/examples/uprbnd1.cpp>

```
#include <stl.h>
#include <iostream.h>

int main ()
{
  int vector[20];
  for (int i = 0; i < 20; i++)
  {
    vector[i] = i/4;
    cout << vector[i] << ' ';
  }
  cout
    << "\n3 can be inserted at index: "
    << upper_bound (vector, vector + 20, 3) - vector
    << endl;
  return 0;
}
```

```
0 0 0 0 1 1 1 1 2 2 2 2 3 3 3 3 4 4 4 4
3 can be inserted at index: 16
```

Example <ospace/stl/examples/uprbnd2.cpp>

```
#include <stl.h>
#include <iostream.h>
#include <string.h>

bool char_str_less (const char* a, const char* b)
{
  return ::strcmp (a, b) < 0 ? 1 : 0;
}

char* str [] = { "a", "a", "b", "b", "q", "w", "z" };

int main ()
{
  const unsigned strCt = sizeof (str)/sizeof (str[0]);
  cout
    << "d can be inserted at index: "
    << upper_bound (str,  str + strCt, "d", char_str_less) - str
    << endl;
  return 0;
}
```

```
d can be inserted at index: 4
```

Appendix

This section includes a description of every event that can be generated by Systems<ToolKit>, together with a list of additional STL resources. For more information about error and panic events, consult the "Error Handling" chapter of the *Systems<ToolKit> User's Manual*.

Error Events

The error events that may be generated by Systems<ToolKit> can be divided into two kinds:

- *System Call Errors* (marked `syscall` in a class catalog entry): these are errors generated by the operating system when called from Systems<ToolKit> classes. Systems<ToolKit> traps these errors and converts them into error events.

- *Other Library Errors* (marked `other` in a catalog entry): these are errors detected by code within Systems<ToolKit>.

The next couple of subsections describe the individual error codes associated with each kind of error event.

System Call Errors

This section contains a list of all of the error codes associated with error events generated by system call failures, together with a brief description.

Error code	Description
E2BIG	Arg list too long
EACCES	Permission denied
EADDRINUSE	Address already in use
EADDRNOTAVAIL	Cannot assign requested address
EAGAIN / EWOULDBLOCK	Resource temporarily unavailable
EALREADY	Operation already in progress
EBADF	Bad file number
EBADFD	File descriptor in bad state
EBADMSG	Not a data message
EBUSY	Device busy
ECHILD	No child processes
ECOMM	Communication error on send
ECONNABORTED	Software caused connection abort
ECONNREFUSED	Connection refused
ECONNRESET	Connection reset by peer
EDEADLK	Deadlock situation detected/avoided
EDEADLOCK	File locking deadlock
EDESTADDRREQ	Destination address required
EEXIST	File exists
EFAULT	Bad address
EFBIG	File too large

Error Code	Description
EHOSTDOWN	Host is down
EHOSTUNREACH	No route to host
EIDRM	Identifier removed
EINPROGRESS	Operation now in progress
EINTR	Interrupted system call
EINVAL	Invalid argument
EIO	I/O error
EISCONN	Transport endpoint is already connected
EISDIR	Is a directory
ELOOP	Number of symbolic links encountered during path name traversal exceeds MAXSYM
EMFILE	Too many open files
EMLINK	Too many links
EMSGSIZE	Message too long
EMULTIHOP	Multi-hop attempted
ENAMETOOLONG	File name too long
ENETDOWN	Network is down
ENETRESET	Network dropped connection because of reset
ENETUNREACH	Network is unreachable
ENFILE	File table overflow
ENOBUFS	No buffer space available
ENODATA	No data available
ENODEV	No such device
ENOENT	No such file or directory
ENOEXEC	Exec format error
ENOLCK	No record locks available
ENOLINK	Link has been severed

Error Code	Description
ENOMEM	Not enough space
ENOMSG	No message of desired type
ENONET	Machine is not on the network
ENOPROTOOPT	Option not supported by protocol
ENOSPC	No space left on device
ENOSYS	Operation not applicable
ENOTBLK	Block device required
ENOTCONN	Transport endpoint is not connected
ENOTDIR	Not a directory
ENOTEMPTY	Directory not empty
ENOTSOCK	Socket operation on non-socket
ENOTTY	Inappropriate ioctl for device
ENXIO	No such device or address
EOPNOTSUPP	Operation not supported on transport endpoint
EOVERFLOW	Value too large for defined data type
EPERM	Not owner
EPIPE	Broken pipe
EPROTO	Protocol error
ERANGE	Result too large
EREMCHG	Remote address changed
EREMOTE	Object is remote
EROFS	Read-only file system
ESHUTDOWN	Cannot send after socket shutdown
ESOCKTNOSUPPORT	Socket type not supported
ESPIPE	Illegal seek
ESRCH	No such process
ESTALE	Stale NFS file handle

Error Code	Description
ETIME	Timer expired
ETIMEDOUT	Connection timed out
ETXTBSY	Text file busy
EUSERS	Too many users
EWOULDBLOCK / EAGAIN	Resource temporarily unavailable

Internal Errors

This section contains a list of all of the error codes associated with error events generated by code within Systems<ToolKit>, together with a brief description.

Error code	Description
os_ambiguous_cast	Casting a derived object to one of its base object is ambiguous.
os_bounds_error	Attempt to access outside of legal bounds.
os_cannot_add_exit_function	No more exit functions can be added to your process.
os_cannot_create_key	A key with the specified path and project code could not be created.
os_class_not_found	An unknown class of object was encountered.
os_directory_not_open	Attempt to operate on a directory that was not open.
os_divide_by_zero	A divide by zero error occurred.
os_empty_error	Illegal operation on an empty object.
os_eof_encountered	End of input was detected.
os_exclusive_create failed	Attempt to exclusively create an object that already exists.
os_framing_error	An object was not written in the same way it was read.
os_illegal_index	Index is outside range.
os_illegal_allocation	Illegal allocation operation.
os_invalid_argument	Invalid argument.
os_invalid_conversion	Attempt to convert to incompatible type.
os_invalid_group	Invalid group name or id.
os_invalid_host	Invalid host.
os_invalid_network	Invalid network.

Error code	Description
os_invalid_process	Attempt to operate on a process with an invalid PID.
os_invalid_process_group	Attempt to operate on a process group with an invalid PGID.
os_invalid_service	Invalid network service.
os_invalid_user	Invalid user name or id.
os_max_args_exceeded	The maximum number of arguments to a program was exceeded.
os_nil_error	Could not write nil as an object.
os_not_implemented	The requisition operation is not implemented.
os_object_exists	Could not add a duplicate object.
os_object_not_encodeable	Could not read or write an object that does not support binary object I/O.
os_object_not_found	Attempt to find non-existent object.
os_pipe_closed	Operation not supported on closed pipe.
os_system_data_unavailable	System data was unavailable.
os_string_debug	An internal assertion failed.
os_string_length_error	Illegal operation which results in a string whose length would be greater than or equal to os_npos.
os_string_range_error	Index out of range.
os_time_or_date_unavailable	Time information was unavailable.
os_type_mismatch	Attempt to read wrong type.
os_unexpected_eof	Object only partially read when eof occurred.

Panic Events

Panic events always cause your program to terminate. Here is a list of all the panic events:

Error code	Description
os_duplicate_class	The class was already registered, two classes have same name or id in the RTTI macros in your program.
os_internal_assertion_failed	An internal systems toolkit assertion failed.
os_no_more_heap	Memory allocation on heap failed.
os_unhandled_event	An handler is holding an event which is neither released nor cleared.
os_uninitialized_class	Incorrect or no RTTI/Binary Stream macro is supplied for the class.

Additional Resources

Here is a list of additional Systems<ToolKit> related resources:

- "http://www.objectspace.com" is the ObjectSpace WWW (World Wide Web) site that contains additional information about Systems<ToolKit>, including a current list of frequently asked questions, software bug patches, and free software utilities.

- Hewlett Packard's public domain version of STL is available from the FTP site "butler.hpl.hp.com" in the directory "stl".

- "http://www.cs.rpi.edu/stl.html" is a WWW site created by Dave Musser, one of the creators of the associative container implementations. It contains some very handy information about STL, some implementations of portions of STL, and some examples.

- "http://www.xraylith.wisc.edu/~kahn/software/stl/STL.newbie.html" is a WWW site created by Mumit Khan, containing excellent resources for those who are new to STL in general.

- *The Standard Template Library*, Alexandar Stepanov and Meng Lee, is a document available from the butler site above. It offers another explanation of STL direct from its creators.

- *Advanced Programming in the UNIX Environment*, W. Richard Stephens, Addison-Wesley, ISBN 0-201-56317-7

- *The Annotated C++ Reference Manual*, Ellis & Stroustrup, Addison-Wesley, ISBN 0-201-51459-1

- *TCP/IP Illustrated, Volume I,* W. Richard Stephens, Addison-Wesley, ISBN 0-201-63346-9

- *UNIX for Programmers and Users*, Graham Glass, Prentice-Hall, ISBN 0-13-480880-0

- *Advanced UNIX Programming*, Marc J. Rochkind, Prentice-Hall, ISBN 0-13-011818-4

- *UNIX Network Programming*, W. Richard Stephens, Prentice-Hall, ISBN 0-13-949876-1